CONCERNING PSYCHOLOGY

Psychology Applied to
Social Issues

Dennis Howitt

OPEN UNIVERSITY PRESS
Milton Keynes • Philadelphia

Open University Press
Celtic Court
22 Ballmoor
Buckingham
MK18 1XW

and
1900 Frost Road, Suite 101
Bristol, PA 19007, USA

First Published 1991

British Library Cataloguing in Publication Data

Howitt, Dennis
    Concerning psychology: Psychology applied to
    social issues.
    I. Title
    302

    ISBN 0-335-09373-6
    ISBN 0-335-09372-8 pbk

Library of Congress Cataloging-in-Publication Data

Howitt, Dennis.
    Concerning psychology : psychology applied to social issues /
    Dennis Howitt.
        p. cm.
    Includes bibliographical references and index.
    ISBN 0-335-09373-6 - ISBN 0-335-09372-8 (pbk.)
    1. Social psychology. 2. Psychology. Applied. I. Title.
    HM251.H73 1991
    302–dc20   91-3309
                                                        CIP

Typeset by Stanford Desktop Publishing Services, Milton Keynes
Printed in Great Britain by St Edmundsbury Press
Bury St Edmunds, Suffolk

CONTENTS

1 Psychology and social issues   1
2 Obstacles to and opportunities for progress   15
3 Values and psychology   35
4 The creation of a social issue: the case of drug abuse   53
5 Taking sides: child physical and sexual abuse   71
6 Internalized ideologies: racism and psychology   95
7 The politics of an issue: pornography and feminism   120
8 Tribulations of real-world psychologists   146

References   167
Author index   181
Subject index   185

1

PSYCHOLOGY AND SOCIAL ISSUES

If common understandings are accepted, then any matter involving controversy or uncertainty over the well-being of substantial numbers of people can be called a social issue ... Viewed from this standpoint, our question may be better put in the form of a negation: What is not a social issue? ... Is there anything from birth through death, from marriage through child-rearing and old age, from gasoline to nonunion grapes or lettuce, that cannot stand plausibly as a social issue?

(Rappoport and Kren, 1975, p. 838)

What use is psychology in the real world? Should one have any great faith in the value of academic psychology for its own sake? Simplistically, this could be described as a book about applied psychology. However, in the light of what is to come, many of the ways in which psychology is 'applied' seem trivial, crude, inappropriate, and even disgraceful. The application of psychology dealt with tries to escape the easy pretence of science and objectivity as the essence of psychology's contribution to understanding real-world matters. Psychology, it is argued, has to drop its defences and recognize the need to develop into an honest, concerned discipline, well aware of its own nature, limitations and history.

One basic assumption is that social issues cannot be effectively tackled by psychologists ignorant of the characteristics of their discipline, which, while purporting to study people in society, often has precious little to do with people or society. Appreciation of what psychology can achieve in the real world depends as much on openness and self-understanding on the part of psychologists as on its methods, techniques and theory. To present psychology as a discipline perfected through 'scientific' objectives is not only to offer a smokescreen, but also continually to reject many opportunities to change.

So what is the proper image for psychology in the real world?

Psychology and the real world

Psychology often dashes the hopes of those seeking an understanding of themselves, other people and society. The goodwill of those exploring psychology for such help is smashed on the altar of an élite academic psychology which wrings out of the discipline concerns about real-world issues. It might not be immediately obvious why this should be the case. Some understanding of the history of psychology as well as its institutional base is required in order to begin to understand the disappointments of psychology. A further side of this mystery is found in the fate of the work of psychologists who show worldly concerns. Psychologists have, without doubt, delved into a vast range of real-life issues, which have benefited from psychological inputs. But where is this psychology? Why does it lie hidden from the public gaze? Is a psychology of real world problems possible?

Many would be surprised at the sheer range of topics which psychologists have explored. These include nuclear issues (Morawski and Goldstein, 1985; Earle and Cvetkovich, 1990), divorce (Kurdeck, 1981), accident prevention (Matheny, 1987), AIDS (Batchelor, 1984; Cumberbatch, 1988), unemployment (Dooley and Catalano, 1988), political violence (Dawes, 1990), deinstitutionalization (Bachrach, 1984, 1989; Shadish, 1984), compensatory education (Weinberg, 1979), sex equality (Klein and Simonson, 1984; Russo and Denmark, 1984) and many others. Some of these will be familiar, some totally unexpected, perhaps. But had the list included perception, memory, cognition, artificial intelligence, mental illness, child development, conformity, leadership, stress, psychotherapy, motivation, emotion, personality, intelligence, thought, language, learning and conditioning, consciousness, and the biological basis of behaviour then most psychology students would have little difficulty in recognizing the bulk of them. They are par for the course – practically any psychology course. Anyone can see why. Surely they are the basic building blocks which, when pieced together, give us a complete picture of psychology? But such a claim adopts lock, stock and barrel one picture of human psychology which deserves to be challenged. The idea that one can piece people together as if they were atoms making up the molecules, making up the cells, making up the limbs, making up the person may be appealing. Nevertheless some might venture that it is a remarkable mind which can join that lot together to glimpse the whole. The list does include a few seemingly 'worldly' matters (mental illness and child development, for example). But can we be sure that they are anything other than tokens or that they themselves are not resolutely abstract?

It should be pointed out, according to Pion and Lipsey (1984), the growth in the social output of psychology in recent years has been largely in terms of service provision – largely counselling and guidance. The social application of psychological knowledge has not shown the same upward pattern. Application of knowledge they describe as being part of the rhetoric, rather than the practice, of psychologists.

The greatest problem is not that there has been a total neglect of applied issues in psychology; to make such a claim would be nonsense. However, there has been a lack of *systemization* of much applied psychology. Most academic psychology is based on anything but the real world. Doggedly, it is committed to the laboratory and the controlled experiment. When it ventures into the real world it is through an intermediary – a structured, multiple-choice, self-completion questionnaire that is 'objective'. Unfortunately these usually do little to come to terms with the real world. While structured questionnaires may often give the appearance of being concerned with real-world issues, one needs to be sure that they are not merely a 'quick and easy' means of getting data without 'muddying one's boots'. There is a place for some questionnaires, but only applied with caution and not as the only means or 'best' means to understanding. Laboratory research deliberately excludes as much of the outside world as possible. To control variables is to take them out of consideration. Real-world psychology ought to be the central material for constructing the body of knowledge to be disseminated as psychology. However, to do so would be substantially to reconstruct the practices of psychologists.

There are many different sorts of psychology, all with different strengths. This book restates one claim as to what the major consideration of psychology should be. This is not to eclipse other forms of psychology as such, perhaps quite the reverse. Neither is the proposed role for psychology a new one. However, applied psychology has traditionally tended to be ignored as a consequence of the institutional or academic power of other forms of the discipline. This has contributed to the under-representation and marginalization of those aspects of the discipline dealing mostly with real-world social problems. Clearly, a 'real-world' psychology has to encompass and then stretch far beyond the psychology of the individual. Such a psychology has to be constructed within a social world which is socio-political in nature with profound moral concerns. Psychology, then, cannot be cocooned from controversy.

Some well-known figures in psychology were never inclined to avoid worldly matters. Sigmund Freud's psychoanalytic psychology, although ostensibly dealing with the innermost recesses of the human mind, in many ways reached out from the individual to society. For example, although the id was a bubbling pot of the unsocial impulse, the superego was the internalization of society. As a consequence, Freud was able to write of war, civilization and anthropological (e.g. Freud, 1950; Dilman, 1983) matters as well as many aspects of individual psychopathology. Skinner (1972; 1976) chose to write of an imaginary utopian (for him) society built on his ideas of operant conditioning. Eysenck (1953; 1954; 1957; 1973; 1977; Eysenck and Nias, 1978; Eysenck and Wilson, 1978; Eysenck and

Gudjonsson, 1989) frequently addressed issues such as whether our national intelligence was declining, political thinking, why smoking is not unhealthy, criminal behaviour, pornography and others, almost always linking them to his theory of personality.

Despite this apparently 'honourable' tradition, much of this sort of work fails as a framework for applied psychology. In particular, most of it tends to adopt an *inside-out* model, where society mirrors the psychological characteristics of individuals. There are problems with this, and in later chapters of this book we will concentrate on the *outside-in* approach, where the key features of psychology are the needs of the outside world beyond the individual and, perhaps more importantly, beyond discipline. From this perspective psychology becomes significant only to the extent that it helps understand matters of real-world interest.

Again, there is nothing particularly new here. Many psychologists have gravitated in this direction – clinical psychology, educational psychology, and prison psychology are just a few examples. However, what does seem to be missing are systematic discussions of the nature, theory and practice of applied psychology as a major arm of the discipline in its own right. This failure is partly a result of the view that applied psychology rides 'piggy-back' on the broad shoulders of pure psychology 'with its many achievements'. To be sure, there are numerous publications dealing with areas of applied psychology. It is more difficult to find attempts to develop the stature of applied psychology in general. There are even fewer theory-orientated accounts of the process of applying psychology.

Part of the problem is the low standing 'applied' psychology has in the psychological hierarchy. Some of the baggage which the label 'applied psychology' carries needs to be jettisoned. Perhaps a 'compendium' view of applied psychology is that it is the pedestrian, uninspired, atheoretical, empiricist, bread-and-butter, workaday, routine and unadventurous dross of psychology which greater minds have shunned. It is held in contrast to the innovative 'pure' work which 'pushes back the frontiers of knowledge', providing the theoretical, conceptual and inspirational context for lesser psychologists.

This implied hierarchy of psychology and psychologists is not only fundamentally offensive but also counterproductive. One reason is that the applied–pure distinction is evaluative rather than descriptive. It bears sufficient justification for many mainstream academic psychologists to ignore applied research. Given that applied research, so conceived, is real-world psychology, often this has the knock-on effect of clawing out of psychology courses much material which is contextualized in the real world. The net effect is to leave behind a peculiarly abstract or decontextualized psychology which can be so frustrating to those hoping to find in psychology some modest understanding of the world as they experience it, not the world of psychological laboratories and sterile self-critiques or auto-criticisms of psychology.

A far more sophisticated view of the processes involved is presented by Abbott (1981). He discusses some key aspects of professions which allow them to operate in a number of paradoxical ways. While psychology is not specifically his interest, his ideas fit the discipline. The criteria of status are different viewed from *within* a profession than from *outside*. Within the profession factors such as numbers of publications, numbers of research grants, membership of the committees of the professional body, and academic status are largely responsible for determining the status of an individual. However, the public at large is much more inclined to judge psychologists in terms of their caring about people, their success in helping clients and others, and their ability to offer good sound practical advice on day-to-day dilemmas. Abbott's (1981, p. 824) explanation of *intra*professional status is that this reflects the degree of 'professional purity' manifested by the individual:

> By professional purity I mean the ability to exclude nonprofessional issues or irrelevant professional issues from practice. Within a given profession, the highest status professionals are those who deal with issues predigested and predefined by a number of colleagues. These colleagues have removed human complexity and difficulty to leave a problem at least professionally defined, although possibly still very difficult to solve. Conversely, the lowest status professionals are those who deal with problems from which the human complexities are not or cannot be removed.

This 'predigestion' shows itself in psychology as over-concern with the minutiae of self-critical theory rather than as concern with the theory of real people in the real world. The idea of 'professional purity' almost pours out of the argot of psychologists. 'Pure' research, 'messy' data, 'barefooted' empiricism, and getting one's hands dirty in the 'field' are all phrases which relate to cleanliness and purity. They are also reflections of status differentials.

What is the consequence of the strain between public status and intraprofessional status? One obvious outcome is that the training of professionals becomes distanced from those matters which non-psychologists would value. This may well explain why psychology education fails to touch on the real-world issues which the general public would think important for psychologists to have something important to say. It certainly provides justification for psychologists' reluctance to tackle the complexities of social issues relevant research.

The myth of applied psychology

The pure–applied distinction is largely built on a convenient myth, one which is defensive and protective of the discipline. There are many reasons for a pure–applied distinction being ossified in psychology. Some of these will unfold directly or indirectly later in this book. Briefly, however, the major reasons for the apparent overvaluing of pure research relative to applied research may be classified as historical, environmental or epistemological.

Historical reasons have to do with the origins of academic psychology. Many of what Farr (1989) calls the founding fathers of psychology such as Wundt (Klein, 1970) specifically discouraged the application of psychology. They were much more concerned with trying to understand the building blocks of human behaviour and experience. (Notice the assumption that there are such basic elements.) Wundt is generally accepted as being the first 'real' psychologist and is credited with setting up the first psychological laboratory. He is an icon for the mainstream psychology tribe. In 1979 the American Psychological Association went so far as minting a gold medallion bearing Wundt's profile to celebrate the centenary of the first psychology laboratory. This is a remarkably clear statement of what psychology regards itself as being. It is interesting, then, to note that Wundt described psychology as 'an attempt to mark out a new domain of science' (Hothersall, 1990, p. 98).

Exceptions to this early 'rule' that psychology should not seek primarily to be useful included, most importantly, Munsterberg. In the 'founding fathers' tradition, he is dubbed the originator of applied psychology. His activities included psychotherapy, eye-witness psychology, jury decision-making, educational psychology and industrial efficiency. Moskowitz (1977) describes how this vital figure was written down to a few short paragraphs in the classic and seminal history of psychology (Boring, 1950). Boring's history of psychology was important in establishing a framework for succeeding ones. Histories of psychology do not simply serve the function of recounting the story, they serve to define what is important in psychology. Such works are likely to be written by academic psychologists and to serve the needs of those psychologists. Inevitably this means that they will have a bias towards those sorts of research and theory that are preferred and developed by academic psychologists. Howitt *et al.* (1989) describe such histories as having a self-serving function. Histories of the kings and queens of England, by analogy, not only reify the status quo but omit the lives of the labouring classes, thus defining them as insignificant.

Institutional reasons have to do with the early allegiance of much of psychology with the physical and biological sciences rather than the so-called social sciences such as sociology, politics, economics and anthropology. This led psychology, which needed little encouragement, to 'ape' those disciplines in its methods. Of course, it would be unnecessary to assume that early psychologists were unenthusiastic about such an organizational structure. Their interests and proclivities already reached in that direction. Furthermore, attempts to make psychology adopt more worldly concerns (such as the setting up of the Society for the Study of Social Issues in the 1930s) were not welcomed with open arms by the 'establishment' represented by the American Psychological Association of the time (Harris, 1986; Stagnar, 1986).

Epistemological reasons concern the sorts of knowledge that psychologists have traditionally seen as acceptable and the ways in which that knowledge can be legitimately obtained. In psychology, the dominant view for much of the twentieth century has been that the precise elicitation of causal links between one 'variable' and another was the essence of a proper psychological science. 'Indisputable' causal relationships can only be established by the use of the experimental method in which participants in the research are placed at random in either an 'experimental' or 'control' condition. Unfortunately, such an assumption about what constitutes 'good' knowledge effectively excludes much research on real-world issues where causal evidence may be scant or problematic. Furthermore, much is squeezed out which would be helpful in understanding the social world as anything other than rods, cogs and levers in a conglomerate of gigantic machines. Many real-world issues can be illuminated by research with more limited and slightly 'mundane' objectives than the creation of 'grand theories'.

Much of the history of academic psychology would not be significantly caricatured by the above description and analysis. But if we examine the recent history of psychology, there may have been a significant alternative. Typically the rump or tail of psychology has been practitioner branches such as clinical, educational and prison psychology – traditionally regarded as not part of the main body of psychology but as virtually an afterthought. After all, most of the applications of psychology came chronologically after the academic. But there has been a growth of the applied and practitioner segments of psychology such that the tail ought to be increasingly wagging the dog. The broad-brush picture is of a discipline which has at its historic core academia which generally has not favoured practice and has seen itself as separated from it. The role of the academic in this context becomes something of a problem. It might be tempting to suggest that changes need to be made in the academic base to make it serve the needs of the practitioner more closely. But even this is to reinforce the view that psychology is for psychologists.

There is no question that a main function of psychology has to be its provision of understanding and ideas – it is the understanding provided which is in question. That these developments may sometimes be utilized is not a necessary requirement but a bonus. Most theoretical and conceptual work in psychology probably has no role to play in terms of any short-term practical utility. Many major 'psychological enterprises' have benefited only to a very limited extent from theory and conceptualization. For example, the development of the notion of psychological testing (in the form of intelligence testing, aptitude and ability testing, and personality measurement) yielded a multi-million dollar industry especially in the United States in relation, for example, to employee selection. But much of this can be seen as largely atheoretical. Another example is psychotherapy. This has attracted a myriad of different theoretical and conceptual approaches. It is far from clear from research that the effectiveness of therapists is dependent on the particular theory they use. Indeed, differences in therapeutic success may be independent of the theory but highly influenced by the 'healing' characteristics of the therapist (Murphy *et al.*, 1984; Cramer, 1991).

By and large the major 'practical' aspects of psychology involve the use of psychology's empirical methods. The application of theory is less common. It would be to stretch the point to suggest that there is no theoretical input. However, most of this sort of applied psychology proceeds 'perfectly adequately' without significant theoretical inputs. The proliferation of scales for measuring everything seems not to have benefited the search for theory in general.

Practically a good theory

In the repertoire of a good many psychologists, especially those who would not be sullied with real-world matters, is one of the few psychological quotations which sticks in practically everyone's mind. When the going gets a little tough and they are asked to justify their particular branch of academic minutiae, they trot out Kurt Lewin's aphorism 'There's nothing so practical as a good theory' (the origin of which seems lost in the mists of time). Obviously the phrase is not retained in the collective folk-memory of psychologists because of its intrinsic wisdom. More important is its pragmatic function in intellectual self-defence. Indeed, so axiomatic is the quotation that it usually passes unchallenged. However, it is a curious statement which would only be supportable if it could be shown that theory leads to real world action or consequences. The generation of further psychological research or theory is not a criterion of practicality. This would be to equate practicality with the self-interests of psychologists. Though it is one of the criteria of a 'good theory' that it generates more psychology, 'practical' is normally taken to mean something else in this context. If there were any truth in Lewin's aphorism, psychologists would not have to resort to its use. They could cite numerous instances of good theories being put into successful practice. That there are not too many examples of this should somewhat limit claims about the praticality of basic theory.

Sandelands (1990) examines the adage very carefully. At virtually every level it is inadequate. However, it should be mentioned that Lewin himself was no stranger to real-world problems. Much of his psychology developed from that interest and so his notion of practicality may well have been significantly different from the rhetoric of many dyed-in-the-wool academic psychologists. Tongue-in-cheek, Sandelands (1990, p. 259) offers the following amendment to Lewin's original comment: 'There is nothing so practical about theory but it may be good to have around.'

There is some 'humbug' in the distinction between pure and applied psychology. Clearly, some psychology has theory as its main objective.

Equally clearly, other psychology is aimed at being useful to policy-makers, decision-makers and others with things to do or matters to sort out. Where the humbug emerges is in the way in which the ideas 'pure' and 'applied' are construed. The intellectual traffic, so to speak, is seen as from 'pure' to 'applied'. It is assumed that 'pure' research feeds 'applied' research, which gives little in return. Potter (1982) writes of an 'ideology of application', taking his conceptual framework from more general social studies of science, not merely psychology. The ideology of application, he says

> is intended to suggest the intimate relation held in scientific cultures to exist between science and technology ... The very language for talking about science encourages these assumptions about the supposed connection between science and utility. What scientists do is said to 'have application in the real world'; bridges and non-stick frying pans are seen to be the 'products' of science. Structurally this ideology suggests a continuum of research from 'pure' to 'applied' with knowledge 'flowing' from one end to the other.
>
> (Potter, 1982, p. 24)

Potter's research evidence shows that there is little utilization of 'basic theory' in at least one area of applied psychology (social skills training) despite it being an area originating ostensibly out of basic theory. Probably other research areas are much the same. But a further concern emerges with the 'ideology of application'. This will probably come as little surprise to most psychologists working in applied fields. But research has shown that mainstream academic psychology fails to inform their research – in terms of theory, concepts, and even substantial findings. It is a failure that has been pointed out frequently (Hovland, 1954, is a classic example from mass communications research). As a consequence, the lack of acknowledgement that the so-called applied areas of psychology are potentially fruitful ground for research and theory is worrying.

So the myth of applied psychology is that it is the application of basic knowledge. It seems not to be. While technology may be seen as the product of applying physical science research, however erroneous that view may be in practice, applied psychology does not normally seek to produce 'hardware' or socio-technologies. Often what is 'erroneously' called applied psychology generates something less tangible – knowledge or under-standing. Usually nothing happens with the output. There is no simple link between the research and creating social change. Typically no such link was intended by the reseachers. While the use of the term 'applied' in these cases may seem inappropriate, it is the curious misnomer given by the psycho-logical community following the 'science' model. We will see that psy-chologists actually mean 'real-life' research as opposed to laboratory research when they mention applied psychology.

Hardware, of course, is sometimes the output of applied psychology – the fields of attitude, personality, intelligence, aptitude, selection, and other forms of testing and assessment have as their main objective the generation of marketable hardware. Notice that here the traffic between pure and applied is largely the reverse of expectations – that is, the testing movement generates formal theory from the hardware, not the other way round. Of course, ideas about the nature of intelligence may be generated from non-applied sources. These, certainly in the case of intelligence testing, inform the process of test construction, but the linkages are generally weak.

It is not the intention to argue that applied psychology is completely synonymous with the term 'real-world' psychology. Indeed, much of what passes for applied psychology says nothing about the real world but deals with, for example, nitty-gritty niceties of measuring grossly abstracted concepts which have no bearing on usable realities. It would appear, then, that there is a second myth of applied psychology: that applied psychology is applicable. It typically is not.

Types of applied psychology

The broad distinction between pure and applied research held in psychology is based on the belief that the former moulds and directs the latter. The blue skies of pure research providing 'hope and inspiration' for the grey, workaday world of applied psychology. This view not only lacks insight but also does great disservice to the potential of applied psychology. In this section some of the varieties of psychology will be discussed in order to refine somewhat our understanding of applied research. It should be made clear from the outset that there is no generally accepted scheme for categorizing different sorts of psychology. Consequently, the framework outlined is a mixture of interpretation of the trends and additional suggestions which might be useful ways of looking at the uses of psychology.

Several different types of psychology need to be described. They reflect different aspects of the pure–applied distinction and elaborate some of the different objectives of psychology. They are not rigidly differentiable categories but they do point applied research in a number of different directions. The types are: pure or basic research; applied psychology; social policy research; social problems research; social issues research; practitioner psychology; and socio-technologies. No one could pretend that there are rigid boundaries between these different types of research, so some fuzziness can be expected at the dividing lines.

In order to give some substance to these abstract categories, each one will be illustrated by reference to an important example. Because relatively little research has been carried out on the pre-menstrual syndrome (PMS) or pre-menstrual tension (Phillips and Bedeian, 1989; see also Kitzinger, 1989b), this is a good instance of a research area which potentially might be approached from the point of view of the different types of psychology. PMS is stated by 20–40 per cent of women to bring about mental or physical incapacitation and is associated with lowering of productivity at work and absenteeism through illness.

Pure or basic research. This is viewed as research which is untainted by 'application'. Indeed, it is something of an anathema to some psychologists that questions of applicability are raised in connection with their work. Genuine examples of where the findings or the theories derived from basic research in psychology are taken and applied to 'real-life' settings through a process of 'research and development' are rare. There are examples, such as the application of basic research on memory to foreign language learning (see, for example, Gruneberg, 1987a; 1987b) or the use of learning theory in the management of therapeutic communities and institutions (Ayllon and Azrin, 1968; Kazdin, 1977), but more often gross over-generalizations from laboratory research are made about real-world events without further research evaluation. It might be a not too fair description to suggest that basic research in psychology is really the psychology of decontextualized settings. In other words, often what is meant by basic research is laboratory research.

Taking our example of PMS, pure or basic research might examine the relationship between sex hormone levels and the extent of the condition.

Applied psychology. It might not be too mischievous to suggest that applied psychology differs from basic psychology only to the extent that it attempts to deal with contextualized settings of the real world. It is rarely the application of basic research and theory. What seems to be applied are the *methods* of psychological research rather than psychological findings. The objective of applied psychology seems to be the generation of real-life theory and knowledge. So, for example, organizational psychology, clinical psychology, and consumer psychology largely appear to be independent of basic psychology.

Applied psychology might investigate how women manage interpersonal relations in the workplace during the pre-menstrual period.

Social policy research. This is a variety of applied psychology but with the specific primary objective of informing the choices of decision-makers. The goals of policy research are in the ideal case totally contextualized by the needs of the policy-maker. A bad example of policy research would be if a research team were asked to investigate means of reducing 'glue sniffing' through educational interventions. To carry out research which, say, demonstrated that structural unemployment and related problems of the capitalist system were causal might be worthless in this context as the policy-maker might be unable to effect any change to the political system.

In the case of PMS, it might be useful to managers and others to know whether the introduction of flexible working times would reduce women's absenteeism in the pre-menstrual period.

Social problems research. This is another sort of applied research, which can be conceived as casting light on matters which are *consensually* defined as ones which society should both address and understand better. The shared feeling that something has to be done is critical. It may well be that there is a broad societal consensus as to what the outcome ought to be – but the means of achieving this or the extent of the problem might be unknown. Instances of such research might include football hooliganism, inner-city riots, illiteracy, AIDS, discrimination in employment, and so forth. It has to be acknowledged that the consensus is in terms of dominant groups in society.

Taking our PMS example, social problems research might look at whether child abuse is commoner in the pre-menstrual period than at other times.

Social issues research. The major significant difference between social issues and social problems research is that the former lacks the consensuality which applies to the latter. Significant differences of opinion are an essential component. In other words, there has to be controversy among substantially opposed views prominent in the community before the description 'social issue' is appropriate. Examples of social issues would then have to include abortion, the death penalty for murder, working mothers, divorce, interracial adoption, suicide/euthanasia, and pornography.

Social issues researchers might be keen to investigate whether PMS significantly affects women's ability to make considered judgements. Any such link would obviously have significant implications for women's promotion prospects. As yet, women in managerial positions remains a controversial area.

Practitioner psychology. Many psychologists work in settings for which research input is often inappropriate or unavailable. As a consequence they develop their own working hypotheses and practices which enable them to function in their work as counsellors, advisers, therapists, trainers, and the like. This is obviously not systematic knowledge and is rarely discussed seriously in the psychological literature.

As for our example, a psychologist may help women with pre-menstrual problems by counselling them on stress management using *ad hoc* procedures.

Socio-technologies. A psychologist might use technologies based remotely on psychological knowledge in dealing with practical problems. Biofeedback apparatus could be used, for example, as a means of identifying and possibly coping with PMS-related stress.

None of these represents a preferred approach to psychology. The classification merely shows the range of different styles of psychology which may be adopted. It should be emphasized again that rigid boundaries between each of these do not exist.

Concluding comments

It was not the intention of this introductory chapter to dismiss the contributions made by academic psychology as useless to psychology. One reason why this should be so is that basic psychology may well supply the sorts of understanding of people which promote interest in psychology. But, unfortunately, it would be ridiculous to pretend that the overwhelming bulk of psychological research and theory has much value. Sometimes the fate of research and theory is sealed not so much by its intrinsic worth but by whether it is picked out and used by the psychological community (or others). The factors which determine this may be the result of the professional structure of psychology rather than the requirements of the discipline itself. The contention of this chapter is that too often psychology avoids tackling important topics in a useful manner because of the premium placed on certain types of approach – particularly pure research with limited or no social contextualization.

Nothing in this suggests that basic or pure research does not have a role to play. What might be questioned is whether or not significant amounts of basic or pure research are ever applied to important issues and problems. Certainly, there is no simple relationship between basic and applied research, but one might ask what sorts of relationships there might be. Six algorithms come to mind to suggest actual or feasible processes. They are:

1   *Basic becomes applied*: The 'classic' relationship in which basic research is taken and put to some sort of 'practical' use.
2   *Applied is basic*: This is the situation in which the development of fundamental psychological theory and research stems from investigations in real-world situations. In other words, the emphasis on decontextualized research is abandoned in favour of developing a fundamental psychology which does not depend on laboratory experiments or obscure questions on a self-completion questionnaire, for example.
3 · *Applied interrogates basic*: In order to question, to extend and to verify applied research and theory, the adequacy of applied research may be established by examining basic research to see the extent to which it lends support for the interpretation based on applied research. Basic research can never *prove* the applied, but it can help examine its adequacy.

4   *Basic interrogates applied*: The reverse of the above. Basic research can
     be extended by examining applied research.
5   *Applied ignores basic*: This hardly calls for elaboration.
6   *Basic ignores applied*: Again, self-explanatory.

There would seem to be a need to take the arguments and ideas of this
chapter and seek what needs to change to enable a fully-fledged applied
psychology which has a degree of sophistication about the world it wants
to embrace.

A danger exists of writing of the pure–applied distinction as if it is
problematic for psychologists when, in point of fact, it is uncontroversial.
While many psychologists might have few difficulties with any of the
points made in this chapter, this is far from true of all psychologists. One
way of demonstrating the reality of the issue is to quote a brief excerpt from
a report on the future of psychology. Not only does this show the reluctance
to forage in applied areas but graphically illustrates the entrenched
arguments:

> The shift towards applied research causes anxiety in some psychol-
> ogists. … [O]ne participant stated the anxieties about applied work
> most strongly. First, because of the way academic departments are
> funded, he claimed applied research could only be carried out at the
> expense of pure research. Second, he knew of little evidence that
> scientific advance arises out of attempts to solve 'real-world' problems.
> Third, pure and applied research, he said, require a 'rather different
> mentality … it is not particularly easy to switch from one to the
> other'. Our ability to do fundamental research would thus be affected
> in the long term. Fourth, without fundamental research, there would
> be a dearth of knowledge to apply. Finally, when it is realised that we
> are not using specifically psychological expertise in solving real-
> world problems, we will find it more difficult to secure funding for
> fundamental research on such topics as object recognition or language
> understanding. He found the claim that no distinction could be made
> between pure and applied research 'incomprehensible'. His main
> contention was that the solution of real-world problems did not
> produce an atmosphere conducive to theoretical advance. This would
> ultimately damage psychology.
>   (British Psychological Society, 1988, p. 20)

It would be useful to close one's eyes and picture this psychologist, then
wonder what he might say of succeeding chapters in this book.

2

OBSTACLES TO AND OPPORTUNITIES FOR PROGRESS

Thousands of researchers down the years have started on projects they really believed in, and which embodied ideas they really cared about. But too often these projects got pared down and chopped about and falsified in the process of getting approval, and the researchers have ended their research soured and disappointed and hurt or cynical. It doesn't have to be this way. Research doesn't have to be another brick in the wall. It is obscene to take a young researcher who actually wants to know more about people, and divert them into manipulating 'variables', counting 'behaviours', observing 'responses' and all the rest of the ways in which people are falsified and fragmented.

(Reason and Rowan, 1981, p. xxiii)

Understanding the nature of dominant forms of psychology aids appreciation of the difficulties psychologists have dealing with significant and socially relevant matters. Obstacles to psychology's progress can be crudely construed as *internal*, that is, to do with the nature of the discipline itself; or *external*, to do with the wider society's acceptance of psychology. No assumption is made that these are mutually exclusive categories: the discipline and society are interactive such that there are no absolute divisions between the discipline of psychology and society of which it is part. This chapter concentrates on the internal factors which hamper progress; some of the wider social factors affecting psychology are taken up in Chapter 8. In some ways, the internal obstacles are the most crucial. It is they which prevent the development of a fully-fledged, worldly psychology. That society might ignore or deride this psychology is less directly influential, though it clearly would be an obstacle to the utilization of psychological knowledge. Furthermore, external factors may restrict the funding of psychology but unless psychology gets its own house in order then these may be irrelevant.

Central to the problems of generating a real-world psychology is the belief that psychology is a science akin to physics and chemistry. Associated with this is the view that there are 'natural laws' which govern human activity. 'Discovering' these laws becomes the major task facing psychology for those who hold the discipline to be a 'science'. While any number of critiques have effectively rebutted this idea, it would be to over-state the case to suggest that psychology has been radically reformulated as a consequence. Perhaps fewer psychologists nowadays admit to seeking for 'natural' laws, but since many still adhere to fundamentally decontextualized sorts of psychology the basic framework remains in place. Attempts to make general statements about human activity from research which excludes the vicissitudes of the real world are tantamount to seeking invariant laws. One simply does not know the circumstances in which these general statements apply, and as a consequence they are treated as universals. A glance at most psychology journals demonstrates the retention of the laboratory experiment as the central methodology. Its pre-eminence is not dependent on its utility in understanding the real world. It is valuable, though, in eliciting cause-and-effect sequences. In other words, the extensiveness of the use of experiments is dependent on the degree to which they help generate 'psychological laws'. That general laws seem to have largely eluded generations of psychologists is irrelevant – experiments having long since generated their own momentum.

So long as experimental psychologists are 'as happy as pigs in muck', what harm do their laboratory games do? Probably very little – so long as defining the objectives, qualities, means and style of psychology is deemed trivial. But they are important. Not surprisingly, there is some pressure to change the face of psychology, exerted mainly from within the discipline.

Psychology and its discontents

Psychology has rarely been short of critics within its ranks (see, for example, Hudson, 1972; Riegel, 1978; Sarason, 1981). Sometimes such criticism has a hint of career posturing in that the arguments turn out to be claims for the ascendance of a particular sort of psychology. That these are equally fiercely questioned by other caucuses is only to be expected. Many of the complaints about psychology fail to articulate an impressive alternative to mainstream psychology that actually undermines that mainstream. Social psychology, which might be expected to generate much of social relevance, is particularly prone to these sorts of critique. Here, rather than being the product of a mature reflection of a lifetime spent in research, often the authors are the young Turks wailing prayers for the smiting apart of psychology. Usually the demand is for a reorientation of social psychology – but in their own image.

An example of a harsh critic of social psychology is Parker (1989), who diagnoses its 'malaise' by claiming that it should be what it apparently is not:

Social psychology should be about changes in the real world. It should also though, be concerned with how people can collectively *change* the order of things for themselves. Unfortunately, social psychology as an academic institution is structured in such a way as to blot out what is most interesting about social interaction (language, power, and history) and to divert attention from efforts to de-construct its oppressive functions in a practical way. This is partly why social psychology deservedly gets such a bad press.

(Parker, 1989, p. 1)

Egocentric as this is, the tone sets social psychology at the hub of society and distinctly over-states the case for the discipline. Why concentrate on change? Do people not successfully change the order of things for themselves without the help of psychologists? – which is in marked contrast to psychologists who seem incapable of changing themselves. Do social psychologists not collectively know an awful lot about language and power, if not of history? What prevents Parker from 'de-constructing' social psychology's oppressive functions in a practical way? And who has read much about social psychology anywhere but in social psychology textbooks? Just what does he want to achieve and why does he not get on with it?

It is easy to sympathize with Parker in abstract. After all, he expresses an ideological commitment to a psychology which does something *for* the real world. Unfortunately, his position tends to be a narcissistic engorgement on 'theoretical' postures which lead to much the same sort of inwardly looking psychology as the empiricists he tilts his lance against. The tone can be made readily apparent from skimming the subjects in his index. The *r*s have, starting well, racism followed by rationality, realism, mundane realism, reflexivity, reification, reified universe, relativism, representation, repression, resistance, rhetoric, rules, rules for radicals, and Russia. The balance is clearly an odd one for a 'real-world' psychology: the 'real world' involved seems to be mainly that of the academic psychologist. Overall, it is nothing more than standard 'critical' social psychological theorizing. But such conceptual obsessions, while being needed, are only useful to a real-world psychology if they generate or help generate such a psychology. Confined to the domain of theory alone they provide little of much significance.

Few modern applied psychologists would have much difficulty in accepting Parker's 'rules for radicals'. Nevertheless, these warrant some attention as they aim to help generate a new sort of psychology. Paraphrasing, plagiarizing and clarifying, some of his 'rules' are as follows:

1   All 'facts' are culturally and historically specific and should be guarded against. Presenting such ideas as facts enables them to serve as deceptions.
2   Social facts cannot be found or discovered as they are best described as inventions.

3   Radical researchers need to think about who they want to help politically
     and to formulate appropriate research goals.
4   Disbelieve points made in writings which are supported by lots of
     reference citations as these are essentially a smokescreen.
5   Ask yourself what the practical effects of the work are on the ability of
     the oppressed to address political issues.
6   Evaluate the findings of research in terms of their likely effects, not in
     terms of what they say.

Unfortunately, the rules for 'radical psychology' do not offer much which
could not improve non-radical psychology if by that we mean establishment-
orientated psychology. Phrases like the state, the establishment, the middle
classes and the like could be substituted in place of Parker's references to
the oppressed. Parker's rules would then be generally applicable and
perhaps beneficial.

A further difficulty is inherent in the question which of the oppressed
would wish the support of radical psychologists. Perhaps the establishment-
orientated psychologist would hold more appeal. Parker is tellingly short
of examples of radical initiatives taken by psychologists. In his single
example, he claims that after the Mexico City earthquake

> the work teams facilitating the reconstruction of the community
> found themselves having to make political choices about *whose* power
> would be deconstructed, and whose power would be developed. In
> cases like these, the political role of the 'researcher' starts to dissolve
> her identity as 'social psychologist': the whole history and political
> function of the discipline starts to unravel.
>
> (Parker, 1989, p. 154)

Whatever else may be said of this apparently key case study, our Mexico
City radical psychologist seems to be in the driving seat. She is making the
decisions leaving some of the recipients of this treatment possibly feeling
somewhat more oppressed! Now they have radical psychologists making
choices for them!

Those seeking a better understanding of real-world psychology might
justifiably feel impatient with both camps – the radical 'chic' with their noses
glued to the minutiae of theory and the 'oppressive' traditionalists with their
horizons limited to the laboratory floor. Collectively, feet cemented in the
same concrete block, they slog out a repetitive battle. The failure of Parker
to come up with the 'goods' is not for want of important real-life issues in
the psychological literature. It is for want of concern that theory should grow
out of real life. In other words, one might wish to be wary of the intellectual 'games' of both the traditional camp and their critics. There is 'fun' to
be had with both approaches. However, siding with either side does little
to facilitate the usefulness of psychology.

Others have dealt with their discontent in a rather different way. For some, the trappings of psychology are indicative of the malaise they find. For Kline (1988, p. 132), much of psychology is simply boring and lacking real interest: 'Most psychology is more powerful than [the sedative] Mogadon.' This is not due to an absence of intellectual curiosity on Kline's part. It is psychology's pretence to being a science pushing back the frontiers of knowledge, shoulder to shoulder with physics, biology and chemistry, which creates the conditions for a largely failed psychology. Abandonment of this approach in favour of something somewhat different (but naturally not too much so) would solve the problem:

> a change in the education and training of psychologists, [to] a nice blend of humanity and science, ... could revitalize the subject and allow powerful investigation of what was truly human. However, at present the panoply of science reigns. Until the voice is heard throughout the land proclaiming that the glorious colours of experimental psychology are but the emperor's new clothes, there will be no progress and psychology will remain ... of interest only to its practitioners.
>
> (Kline, 1988, p. 154)

Again what Kline offers would not be disputed by many – if it were regarded as a complaint against much of what is found in psychology journals.

Westland (1978) expresses a viewpoint on the 'usefulness' issue built on a similar sort of premiss to Kline's. He points out an important difference between psychology and the 'hard sciences' which some expect it to emulate. Normally people in day-to-day life have no view about the issues involved in scientific questions. Not only are people-in-the-street unable to express a point of view on sub-atomic physics, but even those with doctorates in physics are unaffected in their everyday lives by, say, Einstein's Theory of Relativity. Psychologists, though, compete for their subject matter with everybody. Everyone has theories and views, some certainly mistaken, which help them deal with others. For Westland (1978, p. 15):

> If psychology did nothing more than provide negative tests of the wild generalizations we are all prone to, it would serve a valuable function. When in the right mood I derive considerable amusement from a type of encounter which occurs only too frequently: having to listen to someone attacking psychology on grounds such as 'You can't make generalizations about human nature' and 'Human behaviour is unpredictable', only to hear the same person make dogmatic statements about women drivers or university students or black Americans.

Westland (1978, p. 16) goes on to make a rather more formal statement of what this might mean in relation to psychology and the outcome of its stance on the 'science' issue:

(1) ... since the ethos of science is that scientific ideas must be empirically testable and not merely matters of opinion, the scientific pretensions of psychology ... may have done more good in clarifying thinking through *critical reaction* than through substantive achievement.

(2) ... systematic ideas which are unproven, unprovable, or for that matter in some sense plainly wrong, can have value in that they provide a descriptive language which again helps to clarify thinking by offering a means of communication which did not exist before.

These suggestions have largely been neglected but warrant inclusion in any serious discussion of psychology and social issues. Although Westland makes his case in relation to the views of individuals, it is probably more important in relation to more general social knowledge. Groups and organizations frequently operate with collectively shared 'theories' about the nature of people and human activity – for example, that the unemployed do not really want to work, that children need a mother at home, and that women cannot do certain types of job are all theoretical formulations which could be put to empirical test. For psychology to be able to disconfirm some of these may be more valuable than finding trivial laws of human nature.

Positivism

Positivism is essentially the posture of 'hard science' which seeks the same sort of activities aimed at discovering 'laws' in psychology as in the physical sciences. Just what is the problem with the search for universal laws through methods akin to those of physics and chemistry? One would not seriously doubt the success of these disciplines, so why not follow their methods? This approach was adopted readily by the expanding discipline of psychology, especially during the early part of the twentieth century.

John Paull (1980) reports eavesdropping on a conversation between God and an Earthling on the 'laws' of human behaviour. The Earthling clearly has absorbed a smattering of psycho-think and demonstrates a willingness verbally to cross swords with God about human nature. Towards the end of an object lesson in the nature of scientific laws, the following exchange takes place:

Earthling: But surely your very existence implies the existence of laws. I cannot conceive of a God without laws.

God: You mistake the limitations of your imagination for limitations of the universe.

Earthling: You mean you have not imposed laws on the universe?

God: That is for Me alone to know. For yourself, the
              existence of natural laws cannot be established
              empirically owing to (a) the lack of precision in
              measuring instruments, and (b) your lack of free
              access to the time dimension. What pass for laws in
              the sciences are inventions – human artifacts ... The
              world is created so that My laws and hence Myself
              cannot be accessed through reason ... I am perfectly
              just. It would not be equitable for Me to be knowable
              through reason – since under that circumstance those
              with superior reasoning ability would be advantaged.
              Now on the other hand, any imbecile can have faith.
                                              (Paull, 1980, p. 1083)

Psychologists are taught to have faith. They need the world to be orderly
and human activity similarly so. They must be a little circumspect nowadays
about talking as if laws of human behaviour existed, but scratch the surface
and the science ideology seeps through.

What are we to make of God's comments? Even if they are merely the
product of John Paull's fertile mind, they still deserve careful consideration.
They contain elements which the Earthling psychologist should have
understood better than apparently he/she did. If it is not for us to know
whether natural laws govern human activity, too much is at stake to act as
if they did. To seek non-existent laws wastes time. God is adamant that
scientific laws are scientists' laws – it is God's avowed strategy not to
reveal whether or not they are His laws! It is not for mere Earthlings to try
to reveal to God that which He knows already. Thus the only laws seekable
are people's laws. Put this way, psychology's search to discover the laws
of behaviour loses much of its (professionally imposed) 'common-sense'
wholesomeness. Can we really sustain an enthusiasm for positivism if we
are, at best, dealing with understanding made by humans for humans?

Heather (1976, p. 13) gives a simple description of 'positivism': 'a broadly
defined movement in the history of man's [sic] intellectual development,
the distinguishing feature of which is *the attempt to apply to the affairs of man
the methods and principles of the natural sciences'*. But which methods and
principles of the natural sciences? It has been argued (Bevan, 1980) that from
the various ways in which psychology could have developed as a science,
just one became the norm. Not only this; so powerful is professional socialization that it became the norm among those who could not even put a name
to it. It can be described as the Cartesian (after the French philosopher
Descartes) philosophy of science:

   the goal of science is the valid conceptualization of Nature on a grand
   scale. The proper strategy for success is the all-consuming commitment
   of the individual mind. From this perspective comes a whole set of

specific attitudes that define ... the Cartesian scientist's relationship
to work, to colleagues, and to the nonscientific public and its institutions ... Doing science is like running a race, and one's colleagues
in the field can therefore only be viewed as strong competitors.
Science is ... a *consumption good* to be pursued because it is intrinsically worthwhile ... The search for Truth takes precedence over all
other considerations; therefore science is inevitably ethically neutral.
Finally, the public is perceived as having only one role, that of patron
... It can – indeed, it should – provide financial support, but must
otherwise stay clear of the enterprise.

(Bevan, 1980, pp. 779–80)

So close is this description to the 'B movie' scientist that it rings true to
one's own personal conceptions. Images of the world may have many and
varied origins. So much of a stereotype is Bevan's description that it is
tempting to assume its value as a social totem. Paull's God would surely
recognize the Cartesian scientist. Such 'science' is founded on the belief that
there is a true 'nature' which is knowable. However, the Cartesian image
of science encourages selfishness. If the only master is the scientist then the
scientist is the master. In other words, it is a model which allows the
unfettered quest for knowledge – doing what one chooses without any social
obligation. The danger is, of course, that it generates personal intellectual
interests with little social worth. Psychology becomes largely the enterprise
of enhancing one's status over others choosing a similar route through
academic life.

There is an alternative to the Cartesian view which was available to early
psychologists. In Francis Bacon's conception of the role of science:

Science is viewed as a social enterprise, a cooperative activity within
a professional community marked by a clear-cut division of labor but
bound by a single shared altruistic commitment to the promotion of
human welfare. Thus, in this view science is ... an *investment good*. It
has no intrinsic social value, but gains value only as its outcomes give
rise to beneficial application. This is the view predominantly held by
nonacademic scientists. It is also the reason most often advanced for
the public support of academic science.

(Bevan, 1980, pp. 780–1)

Duty to the community, then, is at the heart of this rather than the faith that
there is a permanent reality to be discovered. Bacon's science was neither
for the sake of knowledge alone nor for big research grants to secure rapid
personal advancement. The promotion of human welfare was foremost.
Now there is something subversive about this. After all, how many academic
books and papers can be churned out a year if an eye is kept on their
relevance for human welfare? Psychology's choice of scientific models to

emulate was not arbitrary and maximized the discipline's self-serving potential. Certainly a Baconian approach would have substantially altered the nature of psychology.

There are salutory lessons for psychologists committed to the Cartesian model of science. These are found in the literature on social studies of psychology. Psychology can be investigated as a social system using the methods of the social sciences, much as the organization any other profession can be explored. It would be expected that if knowledge for its own sake were so highly valued then the latest paper by Professor Jones of Harvard University should cause anticipatory flutters of excitement in the hearts of the scientific community. Like the audiences for the latest Dick Francis or Jackie Collins novel, should not the intellectual jaws of psychologists be chomping on each and every morsel of knowledge, picking the bones clean and then sucking on the marrow? The cruel truth is that few seem to care very much. The majority of scientific publications have only a very small readership (Mahoney, 1976).

Williams (1988, pp. 12–13) discusses the nature of psychology as a science in the following characteristically witty fashion:

> A separate issue again is whether psychology is a Science with a capital 's' or in other words whether it belongs with the Faculty of Science rather than Social Science. The expression 'social science' itself suggests the word 'science' is not wholly antipathetic. In collocations it may be acceptable, so long as social science is not necessarily mere qualified science (qualified by being 'social'). A Bombay duck is a fish and not a duck. Even whether social science is predominantly social or predominantly science is open to question. It is certainly not necessarily 'science: social'; a blind Venetian is not the same as a Venetian blind.

In other words, caution is appropriate as to what sort of discipline psychology considers itself to be. Often it seems that being 'scientific' is the final *objective* rather than a means to another goal. Surely the purpose of psychology is understanding people in society better rather than understanding how to apply science better.

Varieties of psychologist

Not all psychology follows the model of the experimental, laboratory-based, people-phobic writer of hard-nosed books and journal articles. Kimble (1984) claims that there are two cultures in psychology, differing essentially along a continuum from tough-mindedness to tender-mindedness. Put into psychologese, the difference is between the scientific and the humanistic. The different groupings of psychologists emphasize rather different values and priorities. This difference in their beliefs about how psychological understanding develops led Kimble to invent the *epistemic differential*. This is a technique for differentiating those who would like humanity in a test-tube from those choked with terminal understandingness. He presents an example of an item from the scale. One merely chooses which of the two statements best approximates one's position:

> All behaviour is caused by physical, physiological, or experiential variables. In principle it is possible to discover exact laws relating even individual behaviour to these variables. Behaviour is understandable, predictable, controllable.

> The concept of causality probably does not apply to behaviour. There is nothing lawful about behaviour except perhaps at the level of statistical averages. Even in principle, behaviour must be regarded as incomprehensible, unpredictable, and beyond control.
> (Kimble, 1984, p. 835)

The most useful parts of the scale consist of six items. These are:

Scientific values – human values
Determinism – indeterminism
Objectivism – intuitionism
Laboratory investigation – field study
Nomothetic – idiographic
Elementism – holism

Determinism is the view that human behaviour follows natural laws; objectivism means relying on clear data rather than feelings or intuitions; nomothetic means that psychological findings concern aggregates of people; idiographic is about the understanding of an individual as an individual; and elementism is breaking people into small elements rather than looking at the total person. The scientifically orientated psychologist tends to agree with the left-hand side of the above six dimensions, the humanistically orientated psychologist with the right.

Kimble found that the scale differentiated between the memberships of various of the then American Psychological Association divisions – broadly speaking members of the Division of Experimental Psychology appeared strongly scientific, members of the Society for the Study of Social Issues tended to be somewhat centrally placed, and psychotherapists and humanistic psychologists on the side of humanism, as one might expect. Things, though, are a little less straightforward than this:

> One one dimension, determinism verus indeterminism, the opinions of all groups of psychologists are in the deterministic direction; the differences are differences in the extremeness with which different groups hold this view. In the case of objectivism versus intuitionism,

... [members of the Society for the Study of Social Issues,] who usually side with the humanists, are on the scientist end of the scale. In still another, data versus theory, the psychotherapists ... join the psychologists interested in social issues and take a stand opposed to that of the experimentalists, who are now in the same camp as the humanistic psychologists.

(Kimble, 1984, p. 838)

But despite these differences, probably of greatest significance was the consensus in the views of psychologists. In particular, *all* of the groups polarized towards determinism. They merely varied in terms of the extremity of the view, not the view itself. Whatever else this implies, there is more than a hint that psychology either socializes its members well to 'proper' thinking or that it chooses the 'right' people in the first place.

Blocks to change

Kline (1988) asks an important, naive question: 'Why do experimental psychologists continue with their work?' This is not the same as asking whether psychology in general is worthwhile. Rather it deals with the usefulness of particular 'scientific' methods in understanding human nature. Unfortunately, half of his answer to his own question is somewhat banal. The prestige generally given to science and technology in Western nations, he suggests, is responsible. But he fails to explain why some succumb to its attractions and others are left relatively cold by it. His second argument is more interesting, perhaps, because it is a psychologist's psychologizing on the psychologies of psychologists:

People in touch with their feelings would hardly be attracted by a discipline which avowedly, in some of its emanations, denies the notion of feelings or at least minimizes their importance ... [T]he type of people who are attracted into experimental psychology make it inevitable that the subject remains as mathematical and precise as it is possible to make it and hence will eschew all those topics which do not easily submit themselves to such treatment and especially those whose emotionality is likely to create anxiety.

(Kline, 1988, p. 26)

Kline's view is that such psychologists need to deny their feelings. While it may well be the case that psychology has its fair share of emotional misfits, surely not all are the same? One can think of examples of psychologists with emotional problems and even one professor of psychology who committed arson in his maturity. However, none of these is the norm. Built into Kline's views, though, is an important paradox. Although researchers in other disciplines may use 'scientific' methods in order to get closer to their subject matter, psychologists use them to avoid getting close to theirs! Mathematically based theory and precise measurement make it possible to know the physical universe better. The existence of some planets, red dwarfs, and the like is only known to us because of this approach. In psychology, the use of 'scientific' methods has left some psychologists no more aware of human psychology than are the passengers on the apocryphal Clapham omnibus.

While sympathetic to Kline's hopes for a better psychology, his analysis of psychology is constrained by typical psychological thinking. It is to stretch disbelief past the snapping-point of incredulity to suggest that psychologists are warped personalities needing to avoid the stress of the emotions which dealing with people would bring, but at the same time basking in the adulation that the Western world has for science. So what are the reasons why experimental psychologists continue with their work?

Productivity may be one reason. Psychologists, particularly academic psychologists, are subject to pressures to increase output – usually in the form of more publications and more research grants. This is obviously to encourage psychologists to stick with a 'winning formula' which helps them meet productivity criteria irrespective of the benefits of the work to the community. Working in the community may be much more time-consuming than running groups of subjects through the laboratory. That is, unless, of course, one uses the ubiquitous self-completion questionnaire to generate vast tracts of data for multiple publications. Also, it should be remembered that work submitted for publication is reviewed by peers committed to the psychological approach. This clearly encourages 'keeping in line'.

Professional socialization may be a second reason. No one expects a person growing up in Birmingham, England or Alabama, to emerge from the process as a Zulu warrior. Consequently, one should not expect people taking a psychology degree to emerge untouched by the 'culture' of psychology. One would expect them to absorb, often uncritically, many of the typical characteristics of psychologists – one of many obvious reasons being that success on psychology degree courses is partly contingent on 'learning all one's lessons' well. One university teacher puts it this way:

> Perhaps we should reflect on organisational cultures, on the messages they transmit about values and attitudes. To what extent do the ways in which we do things project to the students what they think we think is a good student? Not only in the ways in which we teach, or in the communications we transmit, explicitly and implicitly, but in our relationships with them? What are the implicit standards in the organisation, the hidden agenda of rewards, the valued behaviours and beliefs?

> (Gale, 1990, p. 485)

No doubt further reasons could be added. The important matter, though, is that the self-reproducing cycle needs to be broken at some point. How to achieve this is not clear but certain challenges to the classic psychological approaches ought to be promoted to give them greater currency in the psychological community. One approach, social constructionism, is particularly apposite as it provides both a firm contrast and a means of understanding traditional psychology.

The social constructionist approach

Adopting a radically different perspective to positivism, the social constructionist approach offers a great deal of value to the psychology of social issues. Crucially important is that it rejects the idea of natural laws governing behaviour and thought, and positivism in general. The idea that knowledge is uncovered as in an archeological dig is dismissed in favour of the view that knowledge is created or constructed. Consequently, knowledge builds not in a cumulative fashion but in terms of the social forces which demand its creation.

In psychology, the social constructionists have tended to ride piggy-back on traditional research approaches. This is because constructionism is an approach to 'accounting' for knowledge in general. As such, it is as applicable to the understanding of 'scientific' knowledge as any other forms of knowledge. Social constructionism finds fault with many of the assumptions of traditional science. Not surprisingly, then, these traditional views become an object of scrutiny by constructionists. Inevitably, constructionists substitute questions about the nature of knowledge for the traditional positivist problem of finding methodologies which reveal 'truth' or 'facts'. When Gergen (1982, p. 57) wrote that 'Science is itself a lifeform that impinges on other domains of human activity', he perhaps hinted at the necessity of social constructionist concerns about 'scientific' knowledge.

However, not all constructionist and related critiques take 'science' as their substance. An excellent example of how the nature of understanding can be reconstructed comes in Szasz's (1986) discussion of suicide. How suicide is construed does not depend on the nature of the act. Killing oneself has a bearing on a number of different social institutions which might have a vested interest in it. Notice how in the following extract 'science' eventually becomes involved in the social understanding of suicide:

> the end of the Enlightenment – roughly the year 1800 – marks a dramatic change in the perception of suicide. Before that time, suicide was considered to be both a sin and a crime for which the actor was responsible; since then, suicide has increasingly been regarded as a manifestation of madness for which the actor is not responsible ... A

man named Jean Baptiste who killed himself in 1765, was punished by having his corpse tied to the back of a cart and dragged to the public square, where it was hung upside down from the scaffold for 24 hours. Another man, named André Sauvinien, who killed himself in 1752, was sentenced to similar degradations as well as to the seizure of all of his property. Probably because of the latter penalty, Sauvinien's family succeeded in having the superior council of the colony overturn the sentence on the ground that Sauvinien was insane when he killed himself.

(Szasz, 1986, p. 806)

According to Szasz, suicide is nowadays largely conceived as a mental abnormality or a symptom of illness. We are left with an anomalous conceptualization of suicide which leaves it in a no man's land which makes the rational discussion difficult. He asks a number of questions:

If suicide is 'bad' because it injures society, then why is it not a crime (as it used to be) and punished accordingly by the state? ... If suicide is 'bad' because it injures the soul or spirit of the 'victim', then why is it not a sin (as it used to be) and punished accordingly by the church? (Individuals who die by suicide are no longer denied a Christian burial.) ... [I]f suicide is 'bad' because it injures both the suicide and others, like a disease (as people now seem to believe), then why is it not treated as such?

(Szasz, 1986, pp. 806–7)

Szasz believes suicide is constructed in a 'scientific' way largely through medicine. However, ultimately it bears the features of sin, sickness, crime, irrationality, incompetence and insanity. As a consequence, we fail to regard suicide in ways which are similar to other what he calls 'morally freighted acts'. Overwhelmingly we do not see abortion as a sin, a crime, or an illness, but as good or bad, defensible or indefensible, desirable or undesirable, or right or wrong. So why do we strip suicide of this clear status?

Another important example of the social creation of understanding is given in Kuper's (1988) account of those nineteenth-century social anthropologists who invented the notion of primitive society. What they did actually was to take their view of the nature of their modern society and turn it on its head. Modern society was characterized by monogamous marriage, possession of private property, and a political order which had a fixed geographical location. 'Primitive society' was the obverse of this and characterized as sexually promiscuous, communist and nomadic. This constitutes an image which has persisted outside of the anthropological community, if not within it. Certainly such views seem resolutely propagated in Hilgard's *Introduction to Psychology* (Atkinson *et al.*, 1990) which is now in its tenth edition. The treatment heaped on African and certain other societies is one which compares them with a pack of wild animals (Owusu-Bempah, 1990). For example:

> Behavior that is considered normal by one society may be considered abnormal by another. For example, members of some African *tribes* do not consider it unusual to hear voices when no one is actually talking or to see visions when nothing is actually there, but such behaviors are considered abnormal in most *societies*.
>
> (Atkinson *et al.*, 1990, p. 592, emphasis added)

> In another chimpanzee border war observed during the 1970s, a *tribe* of about 15 chimpanzees destroyed a smaller neighboring group by killing the members off one male at a time.
>
> (Atkinson *et al.*, 1990, p. 427, emphasis added)

In contrast, when writing about African cultures in which controls on sexual behaviour are being applied, the word 'tribe' is abandoned – clearly such people do not match the myth of primitive society:

> very restrictive societies try to control preadolescent sexual behavior and to keep children from learning about sex ... And among the Ashanti of Africa, intercourse with a girl who has not undergone the puberty rites is punishable by death for both participants.
>
> (Atkinson *et al.*, 1990, p. 383)

Nevertheless, despite the change in terminology, the Ashanti are still portrayed as murderous even though it is doubtful whether Atkinson or any of the others could name one Ashanti girl murdered in this way in modern times. The point is not merely the messages being transmitted about African cultures, the form of the message is determined by derelict anthropological conceptions – much the same as determined the primal horde of Freudian psychology (Freud, 1950).

One could also mention the myth of the nuclear family (Uzoka, 1979). This myth contrasts the nuclear family (consisting merely of the biological parents and their children) with the extended family. The nuclear family is a false construction of the modern family which conveniently allows it to be seen as pathology-invoking and an easy excuse for social problems. If the fragmented modern family is to blame for social ills then the state can escape its responsibilities.

Gergen (1985, p. 266) lays down the essential objective of social constructionist approaches as follows:

> Social constructionist inquiry is principally concerned with explicating the process by which people come to describe, explain, or otherwise account for the world (including themselves) in which they live. It attempts to articulate common forms of understanding as they now

exist, as they have existed in prior historical periods, and as they might exist should creative attention be so directed.

Among the casualties of social constructionist critiques are the assumptions of 'scientific' approaches to social science. The process of obtaining knowledge about the nature of the world is not the consequence of a process of induction, nor is it the consequence of the testing of general hypotheses about the nature of the world. The knowledge of the world that psychologists generate is not a mapping of reality nor is it understandable if decontextualized from what created it.

> Critiques have been launched against the taken-for-granted character of suicide, beliefs, schizophrenia, altruism, psychological disorder, menopause, and situational causes. In each case, the objective criteria for identifying such 'behaviors,' 'events,' or 'entities' are shown to be either highly circumscribed by culture, history, or social context or altogether nonexistent.
>
> (Gergen, 1985, p. 267)

Different cultures do not necessarily share conceptualizations about the psychological processes. Maoris do not hold the Western conception of the self, for example. As a consequence, constructionist explanations need to explore those institutions (whether they be social, moral, political or economic) which not only support these conceptualizations but also gain benefit from their existence.

Feminists have recognized the importance of the social construction of science and the implication of this for the experiences of women. Hare-Mustin and Maracek (1988) emphasize constructionist influences on feminist theory. The opposition to positivism and its concern with a fixed reality is inherent in feminist critiques of conventional psychology which attempts to promote sex-role differences as reflecting biological differences or the 'natural order'. For them:

> Theories of gender, like other scientific theories, are representations of reality organized by particular assumptive frameworks and reflecting certain interests ... Rather than debate the correctness of various representations of gender, the 'true' nature of which cannot be known, constructivism examines their utility or consequences. How do representations of gender provide the meanings and symbols that organize scientific and therapeutic practice in psychology?
>
> (Hare-Mustin and Maracek, 1988, pp. 456 and 458)

While not set within an overtly social constructionist framework, the following comments of Russo and Denmark (1984, p. 1163) point to some of the ways in which science and its assumed objectivity cannot be distinguished meaningfully from other forms of oppression:

Science and technology are seen as a source of solutions to contemporary problems. Yet, when it comes to women's issues, science and technology are all too often part of the problem itself. Scientific advances, particularly in biology and information sciences, are transforming society in unmeasured and unanticipated ways. Pfafflin (1984) points out that male dominance in scientific and technical fields raises issues of equity, effective human resource utilization, and objectivity in scientific decision making. The prestige of being a member of the scientific community is not sufficient to counteract societal devaluation of women. Patterns of occupational segregation and wage-based discrimination found in society at large are mirrored in scientific fields, including psychology.

Particularly useful is the summary of the approach and the dilemmas it raises provided by Wittig (1985). She suggests that the constructivist 'metatheory' encompasses a number of propositions. The first of these is a statement that positivist views of the acquisition of knowledge are inadequate, while the second is to point out that knowledge gained in controlled conditions (laboratories) is at best incomplete. In addition, she lists four further considerations:

1   Behavior is multiply caused (both with respect to the number of causative factors and the systems involved). Behavior and our knowledge of it are reciprocally related, and the causal relations change in complex, unpredictable ways. This dynamic is the focus of analysis.
2   Although the correspondence of theory and data is sought, verification criteria do not demand such correspondence. For some domains, accurate prediction from rather explanatory principles is largely unattainable. Rather, the truth of a theory resides in how well it represents the domain it attempts to explain.
3   Methods that are sensitive to bidirectional and multiple causality and subjective meaning are likely to advance our knowledge and understanding of the interactional processes involved.
4   Research that coordinates the study of psychological processes with social structural and biological processes is favored. However, explanations derived from research at one level of analysis do not necessarily have validity at another level. Distinct validation criteria may need to be established for different levels of inquiry.
                                                        (Wittig, 1985, p. 803)

Wittig considers that the application of these constructionist principles may well be problematic in practice. She identifies a number of what she terms 'dilemmas' in the metatheory of gender of which the following are the most significant. They are also readily generalizable to other areas of research.

The first dilemma is that of *scholarship or advocacy*. Part of her distinction is that the scholar is formally neutral in the way in which the substantial product of the scholarship is used, while the advocate is most certainly not neutral and instead wishes for particular social outcomes. While there is nothing new in this issue, gender issues have been an area where criticisms have been made concerning advocacy. Her solution is to recommend the avoidance of both ideology and intellectualism! One does not have to abandon the goal of the emancipation of women, she claims, since this may function to guide the nature of the research to be done. Furthermore, once the research has been done it 'can be used as the basis for deciding whether and in what ways to intervene' (Wittig, 1985, p. 804). This may not match the constructionist approach in that it appears to assume that some knowledge is neutral with respect to the social world which generates it. Would, one might ask, feminist psychologists be overly keen to accept findings which are not, by implication, emancipatory of women?

Often it is easy to tease out the latent advocacy in scholarly writing. Later in this book we will come across a number of examples where the advocacy would appear to be the primary aim. Indeed, only in regard to the most trivial of matters is it realistic to regard the scholarship–advocacy dichotomy as reflecting mutually exclusive categories. It is next to impossible to draw a line to say for any individual psychologist where the person ceases and the scholar begins. By the same token, there is nothing in scholarship which ultimately excludes advocacy. There are too many examples of hidden advocacy contained within scholarship to believe otherwise.

Another dilemma she identifies is that of *orthodoxy or schism*. In orthodoxy the researcher acts as an uncritical insider, in schism as outside critic. The resolution of the dilemma for emancipationists is in a 'transformational psychology' which attempts to create a psychology which is an acceptable fusion of the requirements of feminism and the acceptable ways of gaining 'knowledge' of psychology. So 'A transformational psychology of gender attempts to construct a nonsexist psychology from within the discipline, so as to avoid both gender bias and dissociation from psychology' (Wittig, 1985, p. 806). This neatly avoids the issue of what elements of psychology one wishes to retain in this equation. Presumably only that psychology which is free from sexism and not that which serves as a tool for sexism. There is almost a case for 'starting psychology again from scratch', so deeply embedded is its traditional orthodoxy in maintaining social injustice. Chapter 6 deals with related matters in relation to racism.

Finally, there is a dilemma of *subjectivity versus objectivity*. In terms of gender, rather disingenuously, she claims: 'A committed psychology of gender rejects the claim that the psychology of gender must be biased because it involves value presuppositions. It also rejects the conclusion that it is possible to avoid value judgements' (Wittig, 1985, pp. 806–7). Why it is necessary to reject being biased is not clear. Surely the idea of gender equality is not only a working principle – it comes in advance of 'proof' (whatever that term may mean in this context) of gender equality. Indeed, Wittig's views might be construed as a homage to positivistic 'science'. Bias has to be in relation to some 'fixed' reality the existence of which is denied by constructionists. It is difficult to see the point of a psychology which does not acknowledge that part of its foundations has to be a social ethic. Some, hopefully all, psychologists are unprepared to engage knowingly in a psychology which leads to social injustice or results in psychological damage to individuals or groups.

There are advantages in the 'post-modernist' approach of constructionism. Especially in this context is its consigning of 'fixedness' of human nature and society to the wastebin. The spin-off of this is that psychology does not have to be concerned with fixing the boundaries of society, as it has frequently had in the past with its promotion of social disadvantage, racism, and sexism, among other things. There is the possibility of creating previously unimaginable views of people and society. This challenge has not begun to be met.

Concluding comments

This chapter has essentially been about what sort of psychology is needed to enable the discipline to be applied to significant social issues. While elements of 'positivism' have been taken to task, there is no intention to imply that there is not a role sometimes for the classic approaches of mainstream psychology. What is in question is the extent to which they are sufficient in themselves to help develop a significant psychological input to matters of social concern. In many ways what has been discussed is 'an attitude of mind'. It is a matter of what psychology is *expected* to be. The contention is that one cannot fully appreciate the contribution that psychology can make unless one understands the limitation of 'science'. The social constructionist approach lays down a framework for understanding the development of ways of knowing the world in general. By allowing knowledge to be changeable rather than aiming at a fixed reality, it becomes possible to study the real world from a psychological perspective which welcomes variation and change. The dichroism made available by abandoning the excesses of positivism is a welcome bonus.

Take a look at the following statements, and decide which of them are true and which are false. Agreeing with them puts one in the positivist camp, disagreeing with them is essentially a reflection of acceptance of social constructionism (Ungar, 1986a and b; Kitzinger, 1989a):

Most sex differences have an evolutionary purpose.

Science has underestimated the extent to which genes affect human behaviour.

Biological sex, sex role, and sexual preference are highly related to each other in normal people.

Physiological differences limit the degree to which males and females can learn to be similar to each other.

How was the positivist measure of constructionism for you?

3

VALUES AND PSYCHOLOGY

Too often I have witnessed psychologists speaking on education, child rearing, social institutions, and mental health, using what they claim is research evidence as a disguise for advocating a particular public policy. Psychologists and social scientists, more so than other scientists, *need to carefully distinguish between providing scientific data and making policy ... Otherwise, psychology will come to be regarded as a social force rather than a scientific discipline. If that should occur, psychology's potential for helping to solve society's problems will be lost.*

(Atkinson, 1977, pp. 207–8, emphasis added)

A deep fear contrives to prevent psychology contributing fully to understanding the human condition. This is the fear that subjective factors might creep into the psychologist's objective, 'scientific' viewpoint. Paramount among these subjective factors are the risks that one's value system, beliefs, and ideological orientations, will interfere with the quest for scientific 'truths'. To describe someone's argument as a value judgement is a major dismissive ploy in a psychologist's rhetorical armoury. However, what is understood by the epithet 'value judgement' needs discussing since superficially there is no reason why values should not be involved in psychology. Value judgements are seen as antithetical to 'scientific' thinking. The implication is that it is possible for human beings to operate in a value-free manner – provided that they are properly trained in 'scientific' thinking. The following implications need questioning among others:

1 That there is something called 'science' which can avoid value-ridden everyday thinking and that these two things are diametrically opposed.
2 That there is a 'truth' about the world which is out there for the finding – otherwise subjectivity is inevitable.
3 That it is a good thing that science should be value-free.

One problem is that the values of researchers are not always immediately obvious. This is especially the case when, as is probably typical, one merely gives a limited or a cursory reading to their reports. The tendency of psychologists working in a particular area to share similar values and views of the world probably compounds the difficulty. Few psychologists actively proclaim their values in their research publications. It is doubtful that they are even completely aware of them. The desire to avoid value judgements may result in a 'value-less' attitude in which 'anything goes' in research, so long as it does not *appear* to relate to value positions. Of course, it is a pretence (and probably an unnecessary one) to see psychology as such an uncontaminated distillate of the real world. So instead of research being concerned with matters about which the psychologist feels strongly, it becomes an intellectual game which fails to raise the widespread interest of the community. The retreat into basic research, however, does not avoid a moral dimension as it promotes a dehumanizing view of people. Furthermore, basic research may at times have greater undertones of being partisan on values and ideology than is at first apparent. For example, Sampson (1981, p. 742) claims that cognitive psychology basically reflects the ideology of modernity, thus reaffirming much of the current social order, and fails to provide a psychology 'of what may yet be'. In addition, Morin (1977) complained of a heterosexual bias in research on homosexuality.

The operation of values in psychology

It can be a salutory lesson to examine major psychological studies and theories to unravel value positions within them. Sometimes, the contemporaneous revelation of value positions is problematical and the passage of time may be necessary before they become more evident. One good starting point for exploring values in psychology is a classic and highly influential piece of research from the 1930s. Through modern eyes this can be seen to be value-bound. So important were the research and theory to be that they formed the basis an entire branch of industrial theory and practice which emphasized the importance of social relationships in industry (the human relations movement). Furthermore, they contributed 'the Hawthorne effect', a corner-stone of practically every course in research methodology for social sciences students.

The psychologists involved, Elton Mayo (1933) and Fritz Roethlisberger (Roethlisberger and Dickson, 1939), were adamant that the research held vital implications for the organization of factory work. If workers are paid attention on a human level, productivity will improve. In other words, good human relationships equals better cash profits. Initially, the effects of improving the physical conditions of the workplace (for example, the lighting levels) on work rates were investigated. After a while, it became 'apparent' that, no matter what was done either to improve or to worsen the physical conditions, productivity continued to increase. There was no relationship between the physical conditions and productivity. How could these rises in productivity be explained if physical environment made no difference? The researchers theorized in order to explain what became known as the 'Hawthorne effect'. It was the interest and involvement of the research team with the workers which increased productivity. The workers feeling appreciated and worthwhile due to this attention led to a 'better attitude' towards work. The research was a lot more complex than this account can show but detailed descriptions are readily available (see, for example, Argyle, 1953; 1972).

However, the very nature of the way in which the research was interpreted was crucial – or rather, the readiness with which it was absorbed into mainstream psychological textbooks and reproduced for successive generations of students in lectures. Indeed the account given so far violates the research considerably and is to a degree misleading. This has traditionally been the case in the accounts of the Hawthorne studies. Ignoring methodological critiques, typical discussions include the following:

> With striking consistency, these studies revealed that the presence of researchers in the factory, not the actual changes made, had a major impact on the employees. As soon as participating workers were singled out to receive personal attention, they conformed to what they assumed the research team wanted: more productivity.
>
> (Brehm and Kassin, 1990, p. 587)

Sometimes the interpretation seems to have passed well beyond the second-hand to form almost a pastiche of the original ideas:

> novelty itself was causing the change.
>
> (Lloyd *et al.*, 1984, p. 56)

Mayo's (1933, p. 69) account of what happened to the workers involved gives a clear indication of his beliefs:

> At first shy and uneasy, silent and perhaps somewhat suspicious of the company's intentions, later their attitude is marked by confidence and candor. Before every change ... the group is consulted. Their comments are listened to and discussed; sometimes their objections are allowed to negative a suggestion. The group unquestionably develops a sense of participation in the critical determinants and becomes something of a social unit.

One might be forgiven for thinking that the Western Electric Company (and its Hawthorne plant where the research took place, in particular) was a caring and understanding company. Perhaps it was. However, it seems to have been no different from many other American companies of the time in its opposition to organized labour unions. It is known to have used a union-breaking firm as part of its anti-union activities. During this period of American history, violent means of controlling organized labour were not uncommon. At root, Mayo's alternative scenario of keeping workers in harmony with employers was just another way of controlling labour. Psychological methods, it seemed, could be used by management to deal with workers' socio-emotional needs. The 'irrational' hostility of workers against employers could be brought to an end.

In the context of our discussion of values, this is important. Recently it has been argued (Bramel and Friend, 1981) that Mayo, in particular, was presenting a way of seeing industrial life which served the interests of American capitalism. This was incompatible with the search for 'true' or 'objective' understanding of the world. Apparently, Mayo was well aware of the Marxist view which assumes that there is a fundamental conflict between workers and owners. That which is in the best economic interest of workers does not serve owners so well, and vice versa. The key thing, however, is not to choose between Marx and Mayo, communism or capitalism. It is more important to understand the way in which Mayo's ideological stand led to a certain way of establishing 'facts'. One must also appreciate how this is related to Mayo's view of how labour should be managed under capitalism. Bramel and Friend (1981, p. 868) put the issue as follows:

> Marxists believe that capitalist relations of production are exploita-
> tive and necessarily produce resistance and self-organization among
> workers. This individual and collective resistance may or may not be
> expressed at any given time as class consciousness and a political threat
> to the firm or to the system as a whole, but it is always present in one
> form or another ... It is by suppressing the fact of this resistance, by
> trying to explain it away psychologically, and finally, by developing
> human relations techniques designed to prevent workers' development
> of class consciousness that the Mayo group contributed to the attempt
> to save the capitalist system from the fate Marxists said lay in waiting
> for it. We believe that psychologists and others have been insufficiently
> critical of these anti-working-class ideas and practices ... that ...
> seemed to open up endless vistas for employment in the application
> of social science.

A rosy picture of the attitudes of workers at the Hawthorne plant was needed for two principal reasons: first, to demonstrate those 'effective' industrial relations strategies capable of ridding industry of 'irrational' ill feelings that workers expressed through union activity, for example; and second, to show the falsity of Marx's thesis of the conflict of interests between worker and capitalist. For Mayo, bad industrial relations stemmed merely from relatively trivial annoyances (such as those due to the lack of consultation on innovations). But how could the outcome of the research be 'rigged' in such a way? Surely Mayo merely interpreted the data? The answer was simple. 'Troublemakers' – those who were not the happy co-operative individuals which the researchers' ideology demanded – were gradually excluded from the research. Two workers were repeatedly reprimanded for not displaying 'wholehearted cooperation'. After eight months they were dismissed for gross insubordination and low output. Mayo, however, describes them as having 'dropped out', and fails to explain why in published work. However, in a private letter he wrote of a particular worker: 'One girl, formerly in the test group, was reported to have "gone Bolshevik" and had been dropped.'

Even output, a central indicator of morale in this 'human relations' theory, did not show the 'proper' trends. Physical conditions in the workplace *were* important determinants of worker satisfaction despite what was suggested earlier in the 'tidied-up' version. Following extensive discussion of the reasons for and circumstances of a change, rest periods were reduced. However, generally output did not rise but fell. Physical conditions *did* have some bearing on output or workers were *not* the passive 'zombies' that Mayo (and the discipline of psychology) had represented them as.

Bramel and Friend (1981, p. 876) see the failings of the Hawthorne research as part of a more general trend in psychological writing to disparage the working class:

> The view of workers as nonresisting, confused, and irrational that was propagated by the Mayo school ... is, unfortunately, very much still with us in psychology. It is still present in social psychology books and in general psychology textbooks, often as part of a more general tendency to present working class people as second class citizens (i.e., as having lower IQs, deviant subcultures, poor child-raising techniques, racist attitudes, etc.) ... We have found the myth to be so widespread that anyone can easily confirm its presence.

The explanation of such a bias is easily found. Contributing factors include the place of academic institutions in the social class structure and the ignorance of many psychologists of the day-to-day lives of the participants in their research. Major questions raised by Bramel and Friend's critique of the class bias in the Hawthorne research are the following:

1   Why do psychologists so readily ignore the ideological underpinnings of psychological knowledge?
2   How do such debased versions of the original research come to be promulgated?
3   What does it tell us about the 'value'-free science of psychology?

There are other examples which imply that the Hawthorne case is not just an isolated or rare instance of bad psychology. Stretching a little further back into the history of psychology, similar tendencies are to be found in the work of the founder of behaviourism, John Watson. Harris (1979) describes the majority of accounts of a very familiar piece of research as featuring similar fabrication and distortion as facts. This research (Watson and Rayner, 1920) is seen as an attempt to use the principles of Pavlov's classical conditioning to create emotional behaviour in humans. The hapless Albert B., just about the most famous child in the whole of psychology, was nine months old when he was recruited to provide the empirical support for Watson's views about phobias – especially fear of animals. Watson considered that these phobias are due to a child being frightened by an animal, a fear which then generalizes to other animals. Initially Albert was unafraid of a range of different animals including dogs and rabbits. Nor was he afraid of inanimate objects such as a burning newspaper.

Albert was quite happy in Watson's laboratory until his calm was shattered. An unexpected clang was created behind his back by hitting a large steel bar with a sizeable hammer. At this, not surprisingly, he showed signs of fear. A few weeks later, the researchers showed the boy a white rat and at the same time again hit the steel bar behind him. After a few repetitions of this, the poor suckling became afraid of the rat on its own (much as he was of the loud clang). Albert would cry and generally try his level best to escape the beast. When shown other 'animals' such as a rabbit, a short-haired dog, and 'a sealskin coat' or objects such as a bearded mask of Father Christmas and Watson's hair, there was also evidence of modest to strong fear of these. Albert was willing to play with other objects such as wooden blocks and the hair of Watson's assistants and showed no signs of generalized fear of these. In a phrase, Watson had demonstrated the conditioning of fear and stimulus generalization. Next Watson tried to condition fear directly to the dog and the rabbit.

Moving the research into a larger room, he found that the fear of the rat and other animals instantly decreased to low levels. A picture of total chaos then follows. To the cacophony of Albert wailing and metal clashing was added further mayhem ensued when the dog began to bark at Albert. Watson's research required that the clanging first frightened the boy – not the animal itself. Thus the barking of the dog had wrecked the experiment since it frightened Albert itself.

Textbook writers often erroneously insert a significant and misleading revision of Watson's original gospel. Typically, the list of things to which fear generalized was extended. This 'amended' list included a man's beard, a white furry glove and a teddy bear. More bewildering is the fabrication of a cleaned-up version of Watson's research. Remember that he had deliberately created phobias in the child. Despite knowing when Albert's mother intended to take the child home from hospital, Watson made absolutely no attempt to rid the child of the phobias. Not only would this nowadays have failed to pass the university's research ethics committee, he might also fall foul of his professional association. However, some textbook writers describe the deconditioning procedures which Watson used – even though there had been none. There are a number of possible explanations for this.

One is the wish to describe Watson and his work in a favourable light. This generally represents an attempt to promote behaviourist 'science' as capable of significant advances. The cleaning-up of the research is paralleled by the general view that 'science' is a tidy and orderly process.

A second explanation lies in Watson's tendency to shift his own ground in later publications, presenting a version of the research which had stronger implications than a detailed knowledge of the original suggests. For example, in later publications Watson omits to mention that he had tried conditioning fear of the dog and the rabbit in an intermediary stage, thereby creating the illusion that the generalization from the rat to the dog and rabbit was stronger than it actually was. Harris (1979) claims that there was very little evidence of this sort of stimulus generalization.

A third explanation is the desire to make the research fit the theory. Textbooks tend to the view that conditioning should vary along gradients of stimulus similarity. Thus the more similar the new stimulus to the original rat, the more fear there was of it. To this end, writers appear to have 'manufactured' a whole series of conditioned stimuli which did not appear in the original work of the sort already mentioned. Not only do textbook writers fall into these traps, other researchers make similar errors in so far as they retell the story to fit their own theoretical developments.

One cannot dismiss the errors as mere consequences of textbook writers relying on other textbooks rather than reading the original publication. Similar errors occur in very early textbooks as well as in much later ones. They were, therefore, not the consequence of some sort of serial reproduction effect. Samelson (1974) sees such errors as partly a function of the needs of the education system to put over an integrated conceptual approach and a tradition for psychology. Such characteristics would encourage students' interest in and attraction to the discipline. There is no hint in this of scientific objectivity being the crucial characteristic of psychological science.

It is remarkable for such a problematic study as this to reach the dizzy heights of a classic citation. It was probably *the* example of the use of learning theory in the explanation of clinical phenomena. It became so despite warranting consignment to the wastebin for flawed methodology. This says more about the institution of psychology than an objective science. Centrally important is that it demonstrates the less than rigorous quest for 'truth'. If cases like the Albert B. experiment were quickly revealed for their deficiencies, then the role of 'science' in psychology might be seen as important. As it is, 'science' appears to be an ideological posturing, relating more to pragmatic matters. The failure of the research to achieve its objectives was subordinated to what was more in line with scientific ideology, though inaccurate and downright incorrect.

One is reminded of the author of a psychology textbook which was in its third edition (so selling well). He remarked to Henle (1986, p. xviii): 'I have now read at least seventy-five percent of the sources I used in my book.' Some caution though should be exercised before construing the Albert B. example as being the result of sloppiness and sloth. First of all, the 'errors' were very useful for some points of view. Second, it is notable that challenges to mainstream, dominant psychological theories may not be always kindly received. Lubek and Apfelbaum (1987) document the case of John Garcia who followed a successful research career in the 1950s. However, a little later he began to be excluded from the major journals by colleagues in his chosen branch of psychology. The problem was that his research raised major embarrassments for dominant learning theory approaches of the time. Mahoney (1987) gives other examples of what can happen when a researcher 'threatens' establishment psychology.

Both of these examples, the Hawthorne study and the Albert B. experiment, are crucial studies in the history of psychology. They were not chosen from the dusty archives of psychology – they are still much discussed and cited today. That they demonstrate so clearly the influence of subjective factors, and little commitment to precision, does a lot to debunk the myth of an objective, value-free, psychology. What lesser examples would reveal is open to speculation.

A major issue emerges from this. Can the influence of ideology, values and other 'subjective' factors be shrugged off as evidence that psychologists' 'scientific' base needs refinement? Perhaps to train psychologists better would solve the problem. But could psychological 'science' operate in a *value-free* way but for slips? A major difficulty with such a notion is that there is no psychological 'science' which is not the product of psychologists. To pretend otherwise is silly. Psychology textbooks are a ready source of evidence that beliefs, values, attitudes and ideologies influence the way that *ordinary people* perceive the worlds and events. But they usually omit to discuss that psychologists are also 'ordinary' people – even when they pose as 'hard-nosed scientists'. In later chapters we will see more examples of ideological components involved in psychological thinking.

Some psychologists happily rest in the hope that being 'scientific' solves the problem. Getting the methodology 'right' apparently neutralizes the risk that ideology and values pose. Now and then, perhaps, some researchers will perhaps stray and over-generalize or over-interpret their data, but these are exceptions. Some individuals may even fabricate their data (as in the Cyril Burt case: see Hearnshaw, 1979; 1990; Joynson, 1989; 1990) but these are rare, or at least rarely detected. This sort of view of psychology's bad apples should be rejected without undue ceremony as naive.

If psychologists were truly concerned about the role of values and ideology in their thinking then they would try to make themselves aware of such 'biasing' factors. An electrician whose voltmeter has a systematic bias such that it always records 20 volts more than the true value does not have to buy a new one so long as she is aware of the fact and always makes the necessary adjustment. Psychologists, however, are not trained to know themselves in any systematic manner. Numerous techniques are readily available to help us clarify the ideological components of our thinking – equal opportunities training, racism awareness training, training in cross-cultural communication, and other forms of sensitivity and awareness heightening. Few psychologists receive any of these as part of their professional education. Nevertheless, they are supposed to be resistant to letting their personal feelings cloud their professional work. It is no small wonder that they often choose research from which obvious value implications have been squeezed out.

Allied to this is a tendency of some psychologists to be dismissive of psychoanalysis, which has as a core training in personal awareness. While this is not quite awareness of values and ideology, it nevertheless is a form of self-awareness enhancement. Some psychologists have suggested that requiring psychoanalysts to have undergone psychoanalysis themselves is merely a process of indoctrination into a cult (cf. Eysenck and Wilson, 1973). However, it could be equally said that failure to train psychologists in means of knowing themselves better merely facilitates indoctrination into misplaced faith in the objectivity of science. Only knowing psychology textbooks limits the possibility of self-awareness markedly.

Value positions can influence psychological research at different stages. There is no implication here that this is always for the worse. For example, few would argue that many psychological researchers, if they responded more to what they value as being worthwhile topics, might produce more interesting and exciting research. It would be much better than merely doing what is possible in the time available using a new and convenient questionnaire or a 'watertight' experimental method.

In a thorough analysis of the role of values in psychology, Howard (1985) does not see them as an extrinsic nuisance – a 'blip' in the system. He treats them as central to psychology – including its most 'scientific' forms. Following modern trends in the philosophy of science, Howard claims that the question is not *whether* values influence the practice of sciences but *how* they do. Knowledge, in other words, needs to be understood as much in terms of the value systems which shape that knowledge as, say, the methodological, economic, and theoretical contexts of that knowledge.

Theory and values are more intrinsically linked than is normally acknowledged by psychologists. Many tend to see theory as emerging from empirical observation. However, there are choices to be made between theoretical explanations which cannot be based on research evidence alone. There are no events which can be given a single theoretical interpretation. Equally, it is not possible to choose between different theories on the basis of any single empirical observation. Significant theories are not too commonplace in psychology so it is difficult to find convincing instances. For example, Freudian ideas about phobias are radically different from Watson's. Freud (1961, p. 36) wrote that 'the formation of a neurotic phobia ... is nothing else than an attempt at flight from the satisfaction of an instinct'. But it is not possible to refute Freudian ideas using Watson's research. Neglecting the worries about the research itself, Watson may merely have demonstrated an alternative aetiology of phobias rather than having explained phobias *per se*.

The preference for Watson's point of view among numerous psychologists during the decades following the publication of his research cannot be explained by what happened in his laboratory. First of all, what Watson saw was what his theory said he should see – without the theory his perceptions would have no doubt been rather different. Or, to be more precise, his accounts of what he saw might not have been what they were. Indeed, without the theory, what Watson did to little Albert in the laboratory would have been considerably different. Second, the choice of that theory was not determined by what happened in the laboratory since no one saw a stimulus or a response or a gradient of generalization – these were the product of a wish and a willingness to deal with human nature by the use of the metaphor of the machine.

One of the calumnies of mainstream psychologists has been to accuse psychoanalytically orientated psychologists of being unscientific. The accusation is that psychoanalysts rely on a theory which cannot be disproved through research and which is also heavily dependent on the subjective assessment of the analyst as to the theoretical interpretation of the actions of the patient. So closely pinned to science's coat-tail have mainstream psychologists been that they appear oblivious to the possibility that they are similar to psychoanalysts in terms of the influence of 'subjective' factors. Mainstream psychologists simply fail to note that their belief in theories does not emerge from the data collected. No amount of empirical work can tell us what view of humanity is 'best'.

Howard discusses the *epistemic* values of science. Such values are the qualities to be found in a theory which give us faith that the theory is capable of increasing knowledge or understanding – that is, the theory will help us towards the 'truth' or the 'real' laws of nature. These values are perhaps better seen as maxims since they also give what may be described as the rules of proper conduct for theoreticians. Included in the list are the following:

1 Predictive accuracy: does the theory describe what will happen precisely enough?
2 Internal coherence: does the theory make sense in its own terms or is it illogical and inconsistent?
3 External consistency: does it fit in with other theories which are generally accepted?

4 Unifying power: does the theory allow the embracing together of previously separate areas of knowledge?
5 Fertility: does the theory provide a resource for the imagination of the scientist?
6 Simplicity: for some, lack of complexity in a theory is, in a sense, aesthetically pleasing.

Viewed in some lights, these are a bizarre collection. They do not match what we value in other areas of life.

Taking sides

The traditional view of psychology as a value-free enterprise can result in failure to recognize the discipline's location in social structure. The idea of a 'true knowledge' means that it is indepedent of the social system which creates it, otherwise inevitably knowledge is value-ridden and unobjective in a purist sense. In these circumstances the nature of psychology becomes problematic and its weaknesses glaringly obvious. If psychological knowledge is not 'scientific' but emerges from the nature of the social structure which generates it, then awkward questions are unavoidable. Whose perspective is to be taken? Where in the power structure do psychologists' allegiences lie? Whose side are they on?

Not to identify precisely where psychological knowledge lies in the social structure (how, by whom and for whom it was constructed) is to swathe the discipline unnecessarily and unrealistically. To pretend that psychology is mined from a rich seam of nature's truths protects us from professional self-examination. One area needing consideration is that psychology risks serving certain sectional interests. There is nothing novel in this suggestion. It is easily demonstrated by the outrage over some of the arguments psychologists make while claiming 'objectivity'. Often these have every appearance of a fundamental attack on certain groups of people, particularly those already disadvantaged. Indeed, some, with substantial justification, see psychology as part and parcel of the oppression of sections of the community. Obvious examples of this include the debate over whether there were biologically determined race differences in intelligence test scores (Rose *et al.*, 1984), the way in which anything other than heterosexuality is treated (Morin, 1977), and the fundamentally sexist nature of many a psychologist's outpourings. Detailed analyses of similar instances are given in the later 'case study' chapters.

Inevitably psychology serves particular interest groups. Realistically, it is difficult to argue that this could be substantially different. However, to the extent that access to psychology is not available to all interest groups there is a problem. If there are no black psychologists, no women psychologists, no working-class psychologists, for example, then the problem arises as to who is able to make the case for these groups in the psychological debate. But even that does not quite pinpoint accurately enough what is needed. There is no guarantee that black, female, and working-class psychologists will be sufficiently aware of the issues to represent their group effectively. This is not intended to be patronizing. We should not forget, for example, that many women, even those working in professions, accept male definitions of sexuality, femininity and so forth. The stage has only just begun to be reached that awareness of feminist issues is common. So the absence of *aware* black, female and working-class psychologists is the key issue. It should also be mentioned that it is often very difficult for a member of a profession to see disguised ideologies.

The fact that disquiet about the consequences of psychology's position in the social structure is not commonly expressed is one reason to be especially concerned. If psychologists are unaware of the issue then they are also discouraged from examining radically different points of view. Knowing the allegiences of mainstream psychology is as central to understanding the discipline as are method, procedures and other 'technical' details which are invariably freely and regularly reported.

Two different aspects of the 'whose side are you on' issue attract attention. The first is that of the broad moral stance of individual psychologists *vis-à-vis* the representation of minorities. The second is the issue of victimization and the 'discipline' of victimology. Both of these matters are to an extent intertwined with each other but they do contrast at the level of individual morality versus the ideological basis of a discipline.

The case of Nazi Germany

This sort of discussion too easily remains abstract and far removed from familiar issues. It is possible to examine the relationship between psychology and society by asking an extreme question – just for the argument, perhaps. Could psychologists be in favour of fascism? Could there be a scientific infrastructure for fascism? Would German psychology support Hitler's Nazis during the 1930s and the Second World War? While we might like to believe that psychology would reject such views, in reality it did not. One thing that needs to be made clear is the important distinction between those psychologists dismissed from academic life because they were Jewish or in some other way unacceptable to the Nazis and the more general issue of psychology's collusion with the Nazis in Germany. It has been the general tenor of writing about this time to suggest that the Nazis were antagonistic to psychology. This is actually quite difficult to support from documentary evidence. It is far easier to show how psychology 'prospered' during this period.

A number of academics did leave Germany and annexed countries during the 1930s – some to find a more fitting environment for their studies, some because they were Jewish, and one was even released from prison on condition of her emigration. Furthermore, many Jewish academics were removed from their posts because of a German law of 1933 which required the dismissal of Jewish and other civil servants who were politically 'unreliable'. But that this resulted in the dismissal of a number of academic psychologists does not constitute any Nazi attack on psychology. While it might be comforting to believe that psychology was at root incompatible with fascism, this is not true. Indeed, there are numerous examples of fascist psychology (Billig 1979; 1981), but more immediately relevant was the routine involvement of psychology with Nazism and its growth. The number of professorships of psychology almost doubled in Germany in the period 1932–42 (from 13 to 23). Practising psychologists also increased substantially in number. In 1930 there were approximately 30 psychologists working in public institutions in Germany. Half were in vocational guidance, the other half in the army. By 1942, something like 450 people were working as psychologists in the military forces. According to Geuter (1987, pp. 175–6),

> the SS sought to enlist the 'cooperation' of a woman psychologist ... in its 'selection' of Polish children, who were taken from their parents and distributed to German families, public foster homes, or camps. To decide the destiny of these children, which could mean not only the choice of their future quarters but also between life and death, the SS planned to have the psychologist carry out characterlogical assessments.

Psychology grew as a profession in this period – the professional organization of psychologists did nothing to oppose the dismissal of leading Jewish academic psychologists (see also Graumann, 1985). Geuter's (1987, p. 181) conclusions are food for thought, certainly a broadside against complacency:

> Many were willing to legitimize Nazi power with psychology, or at least to offer their expert knowledge to the institutions of the Nazi state ... Psychologists were not forced to rewrite their theories according to Nazi ideology. Some scholars did not do so, and they did not suffer political repression ... But at the same time the party authorities and representatives who were responsible for science policy fostered the professional development of the field.

Fascists in Australia

So psychology was capable of serving the purposes of Nazism. We would perhaps like to believe that it is fundamentally opposed to fascism today. How does psychology now align itself in relation to broad egalitarian principles such as social justice? Are there unacceptable ideologies still hidden in the closet of psychology? Surely only those looking in the closet will find them. Take, for example, the following debate between Ray and Billig over comments made by Billig (1981) about *Conservatism as Heresy* (Ray, 1974). It is claimed by Ray (1985, p. 442) that the book shows 'how various conservatism ideas can be defended from a libertarian perspective'. He continues:

> I believe that people like best those who are most similar to themselves and that genuine differences between people can therefore explain the dislike people feel for one another. Billig regards such a theory as a 'vulgar justification of racial prejudice' but in so doing ignores the fact that Jewish scholars produce similar explanations for antisemitism. Stein even finds that Jews *need* their persecutors and hence provoke persecution. Glock *et al.* found that antisemitism is low where Jews are few and high where Jews are frequent. He concludes, therefore, that antisemitism is an outcome of culture-conflict, i.e. that it has something to do with Jews themselves. Although Stein goes a lot further than I would, it should be clear that both Stein and the Glock group are arguing very much as I do. Are these respected Jewish scholars then giving 'vulgar justifications of antisemitism'? Billig would have to say that they are but the absurdity of so saying is surely apparent.

Stepping lightly past the final comment (which does not follow at all since racism is so pervasive that it can be internalized by members of the minority group and directed against themselves), there is a gloss of reasonableness which characterizes the above passage. This possibly would result in a casual reader concluding that there was little to take exception to in Ray's self-justification. It takes an effort sometimes to tease out embedded assumptions in texts. But, in fact, there is a great deal that Billig (1985b, p. 448) takes exception to following a detailed reading of Ray's writing:

> The key phrase in Ray's present defence is that anti-semitism has 'something' to do with Jews ... Much hinges upon what the 'something' is. However, [elsewhere] Ray argues, not that anti-semitism has 'something' to do with Jews, but it has *everything* to do with Jews. His intention is clearly expressed: it is to offer an explanation of anti-semitism that puts the 'fault squarely in the camp of Jews themselves' ... Ray's methodology is qualitatively different from that of ... any social scientists, Jewish or Gentile, that he cites. The methodology is simple. Ray talks to anti-semites, and then accepts what they say about Jews as factually true. For example, he describes 'a very successful business entrepreneur with an attractive wife and three beautiful small children'. This man holds firm views about both Jews and Aborigines: 'he sees both as grasping – the one by deceit and the other by indolent whining'. Ray assures us that this is not prejudice, because the man 'has come

to know those of whom he speaks' and therefore 'this is an ethnocentric man whose attitudes I believe we must respect'.

Both Ray and Billig have taken sides: Ray with the self-confessed racists whose racism is excused as 'rational' knowledge gained from experience, Billig, perhaps, is rather more circumspect about revealing his allegiences and embeds his argument more closely in precise academic argument – however, it cannot be doubted that his perspective favours minorities who are discriminated against and is motivated by those sympathies. Despite this, there is no sense in which Billig's criticisms are purely emotive – nor do they depend on trivial methodological criticisms. Billig's argument largely rests on drawing out of Ray's work the key assumptions and means by which those assumptions are articulated. It is an exercise in the application of academic care against careless bigotry. Taking sides is not unacceptable bias, rather it is part of being motivated into thought.

Victimology

Ray claims to base his case on the principles of 'victimology' – really a branch of criminology which studies the victim of crime as opposed to the criminal. He sees racism as an interaction between both the victim and the victimizer. This allows him to justify holding Jews responsible for being victims. However, to claim the 'kudos' of victimology as justification for blaming the victim for his/her plight is problematic in itself. 'Victimology' is not necessarily any freer from unacceptable elements than the racism which Ray attempts to justify by reference to it. Victimology has some perfectly acceptable concerns. It is useful to know the relationships or degree of familiarity between criminals and their victims; and the characteristics of people most likely to be victims of crime may help us understand the inequitable distribution of suffering of crime, and which geographical locations are typical of being victimized (Drapkin and Viano, 1974). What is fundamentally unacceptable is the suggestion that victims have any significant responsibility for the criminal acts perpetrated against them.

It is worthwhile exploring the feminist literature in the search for a worthwhile debate on victimology. Sexual attacks on women have often been held to be the responsibility of the women themselves. Clark and Lewis (1977) draw out the some of the typical victim-blaming strategies. Basic in their argument is the observation that rapists are ordinary men – there is no particular mental aberration which is responsible for their actions. Social scientists, who are predominantly men, Clark and Lewis argue, find it hard to reach the conclusion that since rapists are normal men then normal men must be potential rapists. So how can rape be explained? One solution is to blame the victim. If rapists are normal men then it is the fault of the woman that she 'gets what she was asking for'.

If this seems a crude exposition of what might be rather subtle inferences in obscure scientific writing, then examine the following quotation on the matter of the rapist's psychology:

A woman's behaviour, if passive, may be seen as worthy to suit action, and if active, may be taken as an actual promise of success to one's sexual intentions.

(Amir, 1971)

Clark and Lewis (1977, pp. 153–4) write of this:

Therefore, a woman cannot win. No matter how she behaves, she may provoke a rape attack. In fact, it is not her behaviour which precipitates rape at all, but the rapist's *interpretation* of her behaviour. Here, Amir reveals both the fallacy and the male bias in his theory. It may well be that 19% (or more) of all women behave in ways which a male bias would perceive as an invitation to rape, but their behaviour is not classified as 'rape-precipitating' unless they are actually raped. Amir's unquestioning acceptance of the male perspective is not unique ... In *Rape Offenders and Their Victims*, (MacDonald, 1971) suggests that some women 'invite rape' or 'are rape-prone, as others are accident prone'.

Is there such a thing as not taking sides? Probably not. But radically different ways of understanding the issue will emerge according to the viewpoint. To adopt the female standpoint requires the immediate acceptance of a more or less implicit or explicit feminist stance. Less work may be required to adopt the male standpoint – one simply sides with the science establishment which is often another male mouthpiece in a male-dominated society.

Subjects of research

One of the most curious but rarely debated habits of psychology is the use of the word 'subjects' to describe the people who participate in a researcher's study. It is virtually universal and part of the lore of a psychological research report to have a section dealing with 'the subjects'. As a consequence, perhaps not surprisingly, the use of the term goes virtually without question. Such a stance is, however, inappropriate when the choice of term reveals much of the relationships of psychologists with people. A glance at a dictionary will reveal that the word 'subject' has several connotations: theme, topic; that about which something is predicted; conscious self; one under power of another; owing allegiance; and subordinate. Which of these do we mean in psychology? Perhaps the second, about which something is predicted, but are we sure that we do not mean one under the power of the psychologist or the subordinate of the psychologist? Do we mean that these are people part of the kingdom of psychology – the loyal subjects of psychologists?

According to Danziger (1985), the virtual universal use of the term 'subject' was a relatively late development in psychology. In the early days of the psychological experiment, towards the end of the nineteenth century, 'subjects' were described as reactors, observers, participants, individuals under experiment, or experimentees. In American psychology journals by the mid-1890s the term 'subject' was used about half the time, the term 'observer' a quarter of the time, with 'reagent' a poor third. Pertinent to the question why the terminology was rather less abrasive than our modern word is the following comment by Danziger (1985, p. 134):

> We might also note that the participants in these early psychological experiments were never strangers to one another. They interacted outside the laboratory as professor and student, as fellow students, and often as friends. They clearly saw themselves as engaged in a common enterprise in which all the participants were regarded as collaborators, including the person who happened to be functioning as the experimental subject at any particular time.

The sharing of status and interest is hardly typical of most psychological research. A traditional and more or less fair complaint has been that psychology is really the psychology of the American middle-class college student. Perhaps this should be extended to mention that it is the psychology of those students as researched by their professors. Automatically, by virtue of this, power relationships are built into the research. Since, in addition, these students are poorly informed about the nature of the research other than in a perfunctory post-research debriefing, one can see that much of modern psychology is diametrically opposed in these respects to its historical antecedents. It is interesting to note that Danziger regards the psychological experiment as a sort of social world in miniature. Its nature, then, is itself a direct conseqence of the broader social context:

> The social interactions that are necessary for psychological experimentation were not designed from scratch on the basis of purely rational considerations but simply grew out of patterns of interaction that were already familiar to the participants. Medical and educational institutions provided the sources of many psychological concepts ... The point is that methodology is no more free of the influence of social context factors than is the formation of theoretical concepts.
>
> (Danziger, 1985, p. 138)

The suspicion is that modern psychologists use the term 'subjects' not because of a lack of an alternative terminology but because it precisely describes the relationship between the major figures in research. There are two signficant implications of the use of the term 'subjects' that probably reveal more about psychology than a mere word should. First, people become merely objects to which something is done, thereby losing many of the features of their humanity – including having choice of action and being active rather than passive. Second, psychology is the realm of psychologists not of their subjects. So rather than psychology being what people who take part in research give to other people conducting the research, it is separated from people and in the hands of those who *do* this sort of psychology to people. Very clearly this is a power relationship for the production of social knowledge.

Why not speak of 'participants' in the research, as do Howitt *et al.* (1989) in their introductory textbook? This would imply more accurately the nature of the social relationships in research as developed in the social psychological studies of the laboratory experiment (Orne, 1962). Some might argue that the researcher is also a participant in the research – which is surely the case. Given this extensive research tradition on the influence of the researcher, it might perhaps be advantageous to merge the roles of researcher and those researched.

Concluding comments

Rappoport (1984, p. 122) insists on:

> a value orientation emphasizing that future social science cannot place any consideration of objectivity, logic, reason, or method, no matter how these may be defined, above the guiding ideal of a unitary, indivisible humanity. A social science ungrounded in these terms is simply too dangerous ...

Nothing more should need to be added. The next four chapters, then, perhaps do the unnecessary. They are case studies in the application of psychology to social issues. Each was selected to highlight a particular theme in the use of psychology. These themes are: the socially constructed nature of social issues and problems; the problem of taking sides in the perception of research issues; the ideologies internal to the profession which pass as 'science' but ultimately have oppressive consequences, and the broadly political forces which impinge on psychological research from outside the discipline.

4

THE CREATION OF A SOCIAL ISSUE: THE CASE OF DRUG ABUSE

> ... *this custom of sipping tea, affords a gratification, which becomes so habitual, as hardly to be resisted. It has prevailed indeed over a greater part of the world; but the most effeminate people on the face of the whole earth, whose example we, as a wise, active, and warlike nation, would least desire to imitate, are the greatest sippers; I mean the Chinese among whom the first ranks of the people have adopted it as a kind of principle, that it is below their dignity to perform any manly labor, or indeed any labor at all; and yet, with regard to this custom of sipping tea, we seem to act more wantonly and absurdly than the Chinese themselves ... It is an epidemical disease; if any seeds of it remain, it will engender a universal infection.*
>
> (Hanway, c.1756, in Kohn, 1987, p. 16)

A careless reader may well have misread the above as a tirade against opium. More careful readers may have been amused by such a diatribe against the 'innocent cup of tea'. Furthermore, they may have recognized a good deal of racism, sexism, jingoism and, perhaps, anti-gay sentiment. Tea is described in terms which may read like pastiche. However, the deception was intended in all seriousness. Teasing apart the structure of the argument, there is every reason to see a parody of popular sentiment and beliefs about heroin, crack, and any number of other drugs. That it pre-dated any significant articulated social concern about drugs in Western culture by a century or more should perhaps help clarify its rhetorical significance. Hanway's claims hoist sipping tea onto a number of ideological structures – especially the twin modern 'ism's of race and sex. Given this, the passage should alert one to an important matter – that the ingestion of substances relates to wide issues of which food taboos are just another example.

A cursory view of substance 'abuse' tends to regard it as a problem of *individuals* with psychologically *weak characters* who get 'hooked' on chemicals which alter their physiologies and personalities. As such, drug abuse is clearly a medical/psychological problem. It involves psychologists to the extent that they are sometimes skilled in counselling and therapeutic techniques. Psychologists' skills appear to offer the opportunity to do something about the psycho-pathological nature of the drug taker. Why do we think this? How did such ideas emerge in society? Do they constitute the only conceptualization of the matter?

The emergence of drugs as a social problem can be examined in order to demonstrate the degree to which a psychological approach to social problems can be informed by understanding social and historical contexts of ideas. It should become clear that the social definition of an issue depends on a range of different factors. These help form the framework of ideas, beliefs, and assumptions which form the interpretative structure used to understand a 'problem'. This framework not only helps form the views of laypeople but also frequently structures the orientation of professionals working in the field. Drug abuse is a particularly good illustration of the social construction of a problem since it arouses strong feelings, is of major political concern, has serious consequences, and has a well-documented history.

To discuss the British drugs 'problem' as a case study is a particularly useful starting point. One important reason is that it is frequently argued that Britain has had a radically different philosophy of how drugs should be dealt with (Judson, 1973). In this formulation, Britain is seen as a haven of sensible moderation compared with, say, an 'excessively' punitive approach in the USA. Obviously Britain is just one nation among many and it might also be profitable to study other countries (as does a special issue of the *International Journal of Addictions*, 1991). However, the special approach which has been attributed to Britain makes it an especially useful context in which to study the social construction of the social problem of drugs.

It cannot be emphasized too much that it is not inevitable that drugs become defined as a social problem. There is nothing in the taking of drugs which, in itself, warrants the sorts of concern commonly expressed. The fact some people take them does not in itself explain why draconian controls are imposed on their use. That anti-drugs legislation is common throughout the world is not evidence of the inescapable need for such legislation – it is possible that legislation is common because it has shared social origins. In historical terms, drug controls are very recent indeed. Furthermore, it is perfectly possible to envisage benign and accepting 'policies' on drugs. Punitive policies are not the only option. So why one approach dominates rather than another becomes a central question. There is little history in most psychology. Indeed, even historical approaches (as represented, for example, in Gergen and Gergen, 1984) seem to be rather light on historical detail as opposed to arguments about why history is important and ought to be studied in psychology. So indulgence needs to be craved while it is demonstrated why the historical context of drugs use is important.

Historical background

Opium taking was common in nineteenth-century Britain. Not only was it taken for medical reasons, it also had non-medical purposes. There were no governmental controls on supply and distribution. One can understand its medical use given the lack of pain-relieving and other medicaments at the time. Opium was not just available to those who sought it out, it was openly on sale for most of the nineteenth century:

> In the 1850s, opium could be bought in any grocer's or druggist's shop; by the end of the century, opium products and derivatives and opium-based patent medicines were only to be found in pharmacists' shops. Regular opium users, 'opium eaters', were acceptable in their communities and rarely the subject of medical attention at the beginning of the century; at its end they were classified as 'sick', diseased or deviant in some way and fit subjects for professional treatment. It is ... the establishment of a whole new way of looking at drug use which requires analysis.
>
> (Berridge and Edwards, 1981, p. xxvii)

It is possible to translate the use of opium into its equivalent of morphine (an opium derivative with medical uses) for the period 1820–60. During this time, the 'average' person consumed the equivalent of 127 modern therapeutic doses of morphine annually. Despite these levels of consumption, during the early part of the nineteenth century there was no significant social problem associated with drugs. However, by the end of the nineteenth century, there was a growing 'recognition' that drugs were problematic. At the same time, it became more difficult to find signs of significant drug use. This decline in use was not particularly to do with legislation. The only laws in existence at the end of the nineteenth century simply restricted the *sale* of opium to pharmaceutical outlets. It did not make it difficult to obtain the drug from a pharmacist. Perhaps this indicates that drug use need not become locked into society as a social problem. Changes in attitudes towards (and definitions of) drug takers during the course of the nineteenth century cannot be understood without reference the professionalization of medical practice (including pharmacy). Much of the pressure for change lay in the vested interests of doctors and pharmacists. However, this notwithstanding, only in the early twentieth century did any substantial effort to introduce controls begin.

So during the nineteenth century opium use had changed from being little other than a bad habit:

> Robert Harvey, house surgeon at Stockport Infirmary during the 'cotton famine' of the 1860s, when many regular customers could not afford their opium, recalled his surprise that 'the use of the drug

was much more common than I had any idea of, and that habitual consumers of 10 and 15 grains a day seemed none the worse for it; and would never have been suspected of using it'. ... Nor was this habit necessarily a matter of treatment. The early discussions of opium addiction commonly appeared in sections of medical texts dealing with opium poisoning and the treatment of a drug overdose ... it was poisoning and not addiction which was the focus of treatment.

(Berridge, 1989, p. 25)

However, towards the end of the nineteenth century the Society for the Study and Cure of Inebriety formulated a new view of drug use, its first president claimed that inebriety 'is a true *disease*, as unmistakably a *disease* as is gout or epilepsy or insanity' (p. 27, emphasis added). According to Berridge, doctors in the Society:

saw themselves as pioneers, shedding the light of science into the dark ages of vice and crime. Their humanitarianism is not in doubt, nor their desire to subject the drunkard or opium inebriate to a more humane form of control. But we can also see that their views were socially constructed, that disease and science were no more objective than the moral opprobrium they ostensibly replaced. Doctors found professional and social authority in a concept which initially incorporated many of the moral and social assumptions of the temperance and anti-opium movements, and which later gave scientific credibility to fears about racial and imperial decline and to the social measures to arrest this ... (p. 27)

Clearly an important lesson is contained in this for any psychologist believing that their psychological notions reflect a scientific reality.

The history of drug regulation during the early part of the twentieth century (see Bean, 1974) began with a 'moral outrage' of the sort that has stimulated other sorts of moral panic (Cohen, 1974). During the First World War concern was felt about the risks to the war effort from the adverse effects of drugs of addiction. The sale of alcohol through licensed premises was limited drastically. (Not for another 70 years were restrictions significantly loosened to allow drinking with few opening-time limitations during the day.) The panic over drugs was a response to newspaper reports that an ex-soldier and a prostitute were selling cocaine to Canadian soldiers in London. This has all the classic features of a newspaper sensation – it neatly bifuracated good and evil and placed them in opposition. The good side were the armed forces protecting us against the enemy. Evil was represented by the prostitute. These definitions of good and bad pre-existed the news story but the assault of evil against good clearly demanded action.

Very quickly an order was introduced expressly forbidding the supply of drugs to soldiers. Cocaine, heroin, morphine, and Indian hemp were included on the list. An exception to this was that medical doctors could prescribe drugs on a one-off basis; repeat prescriptions were not allowed. Shortly afterwards, similar restrictions were imposed on the general public in a somewhat more limited form through an Act of Parliament. Essentially, only doctors, pharmacists and vets were allowed to possess, sell or administer cocaine. Medicinal preparations of greater than 0.1 per cent strength of cocaine could only be obtained by non-repeatable prescription. Opium received similar treatment, but morphine was not included in the legislation. Effectively, the legislation sought to prevent drugs undermining the war effort. Both military success and industrial strength were needed for victory. The image of drugs as a debilitating evil destroying will and effort was directly in opposition to this.

While the First World War provided the first substantial legislation against drugs in Britain, the seeds of a change in the use of legislation in drugs control had already been planted. Perhaps, from one point of view, this is the most significant event. It involved international co-operation in the control of drugs – a major theme in British activity since that time. Starting with the Shanghai Conference of 1909 and the First International Opium Convention at The Hague in 1912, international co-operation gradually evolved. Britain's involvement was *not* the consequence of a perceived domestic problem. There was no general feeling that Britain's social fabric was being destroyed by drugs or that addiction was a significant social problem. Britain, because of its extensive empire in the Far East where drug use was judged to be endemic, wished to help the Chinese and Indians to deal with 'their' problem. The Hague meeting resulted in a convention signed by all parties to the Treaty of Versailles following the First World War.

There was a requirement in Article 20 of The Hague Convention that the possibility of 'making it a penal offence to be in illegal possession of raw opium, prepared opium, morphine, cocaine and their respective salts' should be explored. Thus the definition of illicit drug use involved the criminalization of the user and a punitive aspect to drugs policy. Inevitably drugs policy, through international agreement, created the image of the drug user as criminal and consequently as deviant. Fundamentally, much drugs use was to be accepted as part of a legal-moral model. It became one of several victimless crimes. In Britain and other Western countries during parts of the twentieth century, male homosexual activity and attempted suicide, for example, were criminal offences which had to wait until well into the second half of the twentieth century to be largely decriminalized. Drug abuse (i.e. possession) is still illegal.

It is worth noting that the USA took a major instigating role in the development of the international effort to outlaw drug taking. To regard drug taking as a criminal offence was a factor of American policy for a large part of the twentieth century. In the USA in 1914, the Harrison Act virtually eliminated the medicinal prescription of opiates. The British situation was to change radically during the 1920s, partially following the American model.

The Dangerous Drugs Act 1920 embodied The Hague Convention's main principle of criminalizing drug use. The distribution of listed drugs was subject to a system of control in which illegal possession could attract a then enormous maximum fine and/or 6 months' imprisonment (which might include hard labour). Reconviction for a drugs offence could attract more than double that fine or two years' imprisonment. According to Berridge (1984), the government sought to increase penalties many times during the 1920s. An obstacle was to be found, however.

The medical profession had an interest in limiting the escalation of the penal approach to drug control. The legislation of the time had resulted in the prosecution of members of the profession for technical offences. At the extreme, pharmacists were prosecuted for inadvertently dispensing forged prescriptions. Furthermore, medical workers were the most likely to be drug takers since they had such easy access to drugs. However, an attempt to make it illegal to prescribe certain drugs to oneself was fiercely opposed by the medical profession. The medical profession had many contacts with government through membership of committees, through the Ministry of Health, and as a consequence of the large numbers of doctors who were Members of Parliament. Self-prescription of drugs was allowed under British law until the 1960s when the medical profession was once again under attack.

What is known as the 'British system' of drugs control was the product of the Rolleston Committee of 1924. Essentially the Committee was a consequence of the struggle between the government and the medical profession. It was indeed a classic compromise. The drug user who obtained supplies independently of the medical profession quite simply remained subject to the considerable force of the law and was criminalized. However, the medical profession and its patients were virtually decriminalized by the recommendations of the Committee. This new legislation gave protection for doctors and certain other professionals from dangerous drugs legislation. Furthermore, clients of these medics could obtain drugs as part of their treatment with immunity from the law. On the other hand, those taking identical drugs obtained from illegitimate sources risked considerable punishment. Howitt (1991, p. 1091) claims that

> the British medical 'model' merely provided substantial immunity from the law for medics and their immediate and privileged clients – the rest were treated in a different fashion. 'Rogue' doctors who were 'over-prescribing' were not exposed to the force of law but to review by a medical tribunal ... The compulsory registration of addicts ... was also opposed by the medical profession and not made a legal requirement at the time.

This bipartite system, then, created a dual view of the drug user – as either a criminal or a sick person being 'helped' by a benevolent and caring medical profession. In truth, neither of these views mattered too much since they dealt with a largely abstract issue – a social stereotype of the drug user rather than a reality. There were very few prosecutions for drugs offences during the period 1920–50 and very few known addicts. In other words, there was a rather cosy 'drugs' scene in Britain which involved few people and seemed well controlled by the law and the medical profession.

Things changed little or not at all until the 1960s when drug abuse dramatically emerged as a local rather than a 'foreign' problem. There was a drastic escalation in the amount of officially known drug use but, more significantly, the typical drug user became a rather more threatening character than before. Drug users were now typically young working-class males – the very group which had come to be a problem in terms of delinquent and other forms of criminal behaviour. (One should not forget the significance of the fact that the word 'teenager' was a social invention of the 1950s.) Taking the decade 1958–68, there was a furious escalation in the number of officially recorded addicts. In 1958 there were 62 heroin addicts, 12 methadone addicts, and 25 cocaine addicts. In 1968 there were 2,240 heroin, 486 methadone and 564 cocaine addicts. While once, most addicts were the product of the medical profession's access to and use of drugs, now non-medical origins became very common. There was scarcely a change in the numbers of therapeutic-origin addicts, but a 36-fold increase in those of non-therapeutic origin. At the end of the 1950s there were no known heroin addicts in their teens; ten years later there were well over 700. In 1958 a slight majority of known addicts were female; ten years later three quarters of addicts were male (Teff, 1975).

In addition to these 'worrisome' changes, growing 'evidence' was forthcoming of a number of 'rogue' doctors irresponsibly prescribing drugs. A former Chief Inspector of the Home Office Drugs Branch wrote in 1970 that 'by far the greatest part of the heroin and cocaine available to create these new addicts undoubtedly came from the quantities prescribed by doctors for existing addicts who exaggerated the amount they were taking' (Jeffery, 1970, p. 67).

The main feature of the consequent legislation was that treatment centres were established. These alone had the right to prescribe heroin and cocaine in treatment of addiction. Furthermore, a three-way classification of drugs was introduced. Class A drugs included opium and heroin. Class B drugs included cannabis (marijuana) and cannabis resin, together with some amphetamines. Class C included other amphetamines and barbiturates. The different classes attracted different penalties for possession: seven, five and two years, respectively. The trafficking of these drugs could result in prison sentences of up to 14 years. Only minor changes have occurred in legislation since then.

Of course, there are other factors which may be involved in the development of policy on drugs as far as this is revealed by the changes in legislation in the 1960s and 1970s. One view is exemplified by Smart (1984). She suggests that at about this time there developed a scientific-cum-technical armoury which allowed for more precise control of drug abusers:

> the manufacture of the synthetic opiate methadone, which was initially promoted as a 'cure' and later as a less harmful substitute for heroin, and the discovery of techniques for urine screening, which could accurately diagnose which drugs a person had taken, provided new methods of processing and regulating drug addicts.
>
> (Smart, 1984, p. 38)

Irrespective of the motives for the changes in the administration of 'drug addicts', the consequence of setting up clinics was to restrict severely the availability of drugs from non-illicit sources. Drugs inadvertently or otherwise 'over-prescribed' by doctors had been a major source of supplies. What was the consequence of curtailing these? According to Leech (1985, p. 8), while the British heroin problem of the 1980s could not have been avoided altogether, 'its extent and its ramifications could certainly have been curtailed had not successive governments and the clinics in effect forced the distribution of the drug entirely on the illicit market'. The consequence was spelt out by Teff (1975, p. 117): 'as the American experience depressingly indicates – profitability is to a large degree dependent on illegality'.

Drugs and psychology

The point of this is not to retell history for its own sake, but to show that drug addiction is substantially a social construction. It provides a framework for perceiving the issue of drug taking which is neither natural nor inevitable – as a medico-legal matter rather than a matter of personal choice. Drug addicts are sick or bad or both, and it becomes extremely difficult to see them in any other terms. Few of us are in a position other than to regard these as appropriate alternatives since what little understanding we have is developed within these broad parameters.

It is difficult to draw the line between the lay and psychological perspectives on this matter. While at first sight referring specifically to scientists' understanding of the natural world, Gergen's (1982, p. 23) comments have an important general message:

> ideas about nature cannot be derived from observation of nature itself. On the basis of senses alone unlimited distinctions could be made among phenomena. In scanning the present page, for example, should one distinguish among groups of lines, individual lines, word

groupings, individual words, letter groupings, individual letters – or should all these possible distinctions be abandoned and attention be devoted to variations in glossiness, or paper texture? Distinctions are possible, innumerable others could be made. Which particular distinctions are made does not seem dictated by or dependent on mere exposure to the stimulus of the page itself.

In other words, there is a theory before psychological theorization.

It should be asked why the changes have occurred so relatively smoothly over time such that what some might see as a 'sickness' is treated as a 'crime'. According to Tyler (1986, p. 21), the answer lies in the symbolic characteristics of drugs which

> repeatedly serve as the most potent metaphor for that which ails us politically and socially … [T]he reputation a drug achieves rarely has much to do with its pharmacological reality but is a product of a culture's topical, often racially-linked panics; or else the reputation is manufactured to serve an imperial or corporate interest.

Not only do the symbolic associations of drug use serve to allow more and more draconian punishments and avoid the questioning of anti-drugs activities, the effects of drugs are presented as a dramatic image which may have its own consequences. Young (1984, p. 13) describes the prevalent image of heroin

> as like a booby trap. First, it portrays heroin as an addictive drug of gothic proportions … second … heroin addiction is caracatured as a terrible degenerative disease rather like tuberculosis … it is hardly surprising that the majority of addicts follow predictions and relapse …

Drugs are alien and it is part of the mythical history of drugs in Britain that they are assumed to be 'foreign'. British policy emerged out of its empire in the Far East and it is a British stereotype of the 'Chinese coolie in his opium den' which reveals underlying attitudes. The opium-smoking coolie is shiftless and lazy, sapped of drive. But is this any different thematically from the more recent ideas about marijuana-smoking West Indian immigrants and, in more recent times, the ideas of international racketeers in human misery peddling their high-priced products (Berridge and Edwards, 1981; Tyler, 1986)?

The reality of drug use in Britain is not dominated by heroin, amphetamines, crack, cocaine and the like, but by cannabis in various forms such as marijuana. In terms of potential criminal charges, the figures speak for themselves. Out of 23,627 such cases in 1988, over 80 per cent involved variants of cannabis. By contrast, the other most common substances accounted for relatively small proportions (amphetamines, 11 per cent; heroin, 9 per cent). At the very least, cannabis accounted for 74 per cent of the drugs involved in drug offences. Cannabis-only offenders accounted for a minimum 71 per cent of drug offences. Not only this, the offences are overwhelmingly 'possession-only' ones, with about 90 per cent coming into this category rather than that of drug dealing.

Just to complete the picture, in 1984 (which is not atypical) 490 people were sent to prison in the United Kingdom for the possession of cannabis, and this included 60 who went to prison for more than six months, and two who received terms of more than five years.

The figures for drugs use in Britain are small compared to those of many other countries (though the degree of punitiveness of the policy is not commensurately low). The precise details of the figures do not matter; what is important is that the taking of certain drugs brings with it a whole canopy of societal beliefs, assumptions, policies, laws, and policies which envelope the act of drug taking. In such cirumstances, how a psychologist examining the issue chooses to define the act becomes profoundly problematic. It is all too easy to drift into a moralistic stance rather than to search for understanding.

So what are the ideas about drugs being fed to psychologists by 'experts'? Two examples taken from recent textbooks for psychology students will suffice. Brehm and Kassin (1990) have little to say on the matter of substance abuse. However, what they do say seeks to adopt a highly principled tone:

> many people under stress turn to alcohol, cigarettes, or drugs for relief. The costs of this type of avoidance tactic are extremely high. When people drink, smoke, or take drugs to make themselves feel better in a stressful situation, they can add serious physical, social, and financial difficulties to the original source of distress. Substance abuse in response to stress is like hitting yourself over the head because you've already been hit over the head. It doesn't solve the problem, and it usually makes matters worse.
>
> (Brehm and Kassin, 1990, p. 658)

In these few sentences the number of disguised value stances is considerable. A few of the value-related themes are as follows:

1 That the use of any of the substances, even on a temporary basis for relief of stress, brings highly undesirable consequences.
2 That to use any substance in times of stress is an 'avoidance tactic' rather than relief from psychological strain that will have to be worked through at an appropriate but different time.
3 Using a mood-altering substance at times of stress is misuse of that substance (otherwise why substance abuse?).
4 That substance use to relieve stress is a self-inflicted *wound* rather than a rational choice for coping with stress.

5   What problem doesn't substance use solve? It may not take away the situation that caused the stress in the first place but it may well be effective at dealing with the emotional effects of stress. For example, in the case of a bereavement where most of the cause of the stress is over, the pain of the bereavement may nevertheless warrant relief.

6   Is taking the substance in itself the source of the physical, social and financial difficulties or society's response to drugs and drug users? If the latter then Brehm and Kassin's (1990) views are already constrained by society's conceptualization.

7   There is an assumption that psychological distress is more benign than physical, social or financial difficulties. It is uncertain how this can be claimed.

The point here is not to defend the use of alcohol, drugs, or tobacco in the relief of stress but merely to highlight some of the assumptions built into such a short paragraph for which the psychological evidence is conspicuous by its absence. It is noteworthy that the substances discussed by Brehm and Kassin do not include medically prescribed substances. This is curious since these are 'designed' to be psychologically active and to help people with various emotional and other crises. There is good reason to believe that 'legitimately' prescribed mood-affecting drugs may be as debilitating or more so than *certain* prohibited drugs for which it is difficult to find evidence of any substantial adverse effects (see, for example, Home Office, 1982).

Atkinson *et al.* (1990) is another 'classic' textbook discussing drugs. While altogether more thoughtful on the topic, it still paints a particular picture which seems well beyond the research evidence presented. Take their discussion of marijuana smoking:

> marijuana smokers do not appear to build up tolerance for the drug, and they experience minimal withdrawal symptoms. Nevertheless, a person who learns to use marijuana when faced with stressful situations will find the habit difficult to break.
>
> (Atkinson *et al.*, 1990, pp. 212–13)

What is this supposed to mean? That a stress-coping mechanism tends to have habit-like properties? – just as perhaps seeking a best friend for an intimate discussion or perhaps knocking hell out of a squash ball. What is wrong with a psychological dependency, if indeed that is what it is? After all, the entire area of social support (see Duck, 1990) is evidence of our resorting to particular coping practices. There is an ease with which a moral tone lacking in-depth intellectual analysis drifts into the discussion of some substances. Notice in the following extract the inability to abandon the 'harm' argument when other tests of it have failed:

> The subjects had used between 2 and 4 ounces of ganja–tobacco mixture each day for over seven years ... Nevertheless, their intelli-

gence levels were unimpaired, they performed adequately on other cognitive measures, and they showed no signs of poor health. However, the long-range effect that smoking may have on these subjects' lungs remains to be determined.

(Atkinson *et al.*, 1990, p. 223)

Contrast these psychology textbook extracts with the evidence that, in 1971, doctors in the United Kingdom issued 13 million prescriptions for Librium, Valium and related pills. This produced 200,000 cases of dependency and the possibility of withdrawal symptoms worse than those of heroin. These drugs had replaced barbiturates which had proven to be toxic and highly addictive, killing 2,000 people a year (Tyler, 1986). The figure for the prescriptions had risen by 10 million to 23 million in 1983 (Griffiths and Pearson, 1988). Women are twice as likely to be prescribed tranquillizers as men. These figures in themselves tell us that there is an ambivalance in our view of relief from stress and distress. So long as it is the medical practitioner who makes the decision then the use of dangerous and addictive drugs produces little condemnation. The moralistic tone of the views of Brehm and Kassin (1990) and Atkinson *et al.* (1990) is almost misdirected. No matter that many psychologists might object to the use of tranquillizers so routinely, the fact remains that the ideas about the use of drugs do not originate haphazardly but are the consequence of a collective cultural history in which the medicalization of drugs as well as their criminalization may strait-jacket thinking. It is no accident that the textbook writers write as they do – they are a part of a culture 'at war' with drugs.

A useful contrast to the easy platitudes of textbook writers who frequently choose to propagate ideologically based morality for knowledge (without identifying it as such – wherein lies the problem) is Shedler and Block's (1990) study. They researched drug use and psychological health in adolescents. They found that although frequent drug users tend to be psychologically unhealthy (alienated from others, controlling their impulses poorly, and emotionally distressed), the reverse was not true. Non-drug users were also shown to have psychological problems – they are described as being anxious, emotionally constricted, and lacking in social skills.

The psychologically healthy individuals tended to be those who had actually experimented to a degree with drugs (especially marijuana) though were not frequent users. Of course, the adolescent experimenters probably reflect a sub-cultural acceptance of marijuana use, so it is not surprising that those with fewest interpersonal problems also reflect the commonest social attitudes of the group.

The importance of research like Shedler and Block's is that it allows us to escape somewhat from dominant social beliefs to approach more closely the nature of drug-using cultures. The social stereotype of the addict does not need to be an accurate reflection of the user, as we can see.

So what – does it matter? What difference does it make? Questions like this may have already missed the point. The history of drugs as a social problem implies that there is a distinctly non-scientific, 'non-objective' frame of reference already for understanding what drugs are, who takes them, what they do, and so forth. Not to be aware of this makes it more difficult to detach oneself from dominant views sufficiently so as to allow one to ask challenging questions – rather than indirectly promoting ideology or morality in disguise. It is disturbing that the ideas of psychologists can be dependent on a moralistic/medical/legal construction rather than a relatively unfettered examination of issues. Psychology graduates may join groups of professionals with extensive contact with drugs. Some become clinical psychologists, some become social workers, others become teachers or educational psychologists, and so on. Their understanding of social issues should arise in an unfettered intellectual context.

Contact with drug users, because it takes place within this broader ideological and moral context, cannot automatically cause revisions of thinking. Griffiths and Pearson (1988) report informal 'research' in which a group of social workers brainstormed stereotypes evoked by the phrase 'drug taker'. The list they produced was young, male, depressed, dirty, hippy, irresponsible, sick, self-destructive, punk, self-indulgent, drop-outs, victims, criminal, doomed, pushers, aggressive, frightened, dangerous, unemployed, inadequate, amoral, working-class, manipulative, rich kids. Griffiths and Pearson suggest that professionals may fail to give drug users the help they could simply because they fail to fit the stereotype.

Thomas Szasz (1990) makes an important argument, not exclusively or especially in relation to drugs, but about the relationship of the medical profession with the state. Szass (1990, p. 7) writes of 'medical despotism' and quotes Rush, the founder of American psychiatry, as suggesting that 'mankind [sic] considered as creatures made for immorality are worthy of all our cares. Let us view them as patients in a hospital.' Rush also conjectured that 'the majority of mankind are madmen at large'. For Szasz, organized medicine has encroached on personal freedom in numerous areas including abortion and contraception, the use of drugs, and others. He contends 'that we now classify many medical acts as scientific when, in fact, they are moral, ... that we classify many psychiatric acts as medical when, in fact, they are religious' (1990, p. 12), and that 'we no longer recognize religion when we see it, demarcating medical from moral institutions and interventions incorrectly and stupidly' (1990, p. 13).

The societal change in conceptions of drugs forced users into categories of morally bad or diseased through drugs. Even language used of the drug user is certainly not value- or assumption-free – 'drug addiction', 'illicit drug use', 'drug abuse' and 'substance abuse' are used almost interchangeably.

A further reason why knowledge about the emergence of conceptions and policies on drugs is important is that they markedly constrain thinking about issues. Indeed, in Britain, though not necessarily elsewhere, the field has been abandoned to sociologists. There is little psychological writing or research other than barefooted empiricism. Perhaps this is a consequence of the way in which the image of 'drug abuse' is constructed. There is evidence of crassness in the approach of some psychologists.

Take, for example, the question of anti-drugs publicity campaigns. The history of social psychology has been dominated by research on attitude and behaviour change through persuasive messages. Psychologists might be expected, therefore, to be sophisticated analysts of effective communication. Indeed, market research and advertising campaigns might be seen as the applied aspects of all of this psychological research and theory. Power (1989, p. 130) describes the recommended strategy of one advertising agency for an anti-drugs campaign aimed at young people:

> Step one: a full page advertisement in a national newspaper, blank except for a small crucifix in the bottom right-hand corner, with the words 'Cocaine kills' beneath it.

> Step two: the same advert the next day, but in the top left-hand corner there is another cross with words such as 'A.N. Other, 25, died from cocaine, 23.3.86'.

> Step three onwards: each day another crucifix is added to the list until the page, like a World War One graveyard, is awash with obituaries and crosses.

The crudity of this proposal is easy to see through, depending as it does on the view that attitudes are formed and changed independently of the social milieu. Advertising campaigns run the risk of 'boomerang' effects through ignoring the social experience of those most at risk from drugs use:

> stereotyping jeopardizes the credibility the campaign might have in the eyes of those young people most at risk of using heroin ... By definition, this group of youngsters is likely to be in direct contact with, or know of, heroin-users; this being the case, they are equally likely to know individuals who manage to control their drug-use, who do not conform to the images of the 'chaotic junkie', and who give positive reasons for using heroin. In short, they will be confronted with real role-models, some of which conflict with those that festoon the billboards and appear on TV screens.
>
> (Power, 1989, p. 137)

Clearly, then, there are dangers in simplistic, warmed-over models of drug use which derive from the medico-legal model. Passive acceptance of this among psychologists who are unaware of the historical development of drugs policy may encourage neglect of the issue. After all, little is to be done from a psychological point of view if drugs are seen mainly as a medical matter. In this context, it becomes more significant that virtually all social scientific writing on drug use in Britain comes from sociologists. While the sociologists have been prepared to come to terms with the social context of drugs use, it is difficult to find examples of psychologists who have. One simple way of demonstrating the risk is to examine the contents of the British psychological publications which deal with clinical and related areas of psychology (the *British Journal of Clinical Psychology* and the *British Journal of Medical Psychology*) for articles on drug abuse. Ignoring papers dealing with alcohol, each journal contained just one drugs-related article between 1981 and 1988. In contrast, alcoholism was dealt with eight times by the clinical journal and three times by the medical journal, which also had one article on prescribed drug dependence.

The first of the articles dealing with drug use was Woolfson (1982), which concerned 'psychological correlates of solvent abuse'. What this actually means is that the *High School Personality Questionnaire* (Cattell and Cattell, 1969) was given to a group of glue-sniffing delinquents and a matched group of non-sniffers. Few personality differences were found between the two groups. Nevertheless, Woolfson (1982, p. 66) seems keen to describe the glue sniffer as 'outgoing, heedless, cheerful, adventurous, alert and extravert'. Clearly the fault is with the glue sniffer in the sense that his or her individual characteristics are held responsible for this propensity to sniffing. However, it would be far more adequate to describe the data as indicating that overwhelmingly glue sniffers are like their non-sniffing controls. This would encourage one to look away from individual personalities to social factors as the explanation of sniffing. In other words, a medical conceptualization restricts explanation of the substance abuse.

The only other article on addiction (Viney *et al.*, 1985) is at first sight more promising. This claims to be about 'The addiction experience as a function of the addict's history'. Couched in terms of personal construct theory (see, for example, Bannister, 1977; 1985), it falls at the first hurdle of selecting the research samples:

> Two comparison groups were used in the study to identify the unique characteristics of the addiction experience. One group consisted of a sample of students attending university who were matched with the addict group on sex and age. They were selected as a comparison group of their full-time and successful involvement in the workforce and/or academic studies which precluded any major involvement with drugs of addiction. The other group was made up of unemployed people, also matched for sex and age, who were chosen to provide a comparison of addicts with other people undergoing the stress of a major life crisis.
>
> (Viney *et al.*, 1985, p. 75)

The assumption in all of this is of the debilitated addict, incapable of holding down a job. Whether this would allow a reasonable understanding of the experience of being an addict rather than being an unemployed addict becomes a moot point. It is intriguing to note that in the study seven out of nine measures differentiated addicts from students. However, only two of these differentiated addicts from the unemployed! Why they did becomes patently obvious when they are examined in a little detail:

1   *Sociality:* This includes items like 'If I keep off it, people help me' and 'I'm starting to get the trust back with my parents'. These might be expected to reflect the addicts experience better than that of the unemployed but they are scarcely earth-shattering differences in the light of that.

2   *Cognitive anxiety:* On this measure, the respondents had to evaluate their most overwhelming experiences by reference to questions like 'I couldn't believe it. It really blew me out', incongruous experiences (using questions like 'I don't know whether he was using me or not'), and strange new events ('I've no idea what's going to happen to me tomorrow'). Again it is not surprising that addicts at a counselling and referral clinic for drugs users answer such questions differently from the unemployed.

In short, the experiences of the unemployed addict and the unemployed non-addict are in the main remarkably similar if the research is anything to go by – except for items which common sense tells us might be expected to be answered differently by addicts. But this is not the message of the original researchers!

The constrained understanding of the social issue of drug abuse by psychologists means that many important aspects of drug use fail to come under the psychologist's purview. For example, Auld (1981) reveals a radically different way of looking at some so-called drugs effects once the viewpoint becomes widened. So distortions of time, feelings of mirth and hilarity, and enhanced appreciation of music are common enough 'effects' of marijuana. In terms of the slowing-down of the passage of time, Auld suggests that this is a consequence of the marijuana user being preoccupied with the analysis of every moment of experience. Such is the uncertainty of the drug-using situation that it needs to be carefully attended to in order to be negotiated. In other words, the 'effect of the drug' is not to be found in a particular biochemical influence but as much more of a social matter to be understood in social terms. That Auld, a sociologist, begins to ask questions which are neglected by psychologists who ought to include among their profession experts on human perceptual experience, is a problem as much in need of understanding as any other to do with drugs.

Concluding comments

According to Gossop (1984, pp. 250–1):

> It would be reassuring to be able to predict a steady, continuous increase of our understanding of drug and alcohol dependence, and a corresponding improvement in the techniques available for the treatment of such problems ... However, there is some room for doubt ... We still have only the most rudimentary understanding of the ways in which drugs are used and abused ... Nor is there any general consensus upon what sort of problem ... drug dependence really [is] ... Although less widely accepted than it was fifteen or twenty years ago, the biomedical model continues to be the most influential view of the addictions, and there is no shortage or research into the physiology, pharmacology and biochemistry of drug dependence ... However, it has not led to any advances in treatment, and it is unfortunate that this sort of research has helped to confirm the supremacy of substance-based views of the addictions.

The argument of this chapter is that the history of the social construction of a 'problem' is of prime importance in understanding it. History provides vital clues as to the social and institutional context in which our modern social views originated. Furthermore, it tells us, for example, why we 'treat' 'drug addicts' and why the 'biological' basis of drug effects dominates.

There is nothing special about drug use in this respect. Many other so-called social problems share similar socio-histories. Psychology has to take note of its close ties and intellectual allegiences to the professions which have contributed these dominant views. Much of the material discussed in this chapter probably fits the description 'social constructionist', which is to say that it treats understanding or knowledge as socially constructed.

Care has to be exercised against assuming that the processes by which social knowledge is created are necessarily subtle or accidental. Zola (1977), for example, discusses the way in which medicine has expanded into dealing with a number of 'life's problems' which do not in themselves seem to be particularly medical in the first instance. He cites the presidential address of a Dr P. Henderson to the British School Health Service Group. This is described as a clarion call for fellow school health workers to involve themselves in such 'health problems' as poverty and slum or new slum housing, behaviour and emotional difficulties, maladjustment, juvenile delinquency, drug taking, suicide, children in care, venereal diseases, teenage illegitimate pregnancies, and abortion. Henderson also mentions other problems such as children with visual, hearing, physical handicaps, speech and language difficulties, epilepsy, dyslexia, and emotional, educational and intellectual retardation. The list is so long that we can share Zola's wonderment about who or what is omitted.

But there is a consequence, some might say a 'social advantage' for medics, of allowing such a wide range of 'problems' to be hijacked by the medical profession as medical issues:

> My concern is what happens when a problem and its bearers become tainted with the label 'illness'. Any emphasis on the latter inevitably locates the source of trouble as well as the place of treatment primarily in individuals and makes the etiology of the trouble asocial and impersonal, like a virulent bacteria or a hormonal imbalance. ... If it has to be handled anywhere or if anyone is to blame it is individuals – usually the carriers of the problem – and certainly not the rest of us, or society at large.
>
> (Zola, 1977, pp. 62–3)

The social construction of the problem in many cases provides the 'means' of dealing with the problem.

The point of this chapter was not simply to examine the drugs issue. It was to establish some principles for the examination of social issues from a psychological point of view. As such, some of the themes raised will reappear in later chapters. The precise detail varies, the broad sweep of the social creation of social concerns is more universal:

> In the act of description scientists establish an essential inventory of 'what there is.' In this sense, such terms as 'repression,' 'socioeconomic class,' 'schizophrenia,' 'learned helplessness,' 'midlife crisis,' 'dissonance reduction,' and so on are not the results of keen observation. Rather they operate as lenses supplied by the theorist to colleagues and society alike. The world is not so constituted until the lens is employed.
>
> (Gergen, 1982, p. 23)

5

TAKING SIDES: CHILD PHYSICAL
AND SEXUAL ABUSE

Initially Freud was quite prepared to accept that women's experiences of childhood sexual interferences were real ... Beneath every case of hysteria, he believed, was 'one or more occurrences of premature sexual experience' ... His paper was ignored or ridiculed by the other members of the Society. Later, after a variety of personal and professional problems, and ... the threat from colleagues that if he pursued this line of thinking he would be ostracized from psychoanalysis, Freud reneged. His new analysis of his patients' experiences was that they were lying to himself and to him.

(Herbert, 1989, p. 156)

This chapter is about a major current issue in what society claims are its responsibilities towards children. Physical and sexual abuse, as the key aspects of the issue, will be the central concern; neglect and emotional abuse are less high-profile matters in the debate and will not be discussed. Although physical and sexual abuse are best conceptualized rather differently in terms of their immediate 'causes', at the same time there are similarities between them in terms of factors like male power which warrant their discussion as a pair. Further, both are intertwined as socially constructed issues of urgent concern.

The Dutch academic, Theo Sandfort, has raised a question concerning child sexual abuse which warrants early consideration since it seems to strike at basic assumptions about abuse. He takes the concept 'sexual abuse' and tries to formulate its various meanings:

'Sexual abuse' seems to be used as an all-inclusive term. Sexual contacts are considered as such *regardless* of the way they came about or the way they have been experienced by the child. Some investigators even included in their concept of 'sexual abuse' events in which no physical contact took place, such as exhibition of the sexual organs, making improper suggestions, showing pornography, talking erotically about sexual matters. Where there was some kind of physical contact, touching the breasts through the clothing and even 'passionate kissing' is sometimes included. These ... may seem morally improper, but do they inevitably cause harm? Does the term 'sexual abuse' not start to lose meaning when it comes to encompass virtually every kind of sexual experience a child can have with an adult?

(Sandfort, 1989, p. 5)

Irrespective of the immediate inclination of some to label discussions like Sandfort's as activist paedophiliac propaganda, it would seem that he, at the very least, performs an important service: he opens up an issue for discussion which has essentially been shut down in recent years. Simply by defining adult–child sexual behaviour as abuse, the impression is created that the child is inevitably seriously harmed by the experience (Howitt, 1990c). Whether or not this is true needs to be submitted to examination. It cannot merely be accepted as axiomatic.

Child abuse and child sexual abuse are recent inventions – so modern, in fact, that they are probably in their earliest stages of proper development as a social issue. Only in the last few years have they become seen as issues fit for the attention of psychologists and other professionals. This does not mean that sexual and physical assaults on children have not taken place by members of their family throughout human history, only that these were not construed as 'abuse', as understood today. Indeed, so recent is psychology's involvement in the field that I can claim with some justification that even as an undergraduate student I was the first psychologist actively to research child sexual abuse. (We are omitting, of course, to mention minor figures such as Sigmund Freud.) However, I thought I was concerned with father–daughter incest as child sexual abuse had not been manufactured as a social issue by around 1964. Incest did not, at that time, carry with it any automatic assumption of direct harm to the child involved. Indeed, one of the most distinguished psychologists of the day claimed that it was *genetic* matters which made the incest taboo necessary to prevent biological degeneracy:

Very simply the formulation I am advancing argues that the biological consequence of inbreeding is a decrease in fitness. This decrement in fitness is present in all animals, but it is particularly pronounced in the case of man [*sic*] for a number of reasons including his slowness in reaching sexual maturity and his limited number of offspring. Given this lowered fitness of a human group practicing incest operates at a selective disadvantage in competition with outbreeding human groups and ultimately would be unlikely to survive. Conversely, a group which prohibited inbreeding (presumably through some form of the incest taboo) would be at an advantage in comparison to groups that permitted inbreeding.

(Lindzey, 1967, p. 1051)

Lindzey also mentions that deformed offspring and infertility were very common themes in incest myths. It is not harm to the victim but harm to society which seems the dominant theme. Of course, if Lindzey's formulation were to be taken seriously it would imply that stepfathers involved in sexual intercourse with their step-daughters commit a lesser crime because genetic 'risks' are not involved.

The literature on incest at the time was not particularly impressive and, on reflection, denied its occurrence in 'normal' families. From memory, the major argument was whether incestuous fathers were mentally subnormal. Early studies suggested they were, but there were big problems about which types of people got prosecuted. Like many other psychologists working in prisons then – or anyone reading the Kinsey reports (Kinsey *et al.*, 1953) on sexual behaviour in detail – I knew that incest was not all that uncommon. But that key knowledge could not be used to generate concern about a major social issue of today – child sexual abuse.

Even Sigmund Freud's psychoanalytic research, as already seen, had identified and then abandoned an acutely accurate insight under outside pressure. Forced into the assumption that incestuous determinants of hysteria were 'fantasy', he might be seen as not only untrue to his observations but also deserving of the later wrath of feminists and others for his consequent undermining of a significant aspect of female experience. But it is question-able that he is more culpable than any of the many professionals who failed to 'do anything about' such adult–child contacts. In a sense Freud was a victim of the patriarchal social structure as much as a defender of that system.

Baartman (1990), in a broad-sweeping look at the refusal to acknowledge child sexual abuse during this century, seeks a systematic explanation of why this should have been the case. Some of his examples almost defy belief. For example, doctors would explain cases of sexually transmitted diseases in children as a consequence of indirect contact. Thus toilets, towels, drinking utensils and bedclothes were the assumed culprits rather than sexually abusing parents. Baartman identifies four separate 'conceptual frameworks' which served as obstacles to the acceptance of children's claims of abuse:

1 The cognitive incompetence of the child – the belief that children were incompetent as witnesses and that their evidence should, therefore, be discounted.
2 The moral unreliability of the child – the view that children may be 'immoral' enough to report fantasies as realities.
3 The disturbed child – children who claimed abuse were mentally disturbed. It was not considered that the abuse caused the disturbance.
4 The erotically seducing child – the idea that the child actively seduced the adult, even when the child in question might be, say, a five-year-old.

These factors may well explain the lack of recognition of 'child abuse' by professionals for so long. This begs the question how the social problem came to be constructed. Is it more than the mere abandonment of the above four 'conceptual frameworks'?

Development of the social problem

Physical abuse

Individual victims of child abuse were well aware of its existence. However, in itself this is insufficient to mobilize society to identify sexual and physical violence against children as being of major concern. Indeed, it may be argued that society had considerably to revise its attitude to domestic matters, and domestic violence in particular, before it could 'discover' child abuse (Gelles, 1979; Gelles and Cornell, 1985). One is reminded that husbands' beating of their spouses was actively condoned in some parts of the Western world until relatively recently. Concern originated in the USA in the mid-1940s with doctors specializing in X-ray work. One of them, Caffey, noted that many of the infants suffering internal bleeding in the skull also had multiple bone fractures of varying ages (Nelson, 1984). Gradually during the next few years the view built up in medical journals that 'bad' parents were responsible. In 1960, the first article written by a social worker discussing such violence appeared. But by and large abuse was a matter confined to the medical literature.

Henry Kempe helped magnify the basic idea into a concept which had the 'right' emotive and descriptive undertones. The concept was 'the battered child syndrome' (Nelson, 1984). This encouraged the more general social recognition of such physical violence against children. From then on action followed very quickly. The media began to take an interest and by the mid-1960s all American states had statutory requirements that medics had to report suspected cases of abuse to appropriate child-care agencies. The scene had changed and it was no longer quite so easy to ignore the possibility of parental responsibility for physical injuries.

The matter may have begun in the USA, but it did not end there. It crossed cultures. How, for example, did it become a British matter of concern? During the 1960s the idea of the battered child syndrome began to filter through the British medical community, albeit at varying rates in different sectors. Child specialists were naturally one major group quickly to recognize the problem. However, many of the key 'frontline' personnel, such as casualty doctors, were not generally alerted to the matter. According to Parton (1981; 1985) the reasons for this might have included a psychological unwillingness to accept that parents could act so extremely violently against their offspring, not liking to violate doctor–patient confidentiality, and not wanting to lose control of the situation to other agencies or to spend time involved in legal proceedings.

The sea change in Britain which finally made parental violence against children into a social problem of high urgency was the case of Maria Colwell, a seven-year-old killed in 1973 by her stepfather. Her aunt had acted as her foster parent for five years. Shortly before her seventh birthday, though, Maria was placed back into the care of her mother and stepfather by means of a supervision order granted to the local authority by the courts. Despite the involvement of several social workers in the case, the child was battered to death. Her teacher and neighbours had expressed concern but were ignored. She was three-quarters the normal weight of a child of her height and age.

Parton chooses to explain the outrage generated at Maria Colwell's death as an example of Stanley Cohen's (1974) concept of *moral panic*. From time to time, a particular person or an identifiable group of persons comes to be perceived as a substantial threat to the majority's values and interests. Such people are characterized by Cohen as being 'folk-devils'. In a sense they form a focus for expressing moral outrage. They provide a foil for goodness. The majority of society form the 'goodies'. But in this case social workers (much more than parents) were the baddies. Parton also raises Hall's concept of *convergence* (Hall *et al.*, 1978) in order partially to explain the moral panic. Convergence describes the situation in which the greater the number of issues relating to the broader concern, the greater the likelihood of a moral panic. The Maria Colwell case primarily involved extreme violence (a major concern after the demonstrations against the Vietnam War, the Festival of Light, campaigns against television violence, and so on). But secondary issues included the perceived 'sloppy liberalism' which caricatured the 1960s left-wing, muddled social worker. Hostility was beginning to be aroused in the 1970s to such an approach with the wind of the new 'political' realism to come. According to Parton (1981, p. 409):

> We can see the panic as part of a broader moral and political reaction to re-establish the traditional virtues and it provided the ideological battleground where certain representatives of 'soft liberalism' could be more readily harnessed to the traditional virtues and the increased emphasis on 'law and order'.

By this he means that social work could be brought in line with the more traditional approaches of state control. The police, for example, and social work begin to share overlapping functions by becoming more repressive in their dealings with people. A new approach to social work was in the making, according to Parton.

Child sexual abuse

Rather different social processes were involved in making *sexual* abuse a focus of concern. Hechler (1988) summarizes the main factors in the USA as: the women's movement, and the victim's rights movement. The treatment of women rape victims by the courts began to be a major focus of concern in the 1970s. Particularly criticized was the process which doubly jeopardized the rape victim by, first, the rapist, and second, the criminal justice system. Many victims felt themselves to be on trial. Lawyers defending their clients tried to undermine the moral standing and character of the women involved. Attempts to change public and political opinion on this matter had the spin-off that the plight of sexually abused children was also highlighted. Children have many difficulties in relation to the legal system. Not the least of these is testifying in court, though this a matter which has changed in many respects. The events and arguments in the USA concerning sexual abuse were paralleled elsewhere, including in Britain. However, this was a 'discovery' which, unlike physical abuse, was not the province of the medical profession.

Physical violence against children in history

There is a temptation to see violence as an accelerating feature of modern life. However, this is to ignore the historical context of violence. For the moment, the special case of homicide (unlawful killing) of children may be considered. Infanticide is a sub-category of this special case. Daly and Wilson (1988) document some of the evidence concerning the great frequency of infanticide throughout history and, particularly, in Britain in the last few centuries. One of the difficulties in establishing the extent of infanticide is that it has held only a marginally illegal status historically. Roman men, for example, had the right to dispose of their descendants however they wished. In Britain between 1856 and 1860, '3901 coroners' inquests were held into suspicious deaths of infants less than 2 years of age' (Daly and Wilson, 1988, p. 67) in London alone. Newspapers of this time typically described as many as five dead babies being found daily in London parks. Modern ideas about the importance of infant life hardly reflect even such recent historical facts. Such infanticide rates did not create then the furore they would today. One reason for this was the appalling treatment that mothers of illegitimate children received in Victorian times. The 'single parent' may not be advantaged nowadays, but employment for single mothers was very difficult then. Being 'in service' was the typical work of young women but was not normally available to those with illegitimate families. Institutions for paupers housed high proportions of single women with 'bastard' children (Daly and Wilson, 1988, p. 67). Obviously the risk of being driven to the workhouse because of an illegitimate pregnancy may have been a strong pressure towards infanticide.

Infanticide, however, legally is not any unlawful killing of an infant. It is a very specially defined crime which only one person can commit. This is the mother who kills her child before it is one year old. So it is a crime specific to the mother–infant relationship.

According to Daly and Wilson's (1988) data, the first year of life is the most dangerous time in the life cycle in terms of death at the hands of another. Furthermore, by far the most likely killer of an infant in this age group is its own mother. The next high peak for deaths is in young adulthood though, of course, mothers are rarely responsible for the deaths of older children. A steady decline occurs in homicide rates as the child's age group increases. Fathers are more likely than mothers to be killers as the child gets older. However, by and large, the frequency of such killings is low, particularly for children over nine or ten years. The differences between fathers and mothers are slight. It is notable that throughout childhood, except for the first year of life, *non-relatives* are generally more likely to kill a child than parents, though again not substantially so. But at about the age of 13 or so (when parents are most unlikely to kill) non-relatives are very many times more likely to be the killers.

The figures for England and Wales (Home Office, 1987) show much the same trends. In the context of beliefs about child abuse these make interesting reading. The figures for the period from the late 1970s to the late 1980s seem remarkably consistent. The numbers of unlawful killings per million children by age group in the year 1987 were as follows: under 1 year, 45 (30 deaths in total); 1–5 years, 10 (26 in total); 5–16 years, 3 (22 in total). Members of the child's family are responsible for about a third of all of these deaths. Although, in this sense, the first year of life is the most dangerous in terms of homicide, the rest of childhood is rather safer than adulthood. The child is also more at risk outside the family than inside. There is a qualification to this. Thus far, natural or biological parents have been discussed. A different picture emerges for stepparents. According to Daly and Wilson (1988, p. 85), the origin of the 'step' in stepparent is not as in 'one step removed' from being the natural parent; rather it comes from an old word meaning 'to deprive or bereave'. Stepparents thus are particularly dangerous. Canadian data suggests that for the 0–2-year age group, a stepchild is 70 times more at risk than natural offspring. Daly and Wilson (1988, p. 90) offer two alternative explanations:

> Much of the popular literature on stepfamilies takes it for granted that the conflict derives principally from the children's rejection of the substitute parent, rather than the reverse. ... [T]his interpretation rings false. Surely it is the stepparent who is likely to resent the pseudoparental obligation thrust upon him, and any rejection by the child may be interpreted as reflecting a well-founded apprehension of that lack of genuine parental solicitude.

They suggest that the two hypotheses mentioned make contrasting predictions about the age of greatest risk of violence. As older children are more in a position to reject the stepparent they should be the most at risk. But they are not – the greater risk is to infants.

The question of sexual abuse is much more problematic in terms of statistical evidence, largely because much of the necessary research has not been carried out properly if at all. It is not wise to take the social work statistics on physical abuse or sexual abuse as evidence. These have been well filtered through a number of different definitions imposed by organizations. Typical social work statistics refer to children 'at risk', which is dependent on social workers' definition of what constitutes being 'at risk'. The level of activity of social workers in the area as well as the number of reports made to them also contribute to the incidence. Criticisms has been made of the telephone 'helplines' which encourage 'malicious' reports of abuse which has not happened. Claims of abuse have even been made as part of divorce proceedings – a high proportion of these appear to have been malicious in order to achieve a particular outcome (McPherson, 1990).

It would seem rather more appropriate to look at specially undertaken surveys (or homicide rates, which are less susceptible to reporting biases as homicide is difficult to conceal). In terms of sexual victimization, a study by West (1985) is useful. One part of this research involved a survey of women aged 20–39 on a general medical practitioner's list. Forty-two per cent of the women replying claimed some degree of sexual contact with adults in childhood. The range of such contacts was wide. The largest category (involving 18 per cent of women) was exposure to 'flashers'. Full sexual intercourse was less common, though one in 50 women made such reports. Approximately a tenth of women had had their genitals fondled by an adult during childhood. West reports a number of other studies which give a similar impression.

By no means all offences were committed by fathers upon daughters. West's (1985, p. 29) figures among those reporting sexual contact with an adult give the following rank ordering of relationships:

1   Strangers (49%)
2   Family friend (24%)
3   Uncle (6%)
4 } Stepfather (5%)
4 } Boyfriend (5%)
6 } Authority figure (teacher, GP, vicar, etc.) (4%)
6 } Father (4%)
8   Brother/cousin (3%)

Nothing in these figures suggests that the primary aim of child protection should be centred upon the immediate family. Indeed, strangers and family friends are overwhelmingly responsible. West does not report analyses for different types of sexual activity. As a consequence, care has to be exercised with the data. An obvious point is that activities against adult abuse of children should not concentrate solely on close relatives. It may be that more serious acts are being perpetrated by close relatives, but it is far from clear that this is the case or what sorts of act are particularly harmful to children. He does report, however, that in a smaller sub-sample who were actually interviewed (not just responding to a self-completion questionnaire) about 1 per cent were sexually penetrated by their natural father and a similar small number by their stepfather. Two per cent were victims of attempted intercourse by their brother. The corresponding figures for fathers and stepfathers are about 1 per cent each.

Of the members of his interview sample, West (1985, p. 70) ranks the long-term self-claimed effects of the experiences were as follows:

1   Pity, amusement (71%)
2   Anger (69%)
3   Indifference, problem worked through (58%)
4   Wary of men (53%)
5   Guilt/disgust (49%)
6   Regret (41%)
7   Hatred/resentment towards adult (36%)
8   Confusion about sexual norms (32%)
9   Anxiety for other children (24%)
10 Emotional/sexual dysfunction (22%)

Clearly these self-reported long-term outcomes are varied and often far from trivial. West's (1985, p. 65) own summary of the literature presents a view which is not fully in accord with his own data:

> Previous research has come to various and conflicting conclusions regarding the effects of childhood sexual encounters with adults. According to one view the very disparity in size and social sophistication between children and adults render[s] such encounters inherently traumatic (Oremland and Oremland 1977). Card (1975), whilst accepting that there are risks of mental or physical harm where very young girls are concerned, states that here any ill effects are generally short term. Kinsey *et al* (1953, p. 121), go further and state, 'it is difficult to understand why a child, except for its cultural conditioning, should be disturbed at having its genitals touched, or disturbed at seeing the genitalia of other persons, or disturbed at even more specific sexual contacts'.

West is able to cite a number of studies which give some support for his comments although the evidence is not very consistent. Some researchers claim that adult–child contacts have no damaging effects (see, for example, Powell and Chalkley, 1988) though there is also evidence to say that they do (see Lynch and Roberts, 1982).

This is an important topic which probably deserves clearer answers than the above, but there is other evidence. Sandfort (1988) found that *non-consensual* sexual activity before the age of 16 was associated with problems in the present (adult) sexual relationship and greater levels of psychosomatic health complaints. However, *consensual* child–adult contact was associated with higher levels of present-day sexual desire and arousability – and with fewer anxieties about contacts of a sexual nature.

In a sense there is a danger of writing the preamble to a paedophile's charter by raising the issue of the harm done by adult–child contacts. One thing is certain. It is not known with any precision which children will be manifestly harmed, and which relatively unscathed. There are obviously enormous problems in defining harm, let alone assessing it. However, what research there is available is of great significance since most child-protection activity functions like a quickly acting emergency service akin to the fire or ambulance service. If speed were not inevitably of the essence, then more considered activity might be possible. In other words, the panic could be taken out of the situation. Given that intervention may create crisis in the family (including a child being taken from its parents), the risks of over-speedy action are not negligible. The processes of being taken into and living in care can in itself be extremely damaging. The balance is not between bad and good, but may be between bad and unsatisfactory.

Preventing child abuse?

It is very easy for psychologists, partly by virtue of their training, to fall into positivistic traps. In the area of child abuse this trap is primarily to assume that psychologists have the skills and techniques for recognizing and preventing potential child abuse. The second aspect of the trap is to assume that interference in 'potentially abusive families' is justified. According to Browne and Saqui (1988, p. 58):

> The risk approach to child maltreatment can be seen as a managerial tool for the flexible and rational distribution of existing resources and their maximal utilization. This is based on the assessment of children and their families as high or low risk for child abuse and neglect. The aim of the risk strategy is to give special attention to those in the greatest need of help in parenting *before* child maltreatment occurs.

'Risk factors' are those characteristics of families or individual family members (as well as those of the offspring) which predict the likelihood of abuse. Previous research (Browne and Stevenson, 1983) had demonstrated that abusing families tend to differ in a number of respects from non-abusing families. On the basis of ratings made by health visitors, abusing families were:

1 Four times more likely to be rated as indifferent, intolerant or over-anxious towards the child.
2 Nine times more likely to have histories of family violence.
3 Two-and-a-half times more likely to suffer socio-economic problems such as unemployment
4 Eight times more likely to have a premature baby with a low birth weight.
5 Seven times more likely to have been abused or neglected as a child.
6 Seven times more likely to have a stepfather or cohabitee present.
7 Five times more likely to have a single or separated parent.
8 Twice more likely to have a mother under 21 at time of birth.
9 Three times more likely to have a history of mental illness, drug or alcohol addiction.
10 Three times more likely to experience the separation of the child from the mother for more than 24 hours after birth.

(Three other characteristics did not significantly differentiate – incidence of handicapped infants, gaps less than 18 months between births of children, and infants never being breastfed.)

On the face of things, this would seem to be good evidence of the possibility of preventive intervention. Several predictors of 'child abuse' have high discriminatory power. Factors of 8 or 9 are common in the above list. It should be noted, however, that the definition of child abuse was that a case conference had been called involving social workers and other professionals. There is no measure of child abuse which is independent of a social process which decides that there is a problem. Thus, believing in the first place that a family with a stepfather is likely to be abusive may help determine that such a family in which a child suffers an injury should be investigated for abuse. In this sense, the 'predictors of abuse' and 'abuse' may well be confounded. This is raised not as a mere methodological criticism but to indicate how misery may be heaped on families who have had it 'rough' in the first place. Indeed, probably not many of the predictors will surprise anyone. This may be a sign that a dominant view of social disadvantage and its effects is well entrenched.

There is something potentially oppressive about Browne and Stevenson's approach. Aspects of this can be seen in the apparent 'screening' potential of the research. A checklist was routinely filled in for 14,238 children born in one English county during 1984 and 1985. The items discussed above (excepting breastfeeding) were assessed by the midwife and then the health visitor on the basis of available information around the time of birth, including documents and observation of the family. Browne sought to relate the checklist factors to the criterion of a case conference within two years of birth.

The data can be used to assess the worth of the 'screening' approach. Table 5.1 shows that there are relatively few mistakes in detecting abusing families as such. That is, families who are subject to case conferences would have been predicted to be abusing by the checklist. However, an awfully high number of *non-abusive families* are wrongly identified as *potentially abusive* – there were about 36 wrong identifications for every correct one!

Table 5.1 Percentages of correct and incorrect cases of abuse identification

Identified in checklist as	Abusing family	Non-abusing family
Abusing	0.33%	11.95%
Non-abusing	0.07%	87.65%

Left as an academic exercise, there is no particular problem which arouses concern about Browne's research – for the moment. However, should the intention be to take preventive action against abuse, then the dangers are great, obvious and disturbing. For example, if it became policy to identify potentially abusing families using the checklist and remove their children, many errors would be made. Twelve per cent of families could lose their children for no good reason and resources diverted from other priorities. If less draconian measures were taken which 'merely' involved social workers, psychologists, and others providing support to potentially abusing families, this remains a massive investment of resources. Its major consequence, however, would inevitably be oppressive and intrusive.

Browne and Saqui (1988, p. 80) do little to enlighten their readership as to the nature of the government whose budget would stretch to meeting the following:

1   All families with a newborn child should be screened perinatally using social and demographic characteristics of the child and its family. This will identify a target group for further screening. However, the remaining population cannot be considered immune to family stress and child abuse. Any change in family circumstances leading to increased stress should be assessed and if applicable the family added to the target group.

2   All parents in the target group should be screened three to six months after birth on their perceptions of the newborn child and those aspects of parenting and family life they consider to be stressful.

3   Approximately nine to twelve months after birth the infant's attachment to the primary caregiver should be assessed together with parental sensitivity to the infant's behaviour.

Their solution seems to shift resources into the coffers of the expert in child-abuse prevention. Wage costs would be the main financial requirement. It seems to ignore that experts have often failed to prevent abuse which was 'as clear as daylight' to teachers and neighbours. Parton (1985, p. 188) is rather more direct in his analysis of what would be appropriate:

> If we are to attempt to tackle the factors associated with child abuse and neglect, the first priority must be a comprehensive anti-poverty strategy. Such a strategy should recognise the need for a more equal distribution of resources. ... a reduction in unemployment would be important.

The fundamental difference between the two approaches is that Browne and Saqui intrinsically accept that there are pathological families. As it is their fault, they deserve whatever intervention is made – even though they deserve whatever they get even if they are merely of the type of family that Browne diagnoses as potentially abusive. Parton argues differently: that politics is responsible for the distribution of wealth and creates the social structure which forces some families into poverty, the breeding ground of abuse. Although interventions are necessary, they are the surgery, not the preventive medicine, of structural change.

Browne and Saqui's approach would encourage errors whereby innocent families would be seen as potential abusers. These are the false positives of the next section.

False positives

It should not be a radical reformulation in a socially equitable psychology to begin to ask questions about professional activity. There is a case questioning not only the faults of families which make them abusive but also the 'errors' of professionals and their organizations. What causes them to make mistakes? There are many cases in which catastrophic errors have been made in the area of child protection. Numerous public enquiries have been undertaken into what went wrong in particular instances (see, for example, Department of Health and Social Security, 1982). The 'errors' of professionals, broadly speaking, are as follows: false positives are diagnoses of abuse when nothing has in fact happened; while false negatives are failures to detect abuse when it has occurred. The former are our major concern in this section.

To accept 'errors' on the grounds that they are inevitable 'hiccups' in the eradication of abuse is naive. First, it assumes that abuse is invariably so serious that dire consequences will follow without intervention. On the premise that 'abuse is abuse is abuse', the dangers of intervention are ignored. Second, it encourages the neglect of justice for all parties. Third, abusers are not allowed to excuse their behaviours as 'errors'.

The likelihood of errors due to over-zealousness or a total commitment to help poor and maltreated children is perhaps higher than it would be without moral outrage associated with the concept of 'abuse' (see also Sandfort, 1989). Can the expert judgement of professionals, including psychologists, be relied on for a balanced view? It is probably to over-estimate the isolation of professionals from 'moral panics' and other pressures. The following example of an outrageous use of psychology or the position of the psychologist is probably sufficient a caution.

The concern about the naivety of academic psychology's treatment of significant social issues needs to be extended to the professional work of practising psychologists. In one well-documented case, the actions of the clinical psychologist were so over-zealous as to verge on irresponsibility. Howitt (1990a) reports how social workers requested a clinical psychologist to prepare a report for a court hearing. This was based entirely on the psychologist's 'clinical' interpretation of a story written as part of the child's schoolwork. It should be stressed that the story was being analysed in connection with a court hearing concerning the child's two siblings. She was about 11 years old at the time of writing the story, which contains all the information that the psychologist claims was available to him. The child's story was as follows:

Christmas Eve

One cold Christmas Eve the white snow began to fall. The wind howled the trees rustled. I moved curtain and peered through the window I saw something running around my snowman. I jumped out of bed put my slippers on and my dressing gown on. I ran down stairs and I opened the door the little men stopped moving and they ran up to me they pulled me into a secret world. There was frost on the green blades of grass. I stood up and I saw white angels prancing around. and I could hear bells. I walked on and I walked past a tree and a man appeared. he walked up to me and stopped me with his walking stick. Luckily I crawled under it I walked on and I saw a may pole. I could see little people dancing. I wish that I could do that. I stood there for hours and hours. as tears began to fill my eyes. Oh I so wish I was a may-pole dancer. I got up and I went back the way I came. I ran in case that man ran after me again. I ran back into the world of our own it seemed like nothing had happened. I couldn't believed what had happened. I went upstairs and I took my slippers off and my dressing gown and got into bed.

The next morning it was Christmas I woke up and I opened one of my presents and it was a walking stick and thats funny I thought. I've seen that somewhere before. My Mum walked in and she wanted to look at my presents. So I showed her she said who gave this one I said I don't know I'll have a look and I said it says watch out I'll strike again don't you worry. I started to cry. My mum was worrying she didn't tell my dad he might worry as well. I went to bed and I left all my presents and when I woke up in the morning the walking stick was hanging on some string. I screamed my mum come in and she said what's a matter and I said I woke up and I found the walking stick in the front of my face. When I sat up Wait a minute my mum said whats this and it was a note it said I warned you didn't I. I didn't know what to do so when my dad came home we told him. We rang the police up and my mum said don't and I said why? because I don't want them involved right. So the next night my dad stayed in my bedroom all night in case the man returned again but he didn't. The next next night my dad didn't bother coming in my bedroom and it didn't bother striking again. It was funny though because my mum was out and when she came back he came to me again. I tried to scream but he put his hand over my mouth and I couldn't recognize who it was. I tried to pull his or her mask off but I couldn't I tried hard. Just then my dad walked in the man disappeared but I don't know where. My dad asked me what was a matter and I said a man attacked me he said what! man attacked me. Right Did you recognize the man No! because he had a mask on and I couldn't see what he looked like. I tried to pull his mask off but I couldn't wait we'll find him then I looked out of the window and I saw those men again and I showed my dad. We went downstairs to have a look they were dancing round my snowman again they tried to pull us in again but my dad stopped them from pulling us into that world again. Then they disappeared.

We wondered what was happening We went back in my dad said wait until we see them again. I'll get him when we see them again I said to my dad Just let me go into that world on my own then you come in. So I opened the door and they ran up to me again and pulled me into the secret world and I went past the angels dancing and prancing. Then I went past the tree then I saw a man stood behind the tree. Luckily it was my dad and we walked further on. We went past a tree with apples on it and I picked one up and I was just about to eat it when it turned into a frog. It jumped off my hand and then turned into a apple. Wonder what this world is coming to [–] a disaster probably.

We went back into our world and my mum come back off her holidays and nothing seen with the man dancing round the snowman. The messages carried on I kept having messages everyday. One night I put some cushions under my covers. So that I could catch who was doing it to me. But they didn't come they had to know I was doing it. and I told only my Mum and dad. So it has go[t] to be my Mum or dad. So I didn't tell any of them but no-one turned up again they must have magical powers. Now my Mum and dad haven't got magic powers well I don't think so anyway I hope not. So I kept trying but for one night. Someone was creeping about in my bedroom so I got a sack and I bagged whoever it was. My pet cat I thought it was small.

Oh no I said why can't I catch whoever it is. This time I'll get her or him don't you worry this time I will and I might o.k. So I got everything ready for the big day I caught who it was it was my mum. I was so ashamed I asked her why. She said I don't know it was all confusing. From that year on nothing else happened. The end.

On the basis of this story only – no interview and no further information – a Senior Clinical Psychologist prepared a case for a court hearing which included the following:

Report on a story entitled 'Christmas Eve'
I have divided my thoughts with regard to the story into the following sections:

Symbolism: Jackie is clearly very imaginative and uses a wealth of symbols, some of which may be derived from her reading or classwork … [T]he walking stick appears as a persistent source of anxiety, if not terror, throughout the story. It is menacing, and intrudes into the girl's happiest moments, eg 'opening presents'. There is a sense in which something which begins, or is projected, outside the family, comes back through into the family again, ie cannot be escaped within the family circle. Clearly this *might* be a phallic symbol. That it appears in front of her face and terrifies her might lead one to wonder whether a penis has been presented to her in this way, and an association between this and oral sex may not be excluded.

Father: I was interested that father needed protecting by mother from 'worrying'. However, father is eventually told. Her father is seen as protecting her by remaining in her bedroom on one occasion. In general, her father is presented in the usual protective fashion, but I was concerned that the man she appears frightened of 'disappears' as soon as father walks in. … It is possible that she has disassociated these two father images as a response to her father behaving in two very different ways.

Mother: Most significantly, she was seen as reluctant to contact the police. I thought it interesting that the girl wished her mother to contact the police, and equally important that she appeared not to want to. Her mother was also described as going out and returning with the man. There was a sense here of mother being involved with the man and perhaps colluding with him. …

Conclusions: I was left in no doubt that Jackie is a deeply unhappy girl and that she feels rather isolated from the peer group. She makes no mention of supportive brothers and sisters, and I wonder whether she is an only child. She certainly sees her mother as being unreliable, secretive and perhaps persecutory. Father is viewed as a positive supportive figure, but this may be a disassociated aspect of his personality, since at other times, he appears to be immediately 'magically' transformed into the man she is frightened of. She clearly understands something of what it is to 'cry for hours'. There was therefore no doubt in my mind that this child should receive some form of help, although, without knowing the parents, it is difficult to know whether they should be directly included or not.

It is also possible that this story represents other stages of conflict in this girl's life, and the direct interpretation in terms of sexual abuse is not the only possibility. The others that came to mind were as follows:

(a) Difficulties in resolving an oedipal conflict. That is Jackie is aware of her mother being jealous of her relationship with her father. Her mother is therefore seen as unreliable and persecuting, while her father is also feared having a more frightening/darker/sexual role. I felt this interpretation was actually contradicted by the girl mentioning the police, since most children who go through a prolonged oedipal conflict would not relate this to matters being reported to the police.

(b) In that mother was seen as very unreliable, I wondered whether she was perhaps mentally unstable and confused, leaving father as the main caretaker. This would make it difficult for Jackie to adopt a female identity, and she may have drifted towards adopting a more male identity for herself. The man with the stick may therefore represent a sexual role that she is attracted towards but fears. What led me to consider this was her fear in that she had no way of being like the other girls dancing around the maypole and that her isolation from them, and their freely expressed sexual role, led her to be very upset. They are able to take their femininity lightly. There also seemed a parallel between the girls dancing around the maypole and the 'little men' dancing around *her* snowman. I thought this interpretation seemed to catch the atmosphere of the story quite well, although clearly this interpretation could also be applied together with the abusive one.

I hope these comments will be of value to you, and hope that you will be able to arrange for this girl to receive the help she appears to need.

This interpretation of the story, to re-emphasize the point, was to be used in a court case, by a social services department, with the intention of preventing two other children being returned to their family. As such, it is not a relatively innocuous theoretical analysis but a speculative interpretation of monumental significance for a family. As a consequence, there are a number of curiosities in the analysis. These include the reference to the Oedipus complex in a girl; the sexing of angels as female by the psychologist, not by the young writer (which probably says more about the psychologist than the girl, and is particularly worrying because substantial elements of the interpretation depend on the angels being female); the suggestion that the evil male turns into the father when in the story there is a person behind a tree which unproblematically turns out to be the father and there is no transformation as such (it is the apple which transforms into a frog); the apparent ease with which the psychologist produces a stereotype of the colluding mother and daughter in incest cases; and the strength of the diagnosis that the girl needs help when she quite clearly ends the story with 'From that year on nothing happened'.

But a reading of the children's book *The Secret World of Polly Flint* by Helen Cresswell (1982) reveals that the child's story and the book written in conjunction with a television series are more similar than the clinical psychologist has bothered to establish, as the following excerpts from the book confirm:

> The man (for she saw that it was a man) went with long bounding strides ... and yet there was a curious dreamlike slowness to his movements ... And raised in his right arm was a long rod ... (1982, p. 59)

> And she saw that he had used the crook of his long stick to trip her, and she stared up into his dark face with terror. (1982, p. 107)

> 'They're practising the May Dances!' she cried, 'and I can't join in!' (1982, p. 57)

The child's story and the book show other close thematic parallels. Polly Flint is extremely fond of her father. He is ill and she is staying with a rather hostile and odd Aunt Em. The mysterious and threatening other world is the central theme of the book. Rather than showing imagination, the child has apparently written a rather mundane version of the television programme and book, though with some inclusions of her own such as the apple changing into a frog. Furthermore, the ambivalence of real-world with other-world characters is an important aspect of the Polly Flint story. A perusal of an earlier version of the child's story shows that many of the elements of the story are attempts to 'make sense' of a rather more fragmentary story.

One should not dismiss this as merely being an example of a less than competent psychologist acting less than competently. It is far more important than that, revealing as it does the ease with which stereotyping processes can be applied in the area of child sexual abuse. It reflects a judgement which is driven by theories and assumptions about the nature of child abuse. These structure an interpretation which is probably unusual in so far as it can be challenged with clear contradictory evidence. Most cases of 'abuse' by professionals are probably not quite so open to independent verification. How social concern about an issue comes to influence professional judgement needs to be understood. Understanding how social problems are constructed has to include appreciation of the professional context of professional work.

It is possible for a professional ethos to develop which matches the public's moral panic and demands for action – the major difference being that professionals *take* action rather than demand it. This is well illustrated by the response to the following letter in a professional journal:

> In 19 years of working clinically with hundreds of adolescents and children, I can recall *not a single case of a client significantly psycholog-ically damaged by sexual experiences.* On the other hand, I can recall several tragic cases of children (and adults) *psychologically devastated by stupid adult reactions to the discovery of sexual relationships.*
>
> (Ryder, 1989)

This awakened a degree of acrimonious response which is not altogether typical of such publications. One writer went as far as to ask whether Ryder was 'trying to provoke discussion by taking the part of the devil's advocate' (Brent, 1989). The overall tone of the critics was disbelief that a practising clinical psychologist could fail to find serious damage as a consequence of adult–child sexual activity. They appear to forget that before about 1980, despite their 'skills', clinical psychologists were ignorant of child sexual abuse and that it was 'the discovery' of women's groups not psychology. Can we expect that their eyes are wider open now than then, despite their changed professional ethos?

Theories of professional errors

It is insufficient for social scientific accounts – even of the activities of child-abuse specialists – to be based solely on research evidence. Understanding has to be built on conceptual and theoretical work. What theoretical sense can be made of the 'mishandling' of child-abuse cases by professionals? Three theoretical viewpoints have been expressed which can be discussed here: one based on cognitive psychology; another on a view of the ideological underpinnings of professional practice in child protection; and a third which dismisses the errors as an attempt to restore the gender-political status quo.

Cognitive psychology and biases in expert opinion

One approach is to regard 'errors' in 'expert opinion' as reflecting general biases in human processing of information. Professional errors are no different from those of anyone else. This view has the advantage of relying on well-established principles of human judgement. The cognitive psychologist, Evans (1989), highlights features of 'expert' decision-making which might encourage errors. These include:

1 Confirmation bias: Evans refers to the idea of 'pseudodiagnosticity' (Doherty *et al.*, 1979). Essentially this is a very common logical fallacy in deductive reasoning. There are many variants but it can be represented by the general form: if *p* then *q*, *q* therefore *p*. Made a little more concrete, this might read: 'All apples are fruits; this is a fruit therefore it is an apple'. In this form the error is obvious. Translated into child abuse it might read: 'Anal abuse causes a reflex response of the muscles of the anus on examination. I observed this anal reflex, therefore anal abuse has occurred' (Evans, 1989).

2 Diagnosticity of signs: Evans argues that evidence is diagnostic to the extent that it discriminates, in this instance, cases of child abuse from cases of non-abuse. If, for example, one-inch bruises are found on the bodies of 90 per cent of physically abused toddlers, the presence of such a sign would be extremely diagnostic if only 1 per cent of non-abused children had similar bruises. On the other hand, should the proportion of non-abused children with such bruises be, say, 85 per cent, the presence of a one-inch bruise on a toddler is virtually worthless as a diagnostic sign. It can be seen that a poorly diagnostic sign, together with the mechanisms which support 'pseudodiagnosticity', could produce an enhanced likelihood of error.

3 Metacognition: Not only do people have thoughts, they are aware that they have thoughts – they have thoughts about their thought processes. They are also aware that they make mistakes and that their cognitions may be in error. Cognitive psychologists have explored the basis of this self-knowledge of error. It is possible to measure this in some cases by asking people to indicate the probability that they are correct in the answers they give and compare these estimates with the true rate of mistakes. It has been found that there is a systematic over-confidence in one's cognitions. This is not a consequence of being an expert – it is a general comment on people's confidence in the adequacy of their thinking.

What practical steps follow from this? According to Evans (1989, p. 114), '[t]he first and major problem is that of convincing people that there is a problem. The problems of metacognition which permit people to maintain illusory beliefs in the rationality of themselves and others create a major barrier to progress'. As practical remedies, Evans emphasizes the need to find effective training methods for 'debiasing' judgements, to look at the possibility of using 'intelligent' computer programs to replace error-prone human judgements, and to develop computer programs of an interactive sort which could interrogate the decision-maker as well as provide an adequate data base to substitute for 'intuition'.

At first sight, Evans's ideas seem not too well founded. They seem substantially ignorant of child-abuse practice and its information base. This may be a premature judgement, based very much on the sorts of error that Evans is trying to highlight. A good illustration of how some of the mechanisms that Evans describes may operate occurs in the following. This was taken from a newspaper report of a High Court judge's decision to refuse an application from the local social services department to have a ten-month-old boy taken into care. The boy had suffered injuries and had been removed from his parents because of the suspicion that 'his injuries were caused by his parents'. A specialist in brittle-bone disease (which results in easy fracturing) told the court that he believed that the boy was probably a sufferer. According to the doctor, between only 3,500 and 4,000 cases of brittle-bone disease had been recorded in Britain. This suggests that most general medical practitioners would see no more than two cases in their entire working lives. The Court's decision established, as well as is normally ever possible, that the boy's was a false positive child-abuse diagnosis.

The comments of the social service's child-abuse consultant are significant from the point of view of the cognitive psychologist:

> Dr Patterson's views on brittle bone disease had been challenged by other leading doctors ... We know there are certain conditions which can resemble non-accidental injury in children. But brittle bone disease is so rare it could be one case in a million ... We accept there may be a few cases in which we are mistaken, but we have considerable confidence in the highly trained medical staff who examine children ...
>
> (Nelson, 1989, p. 5)

The claim that Dr Patterson's views had been challenged is an obvious attempt to reduce the subjective probability that injuries to the child may not have been caused by abuse. This clearly, if accepted, increases the subjective likelihood that physical injuries mean child abuse has occurred. The child-abuse consultant then places a probability on finding a case of brittle-bone disease involved in child-abuse procedures which is extremely small. The phrase 'a chance in a million' is a device in colloquial English, to dismiss possibilities – it refers to a probability of occurrence which is beyond credibility. Finally, the child-abuse consultant also demonstrates the most important principal of metacognition – over-confidence in our abilities. She claims merely that there are *may be* a few cases of mistakes – not that there *are* mistakes.

The ideological struggle

In *The Child Abuse Industry*, Pride (1987) enters a tirade against American social work and other professions which is at the same time programmatic, erratic and stimulating. Unfortunately, it is the sort of book that can easily be dismissed on a superficial reading. It may be seen as journalistic and more concerned with effect than argument. This is probably too dismissive, as there are many theoretical ideas underlying what Pride writes. While much of the argument can be sniped at line by line, the way in which she chooses to conceptualize fundamental issues at least warrants serious attention. Recouching in less sensational language might also help. Her position provides insight into the ideological issues that are at the root of the social work child-protection process.

For Pride, social workers do not operate as brokers of facts concerning child abuse, they operate through 'doctrines'. She also claims that they are 'trained to ignore facts'. Their ideological slogans not only are wrong, they fly in the face of reality (Pride, 1987, p. 41). There is no doubt at all that, for Pride, there is a fundamental truth which is untouched by the ideology of social work. The social work ideology links to a crusade against the family. But really a new word needs to be invented since this crusade claims to be based on the 'scientific knowledge' of child-abuse researchers. Five doctrines are listed by Pride which maintain the ideology:

1   The doctrine of underreporting. 'This doctrine asserts that, although it's true that no evidence exists to prove we have a plague of child abuse, it's only because people are failing to report' (1987, p. 42).
2   The doctrine of underinvestigation. 'This doctrine claims that the only reason so many reports are unsubstantiated is because "we don't have time to investigate them thoroughly"' (1987, p. 42).
3   The blame-the-parents doctrine. 'This declares that parents are always to blame for everything that happens to their children, even if it occurs without their consent or knowledge.' (1987, p. 43).
4   The doctrine of total depravity. '*Every* family, it states, is depraved. *All* families are abusive. Therefore, any and all state interventions are justifiable.' Pride cites a prominent social work text which states that, 'Most parents at some time have abused or neglected their child or a child who was entrusted in their care' (1987, p. 44).
5   The doctrine of the immaculate confession. 'Social workers are taught that anytime a child accuses his [sic] parents (even if his confession occurs under pressure from the worker), this confession must be taken as gospel. However, if he denies everything from the start, or later denies his accusations, his denial means nothing. Here is the Catch-22: *you're only supposed to believe the child if he accuses the parents*' (1987, p. 44).

Pride considers that there is a child-abuse hysteria which serves a particular purpose – it serves as a smokescreen for a radically different set of principles. It is

a self-righteous cover up for anti-child attitudes. Those who don't want to have children and don't want to raise them themselves can use anti-child abuse rhetoric as a way of expressing love for children. It allows them to protect their position in a cloud of outrage. 'Sure, I had ten abortions, but at least *I* don't abuse children.' 'Yeah, I put my child in day care at birth, but at least *I* am not an abuser.'

(Pride, 1987, p. 140)

She discusses a list of 'modern anti-child activities' which encourage abuse of children. These include 'torturing babies to death through abortion', which she claims makes it difficult to understand why unaborted children cannot be smacked after birth; pornography which separates procreation from sex; sexual infidelity, which she claims is present in sexual abuse cases; drunkenness; and no-fault divorce. 'Who is to blame for sexual abuse increase?' she asks.

It is those who *knock the traditional family,* who *oppose traditional religion,* and who hope to cover up their own depraved actions by *forcing depraved standards on the rest of us under the guise of 'mental health' or 'saving the children.'* The root of the problem is social attitudes which disconnect sex from marital responsibility; an increase in unmarried living arrangements and remarriage, with a consequent increase in men living with girls who are not their natural daughters; pornographic propaganda; and the media's desire to cash in on the shock value of child sex. The traditional family stands squarely *against* all these things. Yet the increase in sexual abuse is being used as an excuse to kick traditional families in the teeth!

(Pride, 1987, p. 39)

While some might take exception to the strident tone of Pride's writing and consider it 'over the top', a problem remains: we simply do not know that she is wrong. We do not have the evidence of how social workers and other professionals construe the world, what their ideologies are, and how these may explain what they do.

The gender-politics struggle

In *Unofficial Secrets,* Beatrix Campbell (1988) offers an analysis constructed around the Cleveland crisis in Britain. In this 'scandal', large numbers of children were taken into care following diagnoses of sexual abuse by a very small 'team' of doctors (Bell, 1988; Butler-Sloss, 1988). Her viewpoint is resolutely feminist, though it shares the emphasis on ideology displayed by other accounts of social work errors. Unlike the others, she emphasizes the 'rightness' of these disputed medical diagnoses rather than construing them as errors. Campbell concentrates on the anal reflex test of sexual abuse, which may be seen by most as a purely medical issue but, of course, it is not. The actions of social workers following such diagnoses are a substantial component of the error process, if indeed that it be.

In a remarkable section of her book she discusses the 'politics of the anus'. By this she means several things, but the key element of it all is the role of men in sexual abuse. For Campbell (1988, p. 62), 'perpetrators are typically male and abuse is an expression of a patriarchal sexual culture', and it is this fact which is the key to many things. She treats her comment as if it were a fact hidden from all except women of the 1980s who identified the perpetrators of the problem. Why the anal dilation test was so controversial is that it put male sexuality on the line as the act which is identified as homosexual, buggery, was being done by fathers on their daughters. The politics of the situation was sexual, especially as many of the professionals involved initially in opposing the doctors' diagnoses were men.

Concluding comments

It may be as difficult to strike a balance in professional activity as anything else. While it might be perfectly reasonable to explore the predictors of child abuse as part of the general research activity of academic psychology, the translation of this into social practice can immediately raise issues of justice and judgement. However, contained within most of the discussion in this chapter is the underlying matter of psychology's orientation within the community. Inevitably pipers play tunes called by their masters. This makes it doubly important that psychological training should alert future practitioners and researchers to the nature of psychology's position in society. There are several different ways of doing this, but an examination of the place of psychology in the social structure should help. Also, teasing out the ways in which psychology can contribute to perpetuation of injustice and be a willing partner to that injustice, could also be part and parcel of what needs to be done.

Issues like child abuse can be particularly problematic since it is easy to jump to judgements of what is right and what is wrong in the apparent urgency of the situation. The problems come not only from this but also from the unpreparedness of professionals to deal with the problems raised by such matters. This is hardly surprising given the failure of professions over the years to do anything about abuse – such as recognize it.

6

INTERNALIZED IDEOLOGIES: RACISM AND PSYCHOLOGY

... there is not necessarily a correlation between attitudes and behavior. For example, poor whites are frequently unrestrained in expressing their negative views about black people, whereas those who are better educated are more reluctant to express such attitudes. More frequently, however, the people who are better educated are in positions of power in the society. And although they are less likely to verbalize negative feelings, they frequently profit from America's racism.

(Pinkney, 1984, p. 58)

This chapter presents an unusual argument for a psychology book. It is smug to believe that psychology has made a major contribution to the elimination of racism. Concepts such as racial prejudice, scapegoating, stereotyping, ethnic identity, racial attitudes and self-esteem might seem part of the armoury of psychology to help destroy the edifice of racism. Anti-racism is not the 'jewel in the crown' of psychology's fight for social justice, quite the reverse. Psychology's main function in relation to racism has been its cultivation. This happens in many ways, at different levels, and with various degrees of subtlety. There is an orthodoxy in psychology which has contributed to the promotion of racism. Freed from this, psychology might have much to offer.

Defining racism

The precise definition of racism is no easier than that of any other idea located in society. Choosing a definition creates as many difficulties as it prevents. The following pair exemplify the problematic nature of definitions. Notice how selecting one or the other has radically different implications for both research and theory.

Racism is based in material conditions in that most or all white people benefit from their superordinate position relative to blacks … [R]acism can be regarded as 'culturally sanctioned, rational responses to struggles over scarce resources'.

(Brown, 1985, p. 671)

Racism is the application of 'race' categories in social contexts with an accompanying attribution of invariable characteristics to category members.

(Husband, 1982, p. 19)

Couched in terms which regard racism as a rational choice (Banton, 1983; Hechter, 1986), the first definition (which will be described as 'socio-economic racism') refers to a socio-economic system or a social structure which, in the Western world at least, advantages white people. This leaves black people starved of economic, social, political and other forms of power. What accounts for such a state of affairs is left open. No particular processes are implicated. The second definition (ideological racism), however, is much more restricted. It is dependent on a two-stage argument. First, to be racist requires that the individual sees people as being categorizable by 'race'. Second, 'races' are seen to have invariable and immutable characteristics. Presumably the definition is referring to anatomical characteristics such as skin pigmentation which are assumed to reflect a group's intellectual, cultural and moral worth: that white people are intelligent, energetic and moral; that people of African descent are over-sexed, immoral and indolent; that Asians are fawning, obsessed by money, and smell. The application of race classification is not by itself necessarily wrong (though implying that there are invariable biologically determined characteristics would be factually erroneous). What is racist and noxious is the application of these characteristics in order to establish the relative *social value* of the 'races'. Terms like 'over-sexed', 'immoral' and 'indolent' are not used of black people for their benefit. They do not help black people gain access to privilege. They are intended to justify the placing of black people at the bottom of the social and cultural hierarchy.

The ideological type of definition of racism is dangerous for a number of reasons. First, anyone denying race categories is absolved from racism. Second, anyone making exceptions to the invariable characterisization of racially defined groups cannot be racist by definition. For example, 'My best friend is black' or 'The Asian family next door are really nice' defuses the charge of racism irrespective of the individual's views of 'most black people'. Third, it implies that resources should be concentrated on understanding what the ideologies or value systems of individuals are, that the ideologically laden content talk of racists is the main thing to understand. This type of definition picks up an important theme in the historical development of the concept of racism. Especially during the nineteenth century, it was acceptable among academic circles to claim the biological reality of race. This was then used to justify white political and military dominance throughout the world on the grounds of the biological superiority of white people. 'Finding' basic biological differences accounted for and justified the 'inferior' status of black people together with their exploitation through colonialization. Arguments ranged widely and even included the view that black and white people were so different biologically that they were separate species, incapable of interbreeding! Such views were to a degree reflections of the spirit of the times. A major feature of this were Charles Darwin's ideas on natural selection and the idea of the survival of the fittest. A tempting corollary of the 'only the strong survive' maxim is the belief that whatever is the status quo is the consequence of superior or inferior biological genes. Black people could be assumed to be socially, culturally and morally inferior because of their biological inferiority. This, of course, shies away from many issues – for example, how are superiority and inferiority to be judged?

Biological research has managed only to detect the most trivial of differences between racial groups. Genetically, the variability between individuals of the same 'race' is greater than differences between 'races'. Over 94 per cent of all genetic variation is found within a given 'race' rather than between 'races'. Such massive evidence of virtually complete biological overlap between historically separate races should be the final nail in the coffin of biological racism. However, despite superficial references to biology, 'race' is a social concept, socially not biologically defined. Thus the validity of the biological claims matters little. It is the racial categories which people use which gives race a reality. 'Racism' is part of this social reality. Racial groups are socially defined, usually on gross physical characteristics such as skin colour, facial features, hair texture and the like. This essentially 'false' belief in the existence of different racial groups is all too often used as a basis for formulating policies and for allocating resources differentially – the group presumed superior controlling access to resources and those presumed inferior being denied access to resources through segregation, oppression and discrimination.

South Asians (Indians, Pakistanis, Bangladeshis) would generally be defined as racially distinct from Caucasians (whites) by convention. However, a biological classification will put all three groups of South Asians and white people in the same racial category – Caucasian. Obviously we need to be careful to realize that skin colour is only modestly related to social classifications of race. For example, South African state racism defined 'coloureds' by ancestry rather than skin shade or other features; all that is necessary for a person to be reclassified from white to 'coloured' was the discovery of a distant 'coloured' ancestor.

In a similar vein, Dummett (1984) has observed that in the same schools of Washington DC, native black American children are classified as black, and the black children of African diplomats as white.

Denial of racism is an important technique in ensuring its continuation without change. One means of doing this is to adopt a 'colour-blind' strategy. Such a ploy underlies claims such as 'people are all the same to me'. However, given the centrality of the socially defined concept of race in most societies, to claim to be unaware of this central aspect of one's culture simply begs the question. Furthermore, to ignore the trivial biological difference of skin colour can lead to failure to give attention to the special medical and cultural needs of certain groups (as with sickle-cell anaemia). As a consequence, the health interests, for example, of the white majority may be served best.

Despite these arguments, some researchers toy with the concept of race and are moved to reject it on the grounds that there are no biological races (see, for example, Morgan, 1985). Yet others, while acknowledging that 'racism' derives from the biological concept of 'race', argue that racism is solely ideological in nature, and so should only be applied when all other possible explanations of black people's social disadvantage are eliminated (see Miles, 1989). The latter view is particularly worrying and ignores significant aspects of the question. There are usually alternative explanations which initially seem credible, especially when individual cases are considered alone. The 'true' picture of racism only emerges when an overview is taken.

A concrete example should help clarify this. Miles claims that one should not use the concept of racism to explain the greater rates of unemployment commonly reported in ethnic minority groups without exploring other (more commonsensical?) explanations. For example, black people would be expected to feature in the unemployment figures since they have a tendency to be employed in the textile industry which, for economic/structural reasons, has slumped. But, despite the immediate appeal of this, it is necessary to push the argument further than he does. For example, why should immigrants have been employed in ailing industries in the first place? There is nothing more intrinsically racist than a social system which cynically recruits immigrant labour to do undesirable and economically insecure jobs – the ones which white people do not want because of excessive shift work, bad conditions and poor pay. Furthermore, why are such industries as textiles in decline? One frequently voiced complaint is that this is due to the *exploitation* of cheaper so-called 'Third World' workforces.

Ultimately, it may be that, when we dig a little deeper, racism underlies many of the more palatable 'alternative explanations'. To regard racism merely as a matter of ideology is mistaken, though virtually universal in psychology. Racism is not an abstract concept which academics toy with; to the victims it has a social, economic and political reality. Thus to regard it as a *system* which leads to the social disadvantage of black people is more promising. It allows us to explore far wider than what people say. The consequences of this and other activities for black people become important considerations.

Biological and cultural racism in psychology

Psychologists are not shielded by virtue of their profession from absorbing ideas from the social and cultural climate in which they work. This is as true of racism as anything else. Biological racism has a long and public history in psychology (Billig, 1979). Cultural racism is equally well established but not so well publicized. For this reason biological racism will receive the least attention in this chapter. What is the difference between the biological and cultural racism? One answer is to refer to the authors of the two earliest social psychology textbooks – William McDougall (1908) and Edward Ross (1908). These have been held to reflect the different roots of the psychological and sociological branches of social psychology.

Biological racism

William McDougall was a biological racist believing not only in racial differences in intelligence but also in eugenics (Jones, 1987). This is probably not surprising – McDougall's early career was as part of the British academic community with links with Charles Darwin and his eugenically orientated cousin Sir Francis Galton. Furthermore, his views were not particularly different from those of his American colleagues. For example, a survey of 100 'experts' on race and intelligence (Thompson, 1934) found that only about one in ten of those who responded believed in the intellectual equality of black people and white people. The majority found the evidence inconclusive.

Discussions during the late 1960s and the 1970s of biological racial differences in intelligence ought to be seen as the rearguard action of a defunct branch of psychology. The view is more or less distantly associated with eugenics through leading psychologists including Pearson, Spearman, and Burt, together with others with no such associations such as Jensen. Clear historical connections exist between these British psychologists and Darwin and Galton. The casualties of the debate over racial differences in intelligence, in terms of academic reputations, were unusually heavy.

Great caution has to be exercised not to assume that biological racism is dead. It reappears from time to time in academic writing. For example, just when some psychologists thought that it was safe to look black people in the eye, the work of Rushton (1987; 1990) has appeared to accusations of racism. To repeat what should be unrepeatable, he accepts that there are three biologically identifiable races – mongoloids (basically Chinese type), negroids (African origins), and caucasoids (white, European type) – which differ in terms of their 'reproductive' strategies. The K-strategy involves a greater degree of parental care of each of the offspring. The biological and the 'consequent' cultural characteristics of races using this strategy maximize parental care. An alternative strategy, the r-strategy, emphasizes the production of many offspring which are cared for less intensively. There is no need for intensive nurturance as the 'fecundity' of reproduction ensures the survival of the race. With the K-strategy, the quality of infant care ensures the continuation of the species.

Which races have K-strategies and which r-strategies? Dig deep into your knowledge of racist stereotypes. Which race is claimed to have the biggest genitals, breasts and buttocks, to be sexually permissive and the sexiest, to have the greatest rates of sexually transmitted diseases like AIDS, the least marital stability, and to be the most criminal? Which race is believed to be the most sociable, the most impulsive, the earliest to develop physically, and is the least intellectually and morally developed? For Rushton, this race is the one best demonstrating the r-strategy of maximizing the offspring. The race showing the reverse of these characteristics is the one showing the K-strategy best. According to Rushton, negroids get on with copulating, mongoloids mind the baby best.

Whether or not the theory is the palpable nonsense it appears – and there is plenty of reason to assume that it is – one major concern is whether it is even ethical to raise such questions. If psychology is a discipline intending to help people, what good is done by Rushton's claims? It is difficult to see that such views contribute to humanity's good. To cut a long and unprofitable debate short, it must be recognized that in such discussions, the choice of study, the differences observed and the way they are interpreted say more about the investigator than the investigated. At best they fulfil only the needs of racist rhetoric. The events following the publication of an article by Rushton (1990) expounding his ideas in the 'house journal' of the British Psychological Society are interesting. Clearly worried about the risks of general dissemination of such views, the Society's president wrote to key psychologists requesting them not to talk to the media about the subject of Rushton's article. However, if they chose to ignore this advice, they should be content to reiterate the content of a carefully worded statement enclosed with the president's letter.

Nevertheless, it is most important for psychologists concerned about social issues to note the shared ideological position of those on various sides of this particular debate. A consensus of approach can sometimes mistakenly be taken as correct. For example, take the following extract from the 'party line' (a letter written by Morris on 27 April 1990) to be read to the press:

As a scientific learned society and publisher of scientific books and journals, we are bound by our Royal Charter, Statutes, Rules and Code of Conduct to publish and disseminate scientific papers within the broad spectrum of the science of psychology ... The article by J. Philippe Rushton was submitted to the Honorary Editors ... and like all *scientific* articles it was *refereed* by independent authorities in this particular field. The Honorary Editors then decided to publish on the basis that scientific evidence should not be withheld from the scientific community.

(Morris, 1990a; emphasis added)

Acquiescence to this sort of view, on the other hand, seems particularly dangerous if it is interpreted as implying that anything is fair game in the name of 'science'. Not only is this totally nonsensical, it also ignores the basic ethical concerns of psychologists. There is no question that many activities that psychologists might undertake in order to achieve a 'scientific' understanding are improper, illegal, immoral, unethical, or simply unacceptable. By 1 May 1990, the president had apparently changed his mind. A new letter (Morris, 1990b) was sent out asking the recipients to 'destroy the previous one'. The events leading to the publication were now revised and virtually all references to science expurgated. It also transpires that Rushton's article had not been subject to the independent scrutiny which was claimed (Breakwell and Davey, 1990).

Alternatively, the writing of Flynn, a self-proclaimed adversary of Rushton's position, is a source of similar ideas. It contains a perhaps even more morally bankrupt position on social responsibility in psychology:

Rushton has been the target of much abuse and labelled a racist. There is a real danger that his future work will not get a hearing, thanks to outlets being intimidated by the fear of unwelcome press scrutiny. This is wrong in itself and it is worth remarking that the truth can never be racist, nor can telling the truth as you see it, assuming there is no evidence of wilful neglect of evidence, an accusation Rushton need not fear. Suppressing Rushton's views also means that those who believe they can make a reasoned case against him are silenced, for lack of dialogue, which is to say everyone is the loser.

(Flynn, 1989)

With intellectual enemies like Flynn, does Rushton need friends? To defend racism on the grounds that silencing racist views is to make everyone a loser seems to rely on a naive theory of the real world. Some might prefer to ask who are the long-term beneficiaries from the propagation of racism. 'Scientific' racism has too long a history for the belief that it can be properly laid to rest by rational argument to hold water.

Some modern psychologists have been both resourceful and painstakingly meticulous in teasing out overtly racist thought in the discipline.

Kamin's (1977) views on the fallacies of the argument of inherited racial differences in intelligence are very familiar and will not be repeated here. Equally important is the work of researchers who pick over the ideological bones of those psychologists who have espoused fascist ideologies, sympathized with the eugenics movement, or shown themselves to be directly and overtly racist. Billig's (1979; 1981; 1982) work is an account of historical and some familiar modern figures in psychology who favour racist or other and related and extreme ideologies. For example, he points to the claim of Cattell that a dozen or more major psychological researchers are forced to waste their time lecturing – if only the USA could be relieved of a fraction of the half a million mental defectives it supports, there would be ample finance for these able scientists to become full-time researchers (cited in Billig, 1982, p. 83). Such comments probably set into context Cattell's most famous 'contributions' to psychology – the Cattell 16 Personality Factor Questionnaire and his measures of intelligence (Cattell, 1965). Given the values he expresses, one might wonder as to the value and use of the research that his dozen or so 'wasted' teachers would otherwise have done.

Caution suggests that dangers may arise in the creation of psychological folk-devils based on their scarcely hidden extreme right-wing views. One risk is that a 'holier-than-thou position' camouflages the promotion of equally unacceptable stances.

Cultural racism

Cultural racism is perhaps not as easy to identify as biological racism. It has been defined by Jones (1972) as the individual and institutional expression of the superiority of one race's cultural heritage over that of another race. But it is more adequately described as the process whereby the racist assumptions of a culture/society are transmitted from one generation to the next through its institutions and folklore. Psychology is one of these institutions.

There is little discussion in the social psychological literature of Edward Ross's views on racial matters, though he articulated them very clearly in his early social psychology textbook (Ross, 1908). Though his views were rather different from those of William McDougall (his 'co-founder' of the discipline), Ross's writing contains racist elements:

> Social psychology ignores uniformities arising directly or indirectly out of race endowment – negro volubility, gypsy nomadism, Malay vindictiveness, Singhalese treachery, Magyar passion for music, Slavic mysticism, Teutonic venturesomeness, American restlessness. How far such common characters are really racial in origin and how far merely social is a matter yet to be settled. Probably they are much less

congenital than we love to imagine. 'Race' is the cheap explanation tyros offer for any collective trait that they are too stupid or too lazy to trace to its origin in the physical environment, the social environment, or historical conditions.

(Ross, 1908, p. 3)

So far, so (reasonably) good. Clearly, Ross believes in racial and national stereotypes but he chooses to doubt their biological origins. While not entirely rejecting their possible biological inheritance, he sees their origins as largely to do with circumstances. Despite this, adeptly he picks from a repertoire of racial stereotypes and racist lore:

Social isolation, by hindering contact with contempories, makes closer the contact with the past. The Jews, for ages penned up in the Ghetto and barred from full civil and social equality, came to be obstinately traditional. Confined behind the walls of the Jewry, forbidden to own an estate or practise a profession or intermarry with Christians, they kept alive a jealous, exclusive, tribal spirit, foreign altogether to the demotic character of modern society. As if Canon Law and Civil Law had not done enough, the Jews maintained between themselves and the Christians a hedge of their own, viz., their religious and ceremonial observances. The practice of their rites obliged them to live in closest contact with one another and to shun the uncircumcised.

(Ross, 1908, p. 228)

The discourse of this argument needs teasing apart. Although acknowledging the role of law in oppressing the Jews, gradually the responsibility for being aliens to the rest of society is lain with the Jews – 'they kept alive', 'As if Canon Law and Civil Law had not done enough, the Jews maintained ... a hedge', 'The practice of their rites obliged them ... to shun the uncircumcised.' The same arguments are not made about the oppressing majority – no note is made of them living in closest contact with one another and shunning the circumcized!

But the Jews are not the only oppressed group to be dealt this treatment. Colonized peoples (called 'aborigines') from all parts of the world are held by Ross (1908, p. 150) to be responsible for the reactionary views of their oppressors:

Whites in contact with aborigines let down. Certain of the first trans-Alleghany settlers became so Indianized as to wear a buckskin dress, marry a squaw, and let the scalp-lock grow. Realizing this danger of let-down, an isolated white enveloped by savages becomes intensely conservative. The French Canadians of to-day are French of the seventeenth century, and their conservatism has, no doubt, the same root ... [as] Boer conservatism.

So there we have it – arguing by extension, white South Africans treat black people appallingly to prevent their white culture from crumbling into the 'aboriginal mire'! More adroit blaming of the victim. Ross's argument seems redolent of those in favour of the oppressive treatment of black people already noted in the work of Ray (1974) (see Chapter 3).

Cultural racism is built on imputations about the relative worth of different cultures. It probably comes as no surprise to find that in general white people see Western cultures in a favourable light. On the other hand, they ignore, neglect, distort, disparage and ridicule black cultures. 'Bad' culture is added to the 'biological inferiority' of black people. That is, 'race' still remains the 'phlogiston' (Banton, 1983) of psychology. It matters but little if injustice is justified by arguments about 'bad' genes or 'bad' culture.

It could be argued, quite reasonably, that Ross's writing has long gathered dust on library shelves. Unfortunately, Ross has his heirs in psychology. Whether or not they have read Ross, similar and related forms of thinking have been common enough in recent psychological writing. Howitt and Owusu-Bempah (1990) reviewed the race-related writing of modern social psychologists. They used insights about racism developed from experience of racism-awareness training (group-based methods of facing participants with their racism) to look for covert racist assumptions in this material. Many examples were found which were 'scientifically' couched versions of 'everyday' race thinking. Some of the processes identified include:

1   *Marginalizing racism.* This is the process by which racism becomes categorized as the activities of 'fringe' people rather than being a cultural norm. Chester (1976) describes this kind of approach as 'low embed-dedness'. For example, racism is seen as being largely confined to the activities of right-wing fascists. Repeatedly evidence that racism and con-servatism are unrelated is ignored in favour of seeing racism as part of a personality characteristic associated with general right-wing views.
2   *Avoiding the obvious.* Vaughan (1964) studied attitudes towards their own race in Maori and white children using white or Maori interviewers. The evidence was that, at about 12 years of age, Maori children expressed a more marked preference for the Maori race when interviewed by a white than when interviewed by a Maori interviewer. However, Vaughan (1964, p. 69) concludes that this related to an issue of method: 'the provision of own-race experimenters should be considered an automatic control in ethnic attitude research'. In other words, instead of taking the differences as reflecting an important issue in the racial dynamics of New Zealand society which might indicate a significant indicator of growth of racial pride and antagonism towards whites, the finding is debased to a mere technicality, thus avoiding the exploration of sensitive racial issues.

3   *Blaming the victim.* This refers to the language devices by which we blame the victims of racism for its effects on them. An example of this is Dawson (1969), who claims that Australian Aboriginals come from hunting societies which develop independence to high level. Consequently, '[i]t is thought that Aborigines tend not to do well in modern work situations because of this independent permissive hunting society orientation, which appears to be reinforced by extremely permissive child-rearing processes' (1969, p.139). So unemployment and similar privations are nothing to do with racism in Australia but the consequence of 'permissive' upbringing. Furthermore, would 'permissiveness' of upbringing be used as an explanation of unemployment in other groups? Unemployment in white people is explained in radically different terms.

There are many other examples of these and similar argumentative structures being applied. The difficulty is, of course, that to be sensitive to the underlying meaning of often apparently innocuous-sounding comments requires careful and detailed analysis. Busy readers may be unable to give such attention to every word. Nor should one expect racism to be signalled by overt hostility.

The new racism

Psychologists tend to see racism as a derogating ideology dependent on a strong personal dislike of black people. This is unfortunate since such a view probably helps prevent the profession from recognizing its entrenched racism. Racism theory in recent years has thrown up several conceptualizations of how racism has changed its form of expression. Various related ideas which have similar real-life referents have been described as 'the new racism' or 'symbolic racism'. In many respects the so-called 'new' racism eschews the crude racial bigotry of the past. It does not rely on direct denigration of the biology, the culture, the character, and the personal morality of black people. Simple, overt and offensive racist talk is not part of new racism. Instead the new racism deals with the processes of 'bucking the system' or 'not playing fair'. The new racist objects to black people because they or their actions violate fundamental moral principles of what is proper. The apparent undermining of cherished social ethics results in the expression of antagonism. It may be accompanied by a similar dislike of black people which found its expression traditionally in the more abusive racism, but there are instances where it is quite unrelated to this. In these ideas about new racism are to be found the beginnings of the understanding of the racism of modern psychologists.

So what is this new racism? A number of examples come readily to mind from remarks often made by many white people, including participants in racism-awareness training sessions:

1   In Britain Sikhs wearing turbans are exempt from a law which requires that motorcyclists must wear crash helmets. Repeatedly this is argued as indicating that black people are gaining unfair privileges compared to white people. However, this argument conveniently forgets that Sikhism is a religious category not a racial one, and that a white Sikh would be afforded the same immunity. It also forgets that not every black person is a Sikh and vice versa.

2   It is sometimes falsely believed that a barman refusing to serve a black person on the grounds of drunkenness could be legally prosecuted for racial discrimination, though not if the customer had been white. Although the fundamental argument is one of fairness, the example is totally erroneous and there is nothing illegal in refusing to serve a drunk, irrespective of race.

3   Sometimes the view is expressed that black children in a school class disadvantage the white children because of their inability to speak English properly. Clearly the basic view is that it is wrong for one group to detract from the educational opportunities of others. (Again the argument is based on erroneous premisses and there is no empirical evidence of this disadvantage.)

4   Blacks are cliquish – thus violating the highly valued principle of individualism.

5   'There are far too many immigrants in this area. It's not a question of colour because Asians I don't mind at all, in fact I feel they are an asset to the locality because they are a very cultured people; they keep themselves to themselves; they are quiet; and they embrace a lot of the qualified positions like doctors. Quite unlike the other lot … '.

                                              (Phizacklea and Miles, 1980, pp. 59–60)

Antipathy to black people in the new racism adopts a high moral tone by referring to 'intuitive' rights and wrongs. In this sense, the new racism is no different from crude traditional racism with its rejection of the immoral, dirty, indolent, inferior blacks. What is dissimilar is that some 'new' racists claim to object to crude traditional racial bigotry and find it to be a violation of cherished principles of egalitarianism. The dislike of black people is rationalized through principles which are not clearly directly racist. Given this sort of conceptualization, it is not at all surprising to find that psychology, which tends to align with a broad 'liberal' stance, can express anti-racist sentiments while at the same time blithely expounding subtle racism. Inevitably any psychologist touching on race-related issues risks the charge of subtle racism, possibly with good justification as we have seen. The problem is to sort the words out from the meaning.

Naturally the idea of new or symbolic racism has been debated and criticized by some. Part of the reason for this lies in the inconsistencies among the proponents of these ideas. Kinder (1986) discusses some of these. Sears and Kinder (1971) formulated the concept of 'symbolic racism' following research into an election campaign involving black and white candidates. Suburban whites voted in terms of abstract, moralistic racial resentments – black people 'are too pushy', 'get more than their entitlement', 'are on welfare but don't need the money', and so on. It was symbolic in the sense that the racial views were symptomatic of a wide range of other complaints about society as a whole. But it did involve anti-black feelings. McConahay and Hough (1976) also adopted the title 'symbolic racism' but used it to mean something rather different. Their symbolic racists believed that racial discrimination was a thing of the past and that now modern society was a land of milk and honey for black people. However, both views stressed that symbolic racism is a conglomerate of racial prejudice and traditional values.

Sniderman and Tetlock (1986b) are particularly good at unravelling problems in conceptualizations of the new racism and make a number of interesting points. However, they sometimes shoot themselves in the collective foot:

> [t]here are ... at least four theoretical interpretations of the claim that symbolic racism involves a blend of anti-black affect and traditional values, specifically: (1) anti-black affect may be the cause and the values the effect; (2) affect may be the effect and values may be the cause; (3) both affect and values may be involved, each separately and independently making a contribution; and (4) both may be involved, but interactively rather than independently. These are distinct alternatives, each stipulating a different causal process. Obviously, not all can be correct.
>
> (Sniderman and Tetlock, 1986b, p. 132)

This last sentence is a *non sequitur*. There is no reason why racism cannot be multiply determined. Also the assumption that affect and values are distinct and (more importantly) distinguishable entities is difficult to establish. It is not easy to understand from where the affect comes if not from value-based judgements about black people. Similarly, it is hard to understand the motivation for applying the values if it is not affective dislike of black people. But the choice among the alternatives is meaningless.

Sniderman and Tetlock's query raises one big problem which is, in an indirect way, central to the psychological understanding of racism. The assumption is that the individual has to be motivated to be racist through individual psychological processes such as race hatred or clashes of values, or some variant on this. While there may be such motives in some instances, it is also perfectly possible to act in a racist manner inadvertently or without identifiable malice (Gaertner and Dovidio, 1986). But this is dependent on adopting a definition of racism in terms of consequences rather than ideologies, dislikes or hatred. The industrialist who refuses to employ black people 'because the workforce wouldn't like it' may feel pragmatically justified. However, this merely perpetuates racial discrimination against black people.

There is, in many respects, little merit in trying to distinguish between the 'new racism' and old-fashioned racial bigotry. It makes precious little difference, for example, if some slave-owners were exceptionally cruel and others relatively humane. The fact of the matter is that the slaves were still slaves. It is the racist system and its effects which must be examined and dealt with. A clear-cut example shows some of the futility of separating the new racism of the far right from older forms. A British Member of Parliament articulated the new racism as follows: 'the whole question of race is not a matter of being superior or inferior, dirty or clean, but of being different' (Barker, 1981, p. 20–1). Barker warns that such views are no less racist than earlier views that accepted that race was a question of superiority or inferiority.

Effort is clearly needed to ensure that psychologists understand that the so-called 'new racism' (or 'liberal' pluralism), with its emphasis on individual rights and individual merit, should not simply mask privilege. There is a further idea, that of the 'aversive racist' which has been adequately validated through a variety of psychological research (Gaertner and Dovidio, 1986). Such racists

> sympathize with the victims of past injustice; support public policies that, in principle, promote racial equality and ameliorate the consequences of racism; identify more generally with a liberal political agenda; regard themselves as nonprejudiced and nondiscriminatory; but, almost unavoidably, possess negative feelings and beliefs about blacks. Because of the importance of the egalitarian value system to aversive racists' self-concept, these negative feelings and associated beliefs are typically excluded from awareness. When a situation or event threatens to make the negative portion of their attitude salient, aversive racists are motivated to repudiate or dissociate these feelings from their self image, and they vigorously try to avoid acting wrongly on the basis of these feelings.
>
> (1986, p. 61)

Probably this is a more typical picture of psychologists as racists than any other.

One is reminded of Berry's (1958) 'taxonomy' of people in respect to race as: unprejudiced non-discriminators; unprejudiced discriminators; prejudiced non-discriminators; and prejudiced discriminators. The elimination of prejudice is difficult, so working on discrimination ought to be the major task. Related to this, it should also be mentioned that most psychological views of racism ignore the institutional context in which it takes place. Of great significance is the range of long-established systems, policies, practices and procedures originally conceived and devised to meet the relatively homogeneous society which existed prior to the increasing multi-cultural nature of many societies. Collectively these lead to 'institutional racism'. Institutional racism involves practices that are racist in their effect if not in their intent. White people largely benefit from these practices which at the same time deny black people access and opportunities in relation to power and resources. An excellent example of this is Wrench (1990), in which the pressures on the careers service to discriminate are described.

Committed psychologists and their fate

There is something fundamentally depressing about the discussion so far. It indicates strongly that psychological training is no guarantee of anti-racist views. This scenario ought to be set against the fact that racism research has generated some of the best and most socially committed psychology. But despite the existence of such material, it has sometimes suffered a curious fate. Instead of being an agent for social change, it has become absorbed and transmogrified by mainstream psychological thinking and, in large part, remains part of psychology as an institution.

A major stimulus to research and theory related to racism was the treatment of minorities, notably Jews, in Germany before and during the Second World War. Jewish intellectuals, as was discussed in Chapter 3, were subjected to appalling treatment. Some understanding of their experience can be gleaned from a letter written by Kurt Lewin to Wolfgang Kohler in 1933 (Lewin, 1986). Kohler, a non-Jew, was openly critical of Nazi treatment of the Jews, and claimed: 'Nothing astonished the Nazis so much as the cowardice of whole university faculties, which did not consist of Nazis.' Opposition to the Nazis among academics was minimal. Lewin's letter makes emotive reading:

> When I first heard the National Socialist Argument, 'If the Jews have relatively good jobs, naturally they have them only because they are particularly capable – but that is exactly why we have no choice but to kill them,' I considered it insanity. Since then I have become convinced that broad strata of the population think this ... I cannot imagine how a Jew is supposed to live a life in Germany at the present time that does justice to even the most primitive demands of truthfulness ... Am I supposed to speak as a representative of Germany again on my next trip abroad and 'to encounter the reports of atrocities,' as is tacitly expected of every Jew? ... Perhaps, like many other Jews, a cruel destiny will not spare me this fate ...
>
> (Lewin, 1986, pp. 46–7)

Given the events of the holocaust, Lewin, by being forced to emigrate, was spared the cruellest of fates. It is also worthwhile reflecting some of Henle's (1986) discussion of Kohler's experience of the Nazis and his eventual resignation from his university post. She outlines the considerable pressures on this German academic at Berlin University in the 1930s. However, his despair at the voluntary 'collusion' of other colleagues should be registered. Henle (1986, p. 227) writes: 'Naturally this corroborated the Nazi's contempt for the intellectual life'.

Possibly psychology's major 'advance' in the area of race up until the Second World War was the invention of the *Thurstone Attitude Scales*. Thurstone, as part of the Payne Fund Research into the influence of movies on American youth (Thurstone and Chave, 1929), carried out research on the effects of Griffith's film *The Birth of a Nation* on the racial attitudes of young Americans. By developing a method of measuring social attitudes based on psycho-physical methods, Thurstone provided a central interest for psychologists for decades. But despite the origins of Thurstone's race-attitudes measure, this was no real-world strand of psychological research but a measurement device. Serious work on the psychology of racism was consolidated in *The Authoritarian Personality* (Adorno *et al.*, 1950). The story and fate of this work is a vital one in understanding psychology's response to, and undermining of, a serious examination of an important social issue.

Reich, the Austrian psychoanalyst, had moved to Berlin in 1930 and began to formulate explanations of what he termed 'the mass psychology of fascism' (Reich, 1933). He did not believe that trivial explanations of Hitler's rise to power sufficed. The oratory of Hitler was not enough to explain how fascism could succeed in the prewar German state. Its rise was facilitated by the character structure of lower middle-class and working-class Germans. In a strongly patriarchal society the family moulds the character of a child in a way which reproduces the structure and ideology of the state. The family is a microcosm of the nation. Reich explains this as being a consequence of the repression of sexuality. This generates yearnings for vague and mystical ideas – of nation, duty, honour, religion and motherhood (Samelson 1986). The individual holds the character structure which is both created by the state and supports that state.

The desire to understand how a person comes to be responsive to authority through personality development received a good deal of attention from the Frankfurt Institute, which carried out theoretical studies of the family and authority. Its ideas differed from those of Reich in respect of the underpinnings of sexuality. To cut the story short, several Frankfurt intellectuals eventually moved from Europe to the United States. At this point (*c*.1939) theoretical notions related to understanding fascism became entwined with the issue of racism, particularly in the form of anti-Semitism. Adorno, one of the 'Frankfurt School', was especially involved with a group of critical theoreticians concerned with what was successively called the 'fascist character', the 'anti-democratic character', and finally the 'authoritarian personality'.

Quickly the theoretical underpinnings of the debate concerning fascism became rather 'Americanized'. Gone was the view that historic social forces determined the character and ideology in prewar German thinking. Instead 'amorphous "antecedent sociological and economic factors"' (Samelson, 1986, p. 199) were responsible. In other words, the type of psychology changed to fit the psychological world of the North American academic community – it was a liberal, empiricist, individual psychological framework.

Part of the mechanism by which the enterprise had become so transformed was the work of Nevitt Sanford and Daniel Levinson. Early in 1943 Sanford had received a donation of a few hundred dollars to study anti-Semitism. They set about constructing a psychological scale to measure anti-Semitism. When, according to Sanford (1986, p. 211), they were satisfied with the adequacy of their measure, they asked themselves

> whether or not people who were prejudiced against Jews were also prejudiced against other 'outgroups'; hence our Ethnocentrism, or E scale. After finding that this was indeed the case, and believing as we now did that among the sources of prejudice were deep emotional needs of the personality, we asked ourselves if these needs might be expressed in other ways as well – hence the F (for Fascism) scale.

There is no sense in which these developments were dependent on any grand theoretical design – they simply followed their noses, according to Sanford. Their 'empiricist' work became grafted onto the theoretical 'tradition' as part of the publication of *The Authoritarian Personality* (Adorno *et al.*, 1950).

The almost immediate backlash against the book occurred along two distinct lines. First, the whole issue was distilled down to a matter of method. That is, political/ideological features of authoritarianism, were abandoned in favour of simple methodological issues, such as whether the scale really measured an agreement-response set (Sanford, 1986). This is a sort of tendency to agree with the items of any measurement scale irrespective of its content (as in agreeing with both the statements 'In general I like studying' and 'In general I dislike studying').

The second line of attack was more directly political. Some suggested that the authoritarian personality was no different in essence from that of many other extremists. Eysenck (1954; Eysenck and Wilson, 1978), for example, tried to establish that fascists and communist extremists were similar. At root both are extremely tough-minded. Such a change of language serves almost to make fascism acceptable – what is wrong with being tough-minded? Some modern politicians make a virtue of it. But the onslaught was wider than this. The beginning of the cold war period following the Second World War and the publication of *The Authoritarian Personality* coincided. The USA's enemy was now the communist block not fascist Germany. Criticism of right-wing views could be seen as dangerous since it could be construed as collusion with or sympathy for communism. It was also argued that to imply that the fascist personality could find a happy home in America was to play naively into the hands of the Soviet Union. This view, however, neglected the fact that strong anti-communism was a feature of the authoritarian personality. Witch-hunts directed against communism in 1950s America put great pressure on American scholars:

> Such political attacks in their historical context, including difficulties and dismissals of psychologists for alleged or demonstrated left-wing involvements, apparently put some 'chill' on further discussion and research on this and related issues – although it is, for obvious reasons, hard to find any clear-cut evidence in the journals.
>
> (Samelson, 1986, p. 201)

As a consequence, it is very difficult to find a clear picture of the nature of the relationship between fascism and racism emerging in the psychological debate. Despite the theoretical, empirical, social, political and historical importance of the concept of the authoritarian personality, few psychologists apparently understand it properly. Professional social scientists seem to believe that it refers to the sort of person who in managerial positions is despotic and likes to lay down what should be done and to order subordinates around. But this is mistaken. Authoritarians are defined by their orientation to authority, not by their leadership styles *per se*. Powerless authoritarians still possess this same attitude to authority.

In short, the revised view of the nature of the authoritarian personality was that 'There were no real pre-fascist authoritarians, only agreeable persons without strong opinions, or in one variant of this depolitization process, only a deliberately formal, apolitical (and transhistorical) dogmatism' (Samelson, 1986, p. 203) of the sort suggested by Rokeach (1960). Fascists were not the problem, merely methodology. So an attempt to understand the relationship between social structure, the family, and character was sunk under a mass of different criticisms, many of which were not particularly well founded.

The Americanized version of authoritarian personality theory tends to force attention on a minority of 'deviant' people as if they were the sole exponents of, for example, racist views. However, racism is typical of most people in racist societies. Nevertheless, at a minimum assessment, it reflected an attempt to understand the role of socio-psychological processes in explaining the acceptance of fascism and the racial horrors perpetrated on minority groups in Europe half a century ago. Did the attempt deserve to be smothered by positivist psychology?

Yet although the approach became progressively less politically 'engaged,' as well as more 'empirical,' it would be hard to argue that this improvement in the objectivity of methods succeeded in solving the problem; instead it defined the problem away.

(Samelson, 1986, pp. 203–4)

Textbooks began to write of 'the tolerant' personality free of racist traits thus revealing the broader nature of racism in society. One can only be tolerant of the intolerable, no one has to be tolerant about things which do not cause problems, difficulties or ill-feeling.

Eurocentrism and psychology

Caution should be exercised when describing psychology as 'racist'. There is a risk of assuming that, irrespective of the cultural and racial origins of particular psychologists, they express through psychology racism against other races. It is similarly problematic to describe psychology as 'ethno-centric' since it is only ethnocentric from one perspective – the Western/European position. Consequently probably the most precise term to use is that psychology is *Eurocentric*. This means that it seeks to understand and explain the world in a way which is characteristically Western or European. Joseph *et al.* (1990) claim that a main feature of Eurocentric psychology is the assumption among psychologists that people are significantly alike in all important respects. This might be called 'universalism' – the idea that psychological concepts apply to all people. The concept of mind and the battle for power in toilet training are mentioned by them as major examples. Piaget's theories are the most widely discussed modern ideas about the nature of 'mind' (see, for example, Piaget, 1952). The universalism in these is abundantly obvious. Piaget's theories are essentially asocial in that they assume that cognition develops in more or less invariant stages. If essential stages need to be passed through to achieve the mind's full development then all minds have to develop in similar ways. But Joseph *et al.* (1990, pp. 12–13) claim that despite the aura of universalism, the skills Piaget selected to study the mind are particularly well suited to Western technological culture:

If one assumes, as Piagetians do for example, that there is a 'natural' sequence of development which is universal, with a 'natural' fixed end-point (the attainment of formal reasoning) and that these stages are 'naturally' attained (not through social tutoring) and that this is the path development will take unless there is something lacking in the environment, then the interpretation that some non-western cultures may not be competent at formal reasoning may indeed be seen as ethnocentric.

The other major factor delineating psychology as Eurocentric is its assumption that the minds of individuals are the central focus of psychological understanding. This is probably the result of Descartes' insistence on a distinction between the individual and society, the split between body and mind, and the emphasis that our own mind is all we know with certainty. So psychological characteristics become based on the individual mind not that of the individual as a member of a social group. Consequently, the understanding of, say, morality depends on the individual being the possessor and constructor of moral rules. Morality is seen as a consequence of the conviction with which these rules are held by the individual. It is not seen as the outcome of the support given through social bonds for moral action:

> Studies of morality in India have had the inenviable task of trying to 'explain away' uncomfortable behaviour. Individuals in India appear to act guided by external gratification rather than internal norms alone. The psychoanalytic literature describes this as a failure in the development of internal controls, somewhat akin to the weaker superegos attributed to women generally, and a consequent development of a 'communal conscience' instead of individual conscience ... Rather than accept definitions of deficiencies imposed from without, psychologists from cultures of a more collectivist persuasion need to define their own conceptions of morality and maturity and to recognise the extent to which western developmental psychology has focused on the growth of individual resources in the child or the adult.
>
> (Joseph *et al.*, 1990, p. 15)

Eurocentrism does not only describe much of psychology, together with ethnocentricism, such viewpoints are frequently justified as 'natural'. A good example of this comes from the work of Tajfel (1978; Tajfel and Fraser, 1978) on intergroup relations. He does not go so far as to suggest that racism is a 'normal' or 'inbuilt' human trait. Instead, he suggests that the mere fact of group membership leads to favouritism towards co-members. This is not a consequence of social learning, socialization, or any other socially determined process. Instead, at root, it is a consequence of natural characteristics of the human mind – in this instance to form categories. While this, in itself, might not normalize extreme racism, what it does mean is that the tendency to 'take care of one's own' is conceived as inherent in the structures of human thought. This is not substantially different from the new racism associated with the far right, described earlier. Trivial criteria may be responsible for the self-definition of a group (in Billig and Tajfel, 1973, it is as little as being randomly assigned to a group). Though the following has much more of the flavour of the real world and how ethnic identity arises:

because racial sentiments are not acquired biological dispositions of individuals and groups they can be adjusted and discarded according to changing circumstances ... ethnic and racial mobilization depends on its suitability and expediency in a specific sociopolitical environment ... Ethnic attachments persist only as long as they serve a purpose. Above all it depends on whether there is a perceived need for ethnic identification and how mobilizers capitalize on these needs.

(Adam and Giliomee, 1979, p. 63)

Although in his later career Tajfel was an important figure in social psychology, his intellectual roots in mainstream experimental psychology are manifest in the tendency to see the naturalness of ingroup favouritism resulting from the 'universalism' of mind. Tajfel's approach is often praised as an advance on Sherif's (1966) view that friendship and hostility may develop in groups as a function of shared or conflicting goals. However, Tajfel replaces the potential optimism of Sherif's view (groups can learn cooperation and friendliness) by a depressing cognitive 'innatism'. Furthermore, the reductionist simplicity of his view is alarming. It explains so little, justifies so much. All that is required is the identification of a similarity between people and basic psychological processes take over, leading to categorization. Irrespective of the layers of complexity that can be added to this, its basic logic inescapably regards social divisions as natural. Eventually, such a viewpoint leads to what is known as 'social identity theory', which concerns itself with how groups obtain their identities as groups. This leads to a depressing 'divisionist' view of intergroup relations. Hewstone and Giles (1984, p. 278) present the following as (presumably) a concerned and considered discussion of important matters:

According to social identity theory, individuals define themselves to a large extent in terms of their social group memberships and tend to seek a positive social identity (or self-definition in terms of group membership). They achieve this by comparing their own group with other groups to establish a positively valued distinctiveness between the two groups. Claiming that motivational as well as cognitive factors underlie intergroup differentiation, the theory holds that positive comparisons (intergroup differences seen to favour the ingroup) provide a *satisfactory* social identity, while negative comparisons (differences which favour the outgroup) convey an unsatisfactory identity ... Empirical support for this approach was gained initially through studies using the 'minimal group paradigm', which demonstrated that social categorization alone can be sufficient to engender intergroup discrimination in which the ingroup is favoured over the outgroup ... (emphasis added)

Prejudice is, then, inevitably a consequence of the categorization processes. This is a disturbing theme for any approach to relationships between groups of people. To write of a 'satisfactory' social identity based on apparent inevitably disparaging comparisons with the outgroup is a complacent rejection of important social concerns. Some people gain a 'satisfactory' social identity by raping and otherwise debasing women, by abusing black people, by beating up 'gays', by laughing at the disabled, and other 'satisfactory' means. A social theory such as this is hardly the stuff that those concerned with psychology and social issues should tolerate.

This complacency can be contrasted with a brief paragraph from the writing of Stuart Cook, a psychologist with a lifelong commitment to equality. Writing on the research on school desegregation, the integration of black and white pupils in school, he comments:

> If, in fact, school desegregation has not lived up to its constructive potential, do we as social scientists share any part of the responsibility? My answer – an unpopular one – is that we do. Please understand that I know my answer overlooks the typical constraints of time and money that so often are the determining factors of what we study. Disregarding this reality for the moment, my argument is that social scientists have generally responded to the challenge of desegregation in a reactive rather than an innovative fashion. Their role has been to evaluate the outcome of desegregation experiences just as these have occurred. They have not, by contrast, proposed and studied alternative methods by which school desegregation might be carried out.
>
> (Cook, 1985, p. 460)

In other words, Cook is keen to do the work to *change* society. He does not wish to do the work which sustains and normalizes the status quo. To regard prejudice as 'natural' and, for the individual, 'satisfactory' does not seem to be part of Cook's make-up; nor should it be in the make-up of any psychologist.

The work of a postgraduate student working on her thesis is sufficient to undermine the assumptions of the 'learned' Bristol group who claim to have developed social identity theory. According to Devine (1989), this viewpoint overlooks an important theoretical distinction between *knowing* a stereotype and *accepting* that stereotype. In other words, while being aware of a particular stereotype the individual's beliefs may be totally different. Using ideas from information processing theory, Devine suggests that thought processes can be divided into two types: automatic thought processes, which are mainly involuntary responses; and controlled thought processes, which can largely be invoked voluntarily. Thus we can do something about involuntary thoughts if we so wish. Devine first established that racial stereotypes are familiar to us all, irrespective of our attitudes towards other races. She found that stereotypes of black people held by white Americans included those of criminality, low intelligence, laziness, sexual prowess, athleticism and rhythm. No matter how unprejudiced the individual was, the stereotypes were equally familiar. Devine went on to show that if stereotypes are activated subtly, without the individual necessarily being aware of the fact, stereotypes could be aroused which affect the way an ambiguous passage of text was interpreted. This effect occurred irrespective of prejudice levels. Essentially, it was as if the screening mechanism had been short-circuited. That is, there was no reprocessing of the automatically aroused stereotypes to neutralize them. In this way, the automatically aroused stereotypes had no opportunity to be replaced with non-prejudiced responses.

When asked to list their thoughts about black Americans in conditions conducive to the arousal of controlled thought processes, high- and low-prejudiced individuals differed radically. Irrespective of prejudice levels, participants were equally aware of ways in which black Americans were described. The pejorative descriptions included 'niggers', 'coons', 'spear-chuckers', 'jungle bunnies', and 'jigs'. More neutral terminology was represented by 'blacks', 'Afro-Americans', 'brothers', and 'coloured people'. However, when asked to express their thoughts on black Americans, phrases like 'blacks are free loaders', 'blacks cause problems (e.g. mugging, fights)', 'blacks and whites are equal', and 'My father says all blacks are lazy, I think he is wrong' were mentioned. Some of these are positive towards black people, others negative. The data showed that the *considered* thoughts of the low-prejudice research participants were more positive towards black people than those of the prejudiced participants.

In other words, we can all be affected to stereotypes in some circumstances, but given the opportunity to reflect it is possible to override these and present a more reflected position, if we are so inclined. Vigilance is at the core of anti-racism in a racist culture which has created prejudiced minds.

Another illustration of this comes from anti-racism training. The training is designed to try to make participants aware of the inadvertent racism they carry, as well as to confront overt racism. Group exercises are used to make participants increasingly aware of their racist assumptions, beliefs, attitudes and stereotypes. One exercise is an adaptation of the work of Bartlett (1932) on memory. One person recounts a story to another person, who then tries to reproduce it to a third person, who then tries to tell it to a fourth person, and so on. The Bartlett study is a classic demonstration of information-processing approaches to memory in psychology courses. It is, in fact, a version of what would have been called in colonial days 'Chinese whispers'. The following story starts the sequence (this is a simple variant on Allport and Postman, 1947):

The time was 5.30 pm in London and the underground train was overcrowded as usual at this time of day. In one particularly crowded carriage, a number of passengers were standing up very close to one another. Two men of different ethnic origins were standing up facing each other; one of them had an open double-edged knife and newspaper in his hand. When the train stopped at the next station both men stepped out onto an equally overcrowded platform. There were many young people at the station. In the struggle to get in and out of the train, a passenger stepped on the foot of one of the men. A fight ensued involving a large number of passengers and London Transport staff. Some people were badly hurt. The police were called and they were taken to the local police station. One man rang home and informed his family that he had been remanded in custody at the police station. His wife was furious at the news; she scolded him for his irre-sponsibility and blamed him for what had happened to him that day. The children and some of the people involved were not charged with any offence. The following day one of the men could not go to work so his boss fired him.

Groups almost invariably lose, change or distort parts of the story in a manner which reveals the operation of stereotyped racist (and sexist) thinking. The following is how one group of young people who were overtly anti-racist had reproduced the story after four or five repetitions to another party:

Five thirty on a London Underground station and there were two black people there. One was carrying a rolled up newspaper with a knife partly hidden in the newspaper. There was some kind of scuffle or fight on the tube train itself which involved some people and the police. One person was arrested and the other person got away. And when they got home, the other got home, he was told off by his wife.

Here is another example from a different group:

London underground was very busy and a fight broke between two people of ethnic origin. A double edged knife was used. British rail staff were involved. Someone was arrested. A wife telephoned the police.

The members of the groups are under some stress, having to speak in public into a tape-recorder. The controlled processing, as Devine calls it, should be minimized in this context. Notice how the story is changed in ways which are consonant with stereotypes – racist or otherwise. In the first story, a violent tone to the story has become clearly the responsibility of two *black* men rather than people of different ethnic origins in the original. There is a scuffle or a fight which seems difficult to separate totally from these man-ufactured black men, though this is a little ambiguous. The cause of the fight has become less clearly something of which the black men may be innocent.

Finally, in a classic example of sexist stereotyping, one of the men gets home and is told off by his wife as if 'henpecked'. While the original contains some reference to a man's wife telling him off, the fact that this is retained when much of the rest of the story which becomes lost is of great significance. Virtually none of the processed version reflects reasonably accurately what was said in the original. This sort of transformation is nothing unusual; it is typical of how groups of people respond in such circumstances.

Racism is built by culture into our thinking; without vigilance it guides our words and actions in subtle and elusive ways. It can be faced up to and lessened. It should not be accepted as 'normal'.

Concluding comments

While initially this account of racism might be expected to concentrate on the 'massive' gains in knowledge that psychology has achieved in understanding racism in society, ultimately something different emerged. What was argued was that psychology does not have a rigid boundary which cuts it off from racist ideas. Quite the reverse – the thinking of psychologists reflects racism in a number of important and different ways. This is not simply in terms of overtly racist beliefs but in developing theoretical viewpoints which are more or less directly supportive of racism.

Although some directly racist views expressed by psychologists throughout much of the history of modern psychology have been pointed out, racism is also to be found in the less direct forms of expression. This is not merely in the way in which hidden racist ideas are expressed (cf. Howitt and Owusu-Bempah, 1990) but also in how the thrust of significant attempts to understand racism are neutered and turned into trivial matters of method (as in the case of the authoritarian personality research).

It is not realistic, as a consequence, to seek an understanding of racism from psychological research and theory in general. Psychology is racist but psychologists protect themselves with claims of 'science'. Consequently, the erroneous conclusion is, self-examination is 'not necessary'. It is then both remarkable and completely expected that psychologists are trained but never required to confront their own psyche's latent racism, though they may 'point the finger' at non-psychologists from their position of being psychologists and thus scientifically grounded professionals.

There is some hope that psychology may develop a truly anti-racist stance in practice, theory and research. But that can only be achieved with the realization that nothing is natural in the social order. In other words, we must maximize awareness of creeping racism in the profession by exploring the profession's institutional promotion of racism.

7

THE POLITICS OF AN ISSUE: PORNOGRAPHY AND FEMINISM

The conference, entitled 'Pornography and Sexual Violence' ... was massively oversubscribed ... Potential dissenters were excluded from the afternoon workshops. Women with press tickets were allowed to listen to the series of papers which formed the first half of the conference. A cheer went up when it was announced over the loudspeaker that a group of women who had distributed a leaflet 'against the aims of this conference' during the lunchbreak were 'no longer with us'. The leaflet contained a feminist argument against the dangers of censorship.
(Norden, 1990, p. 1, on a conference held in 1989)

The primarily academic concerns of much psychology have produced some rather anomalous research priorities. This is true even when a significant social problem is chosen for research. A 'classic' example of this is the investigations of American researchers Darley and Latane. These investigations led to the invention of a famous psychological concept, the diffusion of responsibility, inspired by a specific real-life event (see, for example, Latane and Darley, 1970; Evans, 1980; Kitzinger, 1990). This event was the murder of Kitty Genovese during March 1964 in the Queens district of New York. Thirty-eight people either heard her cries for help or witnessed some of the events, but virtually nothing was done to intervene.

Misdirection of theory

Latane and Darley saw the problem as being why witnesses did nothing to intervene in the situation. After theorizing and research, the idea of the diffusion of responsibility was generated. In this, willingness to intervene is determined by the degree to which the individual feels herself/himself to be the only witness. As a corollary, the more people are aware of an emergency, the less an individual feels personally responsible. In a crowd, the responsibility for intervention is shared among all the witnesses, or, in other words, responsibility for intervention is diffused among bystanders. These studies have been included in numerous psychology textbooks as significant contributions to applied social psychology (including Howitt *et al.*, 1989, pp. 96–7). However, Latane and Darley did not investigate why women are violently attacked irrespective of the presence or absence of witnesses.

The details of the Kitty Genovese case deserve more attention than psychologists have given them. Despite the slightly histrionic though nevertheless bland accounts of psychology textbooks, there is a largely unmentioned seamier side to the story. This is far more important than the experiments designed by Latane and Darley in the 1960s social psychology genre could ever be (Howitt, 1990b). One might even forget the name Kitty Genovese since she could have been any woman on the New York streets that night. Winston Moseley was cruising the neighbourhood in his sportscar. Having spotted Kitty Genovese, he chased her, caught her, jumped on her back and stabbed her four times. A bystander at this point shouted for Moseley to leave her alone. Temporarily he did. Wounded, the woman staggered towards her apartment but collapsed outside. Moseley approached her again, knifed her repeatedly and raped her as she was dying.

Moseley had murdered three other women, raped at least four, and attempted to rape yet more. He had a taste for raping dying women. He set fire to the pubic hair of one victim. Imprisoned for the Genovese murder, he escaped from prison only to beat up a man and rape his wife.

While the issue for Latane and Darley was the people who did not intervene to save Kitty Genovese, bystander apathy is not a significant feature of most rapes and murders. On the contrary, the problems were Winston Moseley's 'warped' mind and sexual violence against women in general. To an extent, Latane and Darley can be excused for construing the murder in the way they did. Academic psychology's experiments of the 1960s were a substitute for real-world foci. The major feminist impetus which was to dominate a good deal of academic thinking in the 1970s and 1980s was not anticipated. If Latane and Darley had begun their research, stimulated by a similar murder, in the 1990s, things may have been different. As it is, though, their neglect of the sexual violence in the Winston Moseley case partly reflects social attitudes towards rape at that time. Rape was not a significant social problem. It was socially construed that only some women, usually of questionable morality, were by far the most likely to be attacked by deviant males.

Ideological overlaps between rape and pornography

In the 1970s attitudes began to change and an alternative view took a more central and dominant position. The feminist movement made it more commonly accepted that all women were under threat of male sexual aggression. Indeed, not only was the threat to all women, irrespective of age, class and culture, but the threat frequently became reality. Refuges for women victims of domestic violence, complaints about the way in which the police and courts treated rape victims so as doubly to victimize them, the concept of rape in marriage, child sexual abuse, female circumcision, and sexual harassment at work all served as signs of the more general concern about sexual violence, and its relationship to the maintenance of male power. Why do men perpetrate or seek the perpetration of such acts against women?

In its way, rape provides an encapsulation of critical issues central to gender relationships. Rape is central to feminist theories about male sexuality and male power (Brownmiller, 1975; Faust, 1980; Ellis, 1989). But it is also a much more general issue for psychology. It touches on issues such as differences between normality and abnormality, the origins of deviant behaviour, and the nature of sex as a drive to action. However, when the issue of rape is entrained with that of pornography, an even more explosive combination results. Pornography introduces new ideological debates making the possibility of simple discussion remote. Controls on pornography tap emotive topics such as individual liberty to engage in 'harmless' activities, freedom of speech, the independence of the media from control, and the abandonment of sexual repression. But if pornography adds to sexual violence against women, the equation becomes even more complex.

A joint attack on pornography is possible once the modern formulation of the issues is accepted (Cumberbatch and Howitt, 1989). Part of this is from those individuals and groups who object to the explicit sexual content of pornography (see, for example, Whitehouse, 1967; 1971). The other arm of the attack points to the lessons pornography teaches about relationships between men and women. For the latter group, pornography promotes unacceptable views – such as that women enjoy being treated violently in sexual contexts, that women secretly long to be 'forcibly taken', and that women are to be demeaned. So there is an anti-pornography 'lobby' which 'unites' on a broad front, traditionalists (who believe a woman's place is in the home but dislike sexual 'filth') and 'radical' feminists who see a different role for women and a different problem with pornography. Anything which serves to 'unify' such opposed factions has to be a powerful symbol.

The history of pornography shares similarities with those of other social issues, particularly its lack of fixedness. According to Wilson (1973), pornography has advanced and retreated several times as a social issue over the last two hundred years or so. While, for example, in nineteenth-century America there was a little initial anti-pornography legislation, not until after the Second World War did attention return to the matter. The reasons why this should be the case are relatively straightforward:

> The simple existence of sexual depictions, either verbal or pictorial, does not seem to be a key factor. Such depictions appear to have existed in all times and places. Rather a relatively rapid increase in the availability of such depictions from a relatively stable base (at whatever absolute level) is perhaps the crucial factor. In England, concern about sexual obscenity increased with the widespread use of printing in the 18th century and with the expansion of literacy in the 19th century. In the United States, the passing of obscenity statutes coincided with the drive of universal free education in the first half of the 19th century, and more recently with the advent of inexpensive, high quality color photographic reproduction in the middle of the 20th century.
>
> (Wilson, 1973, p. 9)

There is no sense in which pornography can be construed as a social issue independent of the social and historical factors which created it.

So the question of the effects of pornography is an important one. It is also one which has attracted considerable political utilization of social sciences research. Since about 1970, there have been a number of government commissions, committees and other investigations into the influence of pornography. These include the Commission on Obscenity and Pornography (1970), the Attorney General's Commission on Pornography (1986), the Committee on Obscenity and Film Censorship (Williams, 1979), the Special Committee on Pornography and Prostitution also known as the Fraser Committee (Canada, 1985), and the Joint Select Committee on Video Material (Australia, 1988). We could add to this informal, unofficial investigations of a collective nature such as the Longford Committee Investigating Pornography (1972) and Barlow and Hill (1985). Not only have these often invited input from psychologists, they have also sometimes financed relevant research. Few topics in social sciences have produced such a response and it is difficult to think of a similar involvement on the part of psychology in any other topic – including mass media violence. Nor should it be forgotten that there is a considerable literature generated by psychologists – among the most polemical being *Sex, Violence and the Media* (Eysenck and Nias, 1978). In addition, there are reports produced by psychologists for government bodies. For example, in Britain the Broadcasting Standards Council published a review of the effects of the mass media under the title *A Measure of Uncertainty* (Cumberbatch and Howitt, 1989) which gave special attention to pornography. Furthermore, the Home Office commissioned *Pornography: Impacts and Influences* (Howitt and

Cumberbatch, 1990), a major review of social science research into the effects of pornography with special reference to the European situation.

Prior to the feminist upsurge of the 1970s, the major concern about pornography was that it served to arouse sexual desire which then led to socially undesirable consequences. These included premarital sex, extra-marital sex, illegitimacy and masturbation, as well as sexual crime. Leaving aside issues such as illegitimacy and premarital sex (about which social attitudes have changed considerably since the 1960s), the concept of rape as a sexually motivated crime deserves consideration. Perhaps there are some clues in the Moseley–Genovese case. Moseley's 'sexual kicks' did not come from intercourse particularly but from the stalking and chasing process which was a prelude to raping the totally vulnerable, dying woman. Descriptions of other rapes might clarify things further:

> One of the rapists told the victim he was going to cut her up if she resisted and when she did resist, he hit her in the face with his fist. She was then raped by the men, and they carved the word 'fuck' on her abdomen.
>
> (Sanders, 1980, p. 62)
>
> I asked him what he was doing – told him he didn't have to do it there if all he wanted was a screw … First he tried natural sex; then he insisted on oral sex. I didn't want to but he forced me … Then he said he was going to urinate on me … He rammed his fist up me twice and he bit my breasts. Then he stood up and piddled all over me and said, 'I feel better.'
>
> (Burgess and Holmstrom, 1979, p. 15)

Neither of these examples can be construed as the simple expression of a purely sexual lust. Humiliation and degradation of the victim seem to be the essential characteristics. In the case of the second woman, the victim had fully intended to have intercourse with the man and this must have been clear to him. However, what he wanted was something rather different, as he made manifest by urinating over her. Rape does not necessarily seem to be the natural consequence of intense sexual arousal and the absence of a legitimate partner. Cases of rape can occur very shortly after the man has had intercourse with his regular partner. To think of sexual arousal as the prime motive for rape is perhaps to regard human sexuality as that of a male rabbit attempting to copulate with anything if a female is not available. Following intensive research, feminist-orientated researchers, in particular, have offered the following view of rape:

> sexual desire is not the dominant motive in rape; nor is sexual frustration, for a variation on the myth that the victim has sexually enticed the offender is the view that the offender is a sex-starved male who must rape to relieve his sexual tensions and frustrations … Rape

is ... a pseudosexual act, complex and multidetermined, but addressing issues of hostility (anger) and control (power) more than desire (sexuality).

(Burgess and Holmstrom, 1979, p. 23)

This idea is extremely important. It takes what would at first sight appear to be a criminal activity (rape) and reconceptualizes it in terms directly related to gender relationships in general. The crime of rape takes on a symbolic aspect. It is a representation in microcosm of male sexuality and male power and dominance over women. No longer merely a crime, rape is both a consequence of and a cause of social structures built on gender differentiation and gendered power hierarchies. This view inevitably demands that the rapist and the 'normal' male are indistinguishable. To suggest otherwise reduces the explanatory power of this feminist formulation of rape. Sexual violence is just the dramatic culmination of a gender-related power system which controls women. Pornography, from this perspective, is indicted because it propagates images of women's sexuality which condone sexual violence. The idea is encouraged, for example, that women are sexually turned on by such acts, irrespective of their protestations. All of this is dependent on accepting that rape is not a sexual act *per se* but a violent attack on a woman's self, self-regard and psychological integrity. Nothing could be so radically different from not-so-old views that by depicting sexual organs and activities, pornography stimulates sexual arousal – wherein lies the danger.

Fundamental issues, then, are raised by any discussion of pornography and/or rape. Unfortunately, this is an area somewhat devoid of serious critical examination in the light of research evidence. Because of this, the arguments appear to be more doctrinaire than would usually be the case. While the doctrine may ultimately be supported by research, it is not a proper stance to await contentedly the eventual and casual emergence of relevant research. The search for the evidence needs to go hand in glove with the 'theory', no matter what its doctrinal base.

Rape as normal

A good example of a programmatic rather than sound social scientific evaluation is Russell's (1988) so-called 'causal model' of pornography's effects on rape. Irrespective of personal opinions about pornography's contents and the ideological themes it portrays, neither of these necessarily justify the assumption that men rape as a consequence of using this sort of material. Russell builds her model on the view that the propensity to rape is common among all groups of men. She points to evidence to suggest that over half of a sample of American college males indicated that they might be willing to rape *if* 'they could get away with it' (Malamuth *et al.*, 1979; 1980; Malamuth and Ceniti, 1986). Quite what such answers mean is a matter of conjecture. For example, is it an acknowledgement of the belief that males often are sexually coercive and that one cannot exclude oneself from the possibility? This would be radically different from seeing an affirmative answer as a statement of intent to rape but for the deterrent of punishment. The question does not ask whether the men want to or desire to rape so its precise implications are more obscure than some might wish. For Russell, though, affirmative answers to the question are used to promote the view that there are large numbers of males who *if disinhibited about the consequences for them of rape* would rape (Sommers and Check, 1987). Her model is built on the following assumptions:

1 Someone has to *want* to commit rape, battery, and other forms of sexual assault before they will occur.
2 Internal inhibitions against these desires have to be undermined.
3 Social inhibitions caused by factors such as being caught and punished have to be undermined.
4 The perpetrator has to overcome resistance in the victim.

There are a number of mechanisms claimed in the model which are responsible for these stages being implemented. A brief list of the sorts of evidence she relied on includes:

1 The desire to rape is proven because some rapists claim to have been influenced by pornography.
2 Internal inhibitions are reduced by the thematic material of some pornography that women enjoy rape.
3 Social inhibitions are reduced because rape in pornography goes unpunished.
4 There is some evidence that some sex offenders use pornography to overcome the resistance of the victim by 'demonstrating' the 'normality' of certain acts.

Russell's use of data seems a little selective and frequently speculative. As such, it does not seem to constitute adequate psychological theory. However, in so far as Russell articulates the views of many feminist writers but extends into the research context, her work may help illustrate the strengths and weaknesses inherent in turning feminist theory into psychological theory.

Ignoring peripheral parts of her argument, the crux of her case is that rape proclivity and sexual assault on women are very common. There are good reasons for supposing this from feminist writing since sexual assault is merely the individual expression of the male gender's means of controlling and subordinating all women (Brownmiller, 1975). At the same time, it imposes on our understanding the notion that there is nothing 'different' about sexual offenders. As sexual assaults are seen as common and universally characteristic of male psychology, nothing should separate offenders from non-offenders but 'fate' or 'bad luck'. The convicted offenders are the 'unfortunate' ones who get reported, caught and punished.

This is clearly a radically different view from attempts to explain criminality in terms that, say, some criminologists would use. Instead of characteristics such as social class, age, family dynamics, peer pressure, and personality being implicated in creating the rapist, the sole criterion of male gender is sufficient to predict proclivity to rape. These are extremely different approaches. Inevitably, the big question becomes: who are the men who rape? One answer is to look at the characteristics of convicted rapists. The picture which emerges from this is not supportive of the view that rape is typical of male sexuality. One study (Lloyd and Walmsley, 1989) looked at the criminal histories of a sample of men who were convicted of rape. Virtually all men so convicted during the year 1972 were investigated until 1985. Within five years of discharge, over 50 per cent of the men were reconvicted on at least one fairly serious charge (ignoring motoring offences and the like). But, by and large, these reconvictions were not for sexual offences. About a fifth were reconvictions for theft, about a sixth reconvictions for burglary, about a third reconvictions for an essentially violent offence (that is, a fifth for violence against the person, a tenth for sexual offences, and about a twenty-fifth for robbery).

The picture is very much of a general criminality rather than a rape-prone personality as such. Only 3 per cent of rapists were reconvicted. Of course, financial and other pressures on ex-prisoners may be responsible for the pattern of reoffending. So it is interesting to note that the study also looked at the *previous* convictions of those convicted of rape in 1985. Half had previous convictions for theft and two-fifths for burglary. Just under half had previous convictions for violent offences. Previous convictions for rape were again not very frequent (3 per cent of offenders).

These data cannot be used to dismiss the possibility of there being a rape-prone personality which is different from that of the generally criminal rapist. However, the figures would suggest that these would be a tiny minority, given the low recidivism rate for rape. But the fact that rapists have previous criminal records does not entirely exclude the view that rape proclivity is typical of 'normal' male sexuality. Those prone to act criminally may be willing to express their sexuality through a sexual crime, in a way which non-criminals may not. 'Normal' men may well be coercive in their sexual relations but stop short of a crime. Alternatively, known criminals may be more likely to be prosecuted by the police when a crime is reported, all other things being equal.

Studies of offenders

There is evidence that rape offenders are different from 'normal' men or non-rape offenders. This comes from research showing that rapists are aroused by rape-related imagery. The work was carried out in England at the Broadmoor Special Hospital for the criminally mentally ill (Hinton *et al.*, 1980), using three groups of men. One group had histories of gross sexual offences, another histories of non-sexual attacks on women, and the third consisted of normal men who were not patients. As part of the research the men were shown a number of black and white video films. The first of these featured nudity, mutual masturbation, and intercourse of a heterosexual nature, the second was paedophiliac homosexual activity, and the fourth film included adult homosexual activity. However, the third film shown in the sequence was for our purposes the most significant. It involved a girl, apparently of about 12 years, riding her cycle alone in the countryside. Two men approach her and she is involved in a struggle and chase. The film culminates in a three-minute depiction of a violent rape.

The measurements of sexual arousal in the viewers included physiological measures of the volume of their genitals, a fairly reliable measure of male sexual excitement. With one important exception, no differences were found between normal men and sexual offenders in response to any of the four films. Men who had offended sexually against young girls or women tended to respond sexually to the film in which the young girl was raped. However, it would be incorrect to suggest that the filmed rape caused this sexual arousal since:

> It became apparent early in the testing of sexually deviant patients that offenders against young girls showed a marked increase in penis diameter simply on viewing the first 2 min[utes] of the girl rape film. During this period the girl is seen standing alone fully clothed, being taken, chased, and finally (still fully clothed) struggling with two men.
> (Hinton *et al.*, 1980, p. 215)

This fits fairly precisely with Malamuth and Check's (1980) finding that men who professed a greater likelihood of raping (if they could get away with it) were more sexually aroused by rape pornography than those low on rape proclivity. It would appear that aspects of rape (different from explicit depictions of heterosexual intercourse) are sexually stimulating to some sexually violent men. What these stimulating elements are is unknown – the 'pleasure' of stalking a victim? the fear caused to the victim? or the distress caused in her? Nevertheless, the evidence appears to suggest that sexual offenders have different sexual make-ups from non-offending men.

Further support for this comes from a study of exhibitionists (Kolarsky *et al.*, 1978). On film, a naked actress acted out seductive behaviour in a number of different ways. By recording their sexual arousal physiologically, offenders and non-offenders could be compared. In general, films were similarly arousing to both groups. But careful analysis showed that certain scenes produced more arousal in offenders. The scenes which differentially affected the offenders tended to be those in which 'pseudo-retreat' was absent. Absence of pseudo-retreat essentially involves frontal exposure of the body to the camera, leaving the legs apart, exposing the genitals. While the reasons for this difference are conjectural, the question is raised as to the factors which arouse deviant sexuality. Again this suggests that normal and deviant sexuality are differentiable to a degree.

If this is the case, it needs to be asked whether the psychological and sexual histories of sexual offenders are correspondingly different. If it were established that they are, a further layer of evidence differentiating sexual offenders from 'normal' men would be revealed. One must not assume, however, that all forms of sex offender are similar. Some researchers (Carter *et al.*, 1987) certainly see sex offenders as varying in terms of the aetiology of their deviant sexuality. One important study (Condron and Nutter, 1988) looked at involvement with pornography in the childhood and adolescence of offenders.

Condron and Nutter (1988) used the major criteria for a good study of this subject as laid down by the (American) Attorney General's Commission on Pornography (1986). These criteria were suggested in order to improve the methodological adequacy of research into the role of pornography in sexual offending and to avoid the shortcomings of previous research. They included:

1   The use of non-prisoners to avoid the possible effects of incarceration which might be confused with the factors leading to sexual deviance.
2   Inclusion of the extent to which pornography was used in first sexual experiences (masturbation).
3   The age at which deviant sexual behaviour first happened.
4   The age at which pornography was first used.

The researchers concencentrated on mass-market 'pornographic' material (such as *Penthouse*, *Playboy* and *Forum*). While this ignores extreme forms of pornography, the range of sexually deviant behaviours investigated for pornography's effects ranged from rape and incest to use of enemas in sexual arousal and cross-gender dressing. Four different groups of men participated in the research: non-incarcerated sex offenders, including those who had committed rape, incest and child molestation; men being treated for sexual dysfunctions such as premature ejaculation or loss of sexual desire; men reporting behaviours such as exhibitionism, cross-dressing, and bondage (paraphiliacs); and 'normal' men from a services club. The main findings were that sex offenders and paraphiliacs were the most likely to have begun to masturbate prior to any exposure to pornography. Masturbation occurred earlier than exposure to pornography in 63 per cent of sex offenders, 91 per cent of paraphiles, 47 per cent of sexual dysfunction patients, and 41 per cent of the 'normal' men. The average age of first exposure to pornography was 15 years for the sex offenders, as opposed to 13 years for the other groups of men.

Whatever else these data imply, two things are clear: first, that it is more typical of 'normal' men that they had been exposed to pornography prior to starting first masturbation during childhood and adolescence than 'abnormal' groups; and second, that, if anything, sex offenders are more naive of pornography during adolescence than other groups, including normals. However, masturbation first occurred at a younger age in sex offenders and paraphiles than in the other two groups. Condron and Nutter (1988) raise the possibility that early sexual maturity itself might play a part in the development of unusual sexual behaviours.

Nothing in these data suggests that sexual offenders are merely 'normal' men who had simply been 'unlucky' enough to get caught for their offences. They seem to demonstrate some clear developmental differences in their psycho-sexual histories from those of 'normal' men.

As we have already seen, an alternative to suggesting that rapists are different from other men is the view that rape is an extreme expression of the general attitude of men towards women. This hypothesis takes a number of different forms. One which is common in the feminist, as well as the social scientific, literature is the concept of 'rape myths'. These myths are the beliefs about rape which shift the blame away from the rapist onto the victim. Examples include 'many women who say "no" mean "yes"' and 'she was asking for it because of the way she dressed'. Several psychologists have sought to measure acceptance of these myths (Burt, 1980; Donnerstein *et al.*, 1986; Intons-Peterson and Roskos-Ewoldson, 1989; Padgett *et al.*, 1989). As is usual with psychological measurement, the assumption is that some people accept the 'myths' more than others. So rather than being a universal cultural view of the nature of rape (or a social representation of rape), the myths are seen as more or less accepted by some and less accepted by others.

One important question follows from this: how are rape-myths learnt? An obvious source is that the socialization of females, in particular, discourages them from being in 'dangerous' places when alone and, particularly, at night. Thus the freedom of women to go to the cinema, public houses, walking, fishing, and so on is severely constrained. This is not because a car will accidentally run them over or because wild animals will attack them. It is the fear that men will assume that they are available for easy sexual intercourse. The reverse of this is the view that if a woman is assaulted in such circumstances then she must have encouraged that attack. Another possibility is, of course, that men are taught the rape myths by pornography.

Contents of pornography

There have been numerous suggestions as to the messages conveyed through pornography and what precisely it is. One of the claims is that the frequently violent nature of pornography encourages sexual violence against women. Among other claims are that pornography contributes a view that women have worth solely as physical objects of male sexual desire, and that the physical degradation shown in pornography leads to the social degradation of women in real life. Theories about pornography's effects are thereby varied and rather imprecisely defined. Indeed it is sometimes virtually imposible to turn such claims into social scientifically meaningful statements. For example, take the claims that pornography degrades women. Just who or what is degraded? The women taking part? If so, in whose judgement? All women in the eyes of men? The women who view it? Just what does 'to degrade women' mean? In terms of their morality? Their social worth? The nature of female sexuality?

Answers to some of these questions might emerge from content analyses of pornographic material. These have been rather infrequent and not particularly thorough. A typical finding is that the level of violence in pornography has increased over recent years or is high (Smith, 1976; Malamuth and Spinner, 1980; Cowan *et al.*, 1988; Itzin and Sweet, 1989; Baxter, 1990). However, it has been demonstrated, using archival material from the Kinsey Sex Research Institute, that there has always been a degree of violence in pornography. This proportion has remained consistently low, at about 10 per cent of output (Slade, 1984). Indeed, many of the films which mix sex and violence are relatively mild in both respects. Those featuring sex or violence alone tend to be more extreme. Obviously one might well find certain extreme examples of sex combined with violence. Barlow and Hill (1985) present several synopses of video-nasties. Further studies showing low levels or declines in violence in pornography include Howitt and Cumberbatch (1990); Kutchinsky (1985); Scott and Cuvelier (1987); and Soble (1986).

Content analysis does not seem to supply particularly useful information relevant to pornography's *effects*. This is not surprising since it is largely designed to paint a broad picture of contents. Notwithstanding this, content analysis is frequently used as part of pressure-group campaigns. The feminist is well served by analyses of the media's sexist content (Signorielli, 1985; Livingstone and Green, 1986; Brette and Cantor, 1988). For example, gender differences are commonly observable in media portrayals, particularly ones in which symbolic representations of male superiority are to be found. As a point of focus of feminist issues, the media present common knowledge upon which to construct a debate. However, the evidence that the media portrayals actually contribute to a hierarchical gender-structured society is scant or missing (Howitt, 1982; Durkin, 1985).

It is a major theoretical problem to specify just how the contents of pornography are turned into beliefs conducive to rape. This needs a research methodology atuned to how viewers mentally process pornography. Is it satisfactory to assume that the content of pornography will be interpreted as representing reality if it does not correspond to the reality of the viewer's world? But if it does correspond to the viewer's reality then how can pornography be construed as causing these views of reality? However, if pornography is a source of fantasy, how does this fantasy become translated into real life? In this context, a study by van Naerssen *et al.* (1987) is apposite. The content of a number of gay 'pornographic' magazines published between 1970 and 1983 was analysed. About a third of the stories were classifiable as sado-masochistic pornography. They included such activities as eating from a dog bowl, bondage, and flagellation. There appeared to be a gradual increase in the amount of sado-masochistic material over time. New sado-masachistic activities were introduced which increased in frequency – for example, bestiality and sexual activities involving urination. This was largely responsible for the increase in sado-masochism in the magazines. Some types of activity decreased – coercion was present in 50 per cent of early stories but reduced to 20 per cent later. Extreme forms of violence also waned a little over the period. Severe mutilations, rapes and injury declined.

However, the same authors interviewed gay men with sado-masochistic proclivities. The trends in pornography did not accurately reflect changes in the men's relationships:

> in practice there was always talk of domination, submissiveness, violence, and inequality being *acted*. Irrespective of their roles, persons taking part in sado-masochistic interactions must subject themselves to a social code which does justice to the expectations and desires of all partners involved.
>
> (van Naerrsen *et al.*, 1987, pp. 118–19)

This points to a substantially less than automatic link between pornography's content and the sexual activities of its viewers. Probably a similar sort of story could be told about heterosexual relationships. While this might be the case, it is not definitive proof that pornography is harmless. There may merely be some instances where the effect is not apparent.

One study adopted a careful case-study approach. Kutchinsky (1976) explored the psycho-sexual history of a Danish peeping Tom. However, this study did little to demonstrate a link between pornography and acting out its contents. The man in question had a long history of peeping which altered when the Danish law changed to allow greater availability of pornography. He explains:

> it had gotten such a strong grip on me, this peeping, that I couldn't stop. My wife wasn't much interested, or rather not at all, in sex, so

we don't have any sexual relations. But I was much more engaged in
[peeping]. I still am today, but in another way, because now I think
of live-shows, and I go to see shows and then I don't feel any need for
[peeping] ... You feel almost like a drug addict or a drunkard – you
can't really do without it

(Kutchinsky, 1976, p. 146)

For this offender, pornography served to substitute precisely for what
otherwise would have been an offence. Other offenders (Marshall, 1988),
however, seem to use pornography as part of the commission of their
offences. For example, some use it to demonstrate the 'normality' of
adult–child intercourse to their victims, thus encouraging the children in
social acts. Others use pornography to arouse themselves sexually prior to
offending.

However, none of the evidence actually provides proof that offenders
have in some way been affected by pornography to accept a particular
world-view which promotes sexual attacks. Whether they do or not is
insufficiently researched to provide much of an answer. There is a little
evidence that convicted rapists have different 'rape myths' from 'normal'
men. However, there are several studies (Overholser and Beck, 1988;
Stermac and Quinsey, 1986) which suggest no such differences.

Demographic studies

An alternative approach concentrates on the relationship between
pornography and sexual offences. One way of doing this, of course, is to
look at the pattern of sexual offences in crime statistics over time. While this
might appear to be the obvious thing to do, it is fraught with dangers. No
'pure' indicators of crime rates exist since recorded crime is reported crime.
Virtually all crime statistics depend on the number of 'crimes' police put
on record. This is subject to numerous biases or distortions – the victim being
unwilling to report the crime, the police not being prepared to record a crime
as such, and changes occurring in the legal definition of a particular crime.
None of these is necessarily constant over time. So it is possible that
changes in recorded crimes are artifactual rather than demonstrating the
'true' situation. This is as true for rape and other sexual offences as for other
types of crime.

Rape is a crime which involves extreme humiliation of the victim.
Naturally it may be difficult for her to report the crime because of this,
especially as society has often held the victim responsible. This encouragement not to report can be compounded by courts 'washing the victim's
dirty linen in public'. Increasing sympathy for rape victims may change
reporting habits, help improve policing methods, and aid improvement in

criminal justice procedures. All of these would result in higher levels of recorded crime. Consequently published statistics appear to soar while the underlying 'reality' remains constant. Given these possibilities, it is not surprising that recorded rapes have generally risen in recent years. The success of the women's movement in changing attitudes and practices may have thereby, paradoxically, given the impression of a 'lost battle' against sex crimes because of the rise in reported rapes. It needs pointing out that rises in sexual crime rates are rather slower than general rises in crime. Rape, however, may not follow this trend (Lloyd and Walmsley, 1989; Howitt and Cumberbatch, 1990).

An alternative approach is to investigate regional variations in the levels of sexual crime and relate them to possible causal factors. For example, if the areas with the greatest levels of sexual crime also have the highest circulation rates for pornography then this may suggest a causal relationship. Research of this sort has been carried out in the United States, where there are obviously great geographical and cultural variations. The study by Baron and Straus (1987; 1989) is an important one (but cf. Baron and Straus, 1984). Surprisingly, it has been cited as evidence against pornography (Baxter, 1990) though its authors interpret their work in totally different terms!

Using readily available statistical data, Baron and Straus (1987) created 'league tables' of rape rates and circulation of 'pornographic' magazines such as *Penthouse* and *Playboy* in the various US states. These tables reveal that the states with the highest rape rates include Alaska, Nevada, and Florida; those with the lowest rape rates include Maine, South Dakota, and North Dakota; those with the highest pornography circulations include Alaska, Nevada and Wyoming; and those with the lowest pornography circulations were Mississippi, Arkansas, and West Virginia. Baron and Straus aimed to do more than merely examine statistical relationships. Specifically they tested the relative adequacy of four different theories of rape. These were:

1 *Gender inequality theory*. Rape and the fear of rape are part of the means of maintaining women's subservience. Baron and Straus used as an *index of gender equality* various measures of economic status, legal status, and political status of women relative to men.
2 *Cultural spillover theory*. High levels of violence and aggression within a culture generalize to other activities. So a violent society will have high levels of sexual violence as exemplified by rape. An *index of non-criminal violence* for socially approved ends was developed based on the legitimacy of corporal punishment in schools, capital punishment for murderers, and others.
3 *Social disorganization theory*. Deviance (including crime) is a consequence of social and community ties breaking down. This destroys control of behaviour through consensual social norms. It follows that rape will be

more frequent in areas of high social disorganization. An *index of social disorganization* was used, which included rates of geographical mobility, divorce, religious affiliation and single-parent families.

4   *Pornography theory.* By providing models for sexual violence, sexism and male dominance and by treating women as sexual objects, pornography provides the foundation of rape-proneness. A *pornography circulation index* was developed based on the sales of various mass-circulation magazines of a sexually explicit nature.

Only the cultural spillover theory was rejected by the evidence. As such, rape was unaffected by the culturally accepted and legitimized forms of violence in the community. The remaining three theories do not necessarily compete, they could be complementary. That social disorganization theory found empirical support is not surprising, given the close association between rape and other forms of criminality. Neither should one be surprised at the support for the gender inequality theory. There are elements of the expression of male superiority and the humiliation of women to be found in rapes.

This leaves the pornography theory which, despite the data, Baron and Straus dismiss. Inevitably, in research on social issues, evidence emerges which is 'not to the taste' of the researcher. The researcher may feel that to assume that reading men's pornographic magazines causes rape is an affront to people's ability to separate reality from fantasy. The problem is not so much the clash with personal judgement itself, as just how to respond to the disparity between the two. One solution is to seek evidence which reconciles the mismatch between data and private views. However, recall that Baron and Straus's data have been interpreted by others as indicating the adverse effects of pornography. Consequently, the basis of Baron and Straus's rejection of such a causal explanation needs careful scrutiny.

One prime reason involved the circulation of the female-orientated sex magazine *Playgirl*. Readership of this correlated with the rape rates at a higher level than any magazine aimed at male consumption. Since men, not women, commit rape it is difficult to see how female-orientated 'pornography' causes this. Because of this problem, Baron and Straus attribute the rape–pornography correlation to a confounding third variable. They suggest that this may be 'hypermasculine' or 'macho' cultural patterns. These cultures 'might include such conditions as normative support for violence, the use of physical force to settle quarrels, the belief in male supremacy, endorsement of rape myths, and approval of sexual coercion' (Baron and Straus, 1978, p. 462). In other words, hypermasculine cultures use pornography more – they are not created by it. Clearly this is somewhat conjectural and dependent on the tacit view that pornography is not responsible for social disorganization and sexual inequality. That *Playgirl* circulation correlates with rape rates may simply indicate that women are just as prone to pornography's adverse influence as are men. If pornography causes rape because it destroys society's 'moral bedrock' then this may be as much through its influence on women as on men. It is difficult to accept Baron and Straus's argument about hypermasculine cultures with little more than supposition in its favour.

Tentative evidence that pornography may not have a causal influence on rape is provided by Howitt and Cumberbatch (1990). They reanalysed data presented in a study by Jaffee and Straus (1987) which adopted virtually the same methodology as the Baron and Straus (1987) research. A correlation of about 0.5 was found between rape rates and sex magazine circulation. Again this is evidence of a possible causal influence of pornography on sexual violence. Howitt and Cumberbatch found that the best predictor of rape rates in the Jaffee and Straus data was the percentage of *divorced* males over 15 years of age in the community. That is, rape was frequent where male divorcees were the most common. This correlation was approximately 0.7. Simple statistical techniques can control or eliminate the influence of this 'divorcee variable'. After this is done, the correlation between rape rates and sex magazine circulation becomes small and statistically unreliable. Why the numbers of divorced males should have such a decisive influence is not known. It could be that Baron and Straus's idea of hypermasculine culture relates to the percentage of male divorcees. Nevertheless, this reanalysis provides better support for Baron and Straus's position than they provided for themselves.

Psychologists and punditry

To reach a firm conclusion about the influence of pornography on sexual crime is too great a task in this context (though Howitt and Cumberbatch, 1990, present an in-depth review of the research). The findings and interpretations of several of the committees and commissions would have to be disputed. Social scientific research does not lead inevitably to simple conclusions which can inform social policy. Research which might have its own inexorable logic in terms of psychological theory may be considerably flawed as a means of formulating policy recommendations. Social research proceeds in its own dominion which does not always translate directly to policy. A classic example of this is the work of Donnerstein on pornography (Donnerstein, 1980; Donnerstein and Berkowitz, 1981; Donnerstein *et al.*, 1987). He researched largely from within the framework of laboratory-based experimental psychology. A presumed advantage of laboratory experiments is that they reduce certain interpretative problems of other forms of research. In a few words, if one randomly allocates people to experimental and control conditions varying solely in terms of whether pornographic films are shown, any differences that emerge are due to the different treatments given. A big problem is whether one can generalize laboratory findings to the effects of pornography in the real (that is, non-laboratory) world. There is a sense in which the academic base of psychology serves to fill researchers with a warming, comforting soup of shared backgrounds, assumptions and influences. It is a little too thin to protect from the harsh winters of the real world.

Typically, in Donnerstein's studies, participants have the opportunity to give an electric shock to a male or female 'stooge' who had, or had not, caused that participant some annoyance. It is the classic electric shock machine approach to mass media research (see Buss, 1961; Howitt and Cumberbatch, 1975). While such research is no better or worse than much laboratory work, the pertinence of the approach to real-life issues as such is in severe doubt (Cumberbatch and Howitt, 1989).

Undeterred by any of these issues, Donnerstein secured wide publicity for his beliefs about the implications of his research on policy. For example, he was a prime and 'expert' witness at the public hearings of the Minneapolis City Council in 1983. These were eventually published as *Pornography and Sexual Violence: Evidence of the Links* (Everywoman, 1988). He described the outcome of the research, including his own, as showing:

> that short-term exposure to [pornography of] very normal, sociable, intellectual young males is going to have an effect. It is either going to reinforce already existing predispositions about rape in women and maintain these callous types of attitudes or worse than that, in fact, change them in a very negative direction and that is the majority of the subjects. Unfortunately there is out there a small percentage – and I hate to use the word minority – who are so influenced by this material that it becomes the ultimate sexual turn-on. Individuals are becoming sexually aroused to the trivialization, the degradation, and the use of women. The data, I think, it speaks for itself. I am not a lawyer. I am not an advocate. I am unfortunately an 'ivy tower' professor that does his research. I think that the data is a little too clear, not only from myself but dozens of professors acrosss the country. I doubt that anybody disputes the data. There are effects.
>
> (Everywoman, 1988, p. 22)

What Donnerstein is saying seems clear. 'Normal' men become capable of degrading women through rape by seeing pornography. No wonder that Donnerstein's evidence was welcomed by those opposed to pornography. It seems unequivocating, clear and directive. If pornography does this to men so readily, there seems to be no argument that censorship and control would be justified irrespective of the issues of freedom of speech and individual liberty. Donnerstein is even reluctant to use the word 'minority', implying that really his small percentage is the majority.

A few years later, the Attorney General's Commission on Pornography (1986) in the USA examined the available evidence and concluded that certain types of material were harmful. Donnerstein (Linz *et al.*, 1987) seems to have undergone some sort of volte-face. He turns on the Commission using language which his own critics may well have used of his comments at the Minneapolis hearings:

> the commission ... failed to exercise proper caution in generalizing these studies to sexual violence outside of the laboratory. Despite the higher level of causal certainty accorded the laboratory experiment relative to other forms of investigation, laboratory assessments of the media's effects on behavior, particularly in relation to the violence prevalent in mass media programming, are susceptible to many criticisms concerning external validity.
>
> (Linz *et al.*, 1987, p. 950)

Page (1989) comments on the way in which some psychologists have recently tried to present their approach as a model of constraint compared to the political postures of the Commission. Perhaps one of the most curious passages in Donnerstein's writing is the following:

> It is misguided to single out pornography because of its negative message against women. This leaves the impression that if we could eliminate pornography we would eliminate that material that most harms women in our society. Why limit ourselves to objecting to the demeaning depictions of women that appear only in a sexually explicit context? Our research suggests that you need not look any further than the family's own television set to find demeaning depictions of women available to far more viewers than pornographic material.
>
> (Linz and Donnerstein, 1988, p. 184)

Donnerstein could have known this without embarking on any formal research. He may have decided that pornography is best left alone despite his earlier proclamations of its harm. The difficulty is not so much the shifting sands of his position. After all, he cannot be criticized for changing his stance in the light of newer research. That, indeed, would be commendable and exemplary. However, the changes are not in the light of new evidence since there has been little in his style of research. The changes seem more to be a consequence of political forces intruding into the cosiness of his 'ivy tower' world. It may be fine to appear illiberal in the clubroom of academic psychology, but not in comparison to the outside world. From supporting an extreme feminist position as in the Minneapolis hearings, exactly the same research had been shunted to serve a significantly different purpose. Shifting positions according to one's audience is very different from having a value position which is exercised through research findings.

Writing of the experts who provided them with testimony, the Attorney General's Commission on Pornography (1986, pp. 350–1) commented:

> At no time have we suspected any scientist of deliberately or even negligently designing an experiment or reporting its results, but it remains nevertheless the case that there is room for judgement and room for discretion. Where a researcher has taken on the role as active crusader, one way or another, on the issue of governmental control of pornography, we are forced to question more than we would otherwise have done the way in which this judgement and discretion has been exercised ... [T]he more that is expected to be taken on trust, the more likely it is that active involvement with respect to what is to be done with the results of the research will decrease the amount of trust.

While it is easy (and probably unfair) to express the issue in terms of the individual characters of researchers, the question of active crusading warrants more serious analysis. That researchers can fundamentally disagree on what the broad social implications of research are is a sign of the failure of psychological theory. This is due to the lack of well-developed criteria for deciding what research provides information pertinent to policy. Too often research appears to follow well-tried procedures rather than designing them to meet the requirements of policy. More generally, Cumberbatch and Howitt (1989) have suggested that most research on mass communications fails to examine the design of research with the needs of practitioners in mind. Often, in the research on pornography, certain kinds of studies are ignored. Detailed investigations of sexual offenders give way to convenient questionnaire studies of prisoners at best, or studies of college students at worst.

Once psychologists enter a manifestly political world, the weakness of their approach can be seriously exposed. Psychological research is often not based on the needs of understanding a social issue but on the typical resources provided by the practice of psychological research. Suddenly, instead of scholarly arguments about the intricacies of research, the researcher may find that cherished research findings are being used to create a society which is not to his or her taste. But what is this political world?

The politics of pornography

Pornography, we have seen, has attracted much government attention in the form of commissions and committees. This is not surprising. It is a matter which involves issues of state censorship in areas for which freedom has long been fought. Particularly, the control of pornography is simply another way of controlling the freedom of speech enshrined in the constitution of, for example, the USA and the liberal tradition in other countries such as

Britain. Whether or not one approves of the content of pornography, and whether or not one is prepared to tolerate it at a personal level, serious questions concerning the wisdom of state censorship of that material inevitably arise. Consequently there are, built into the system, pressures encouraging governmental investigations of pornography.

Nevertheless, it should not be assumed that the resources of governments are sufficient to ensure that the highest quality of interpretation ensues. In this context it is worthwhile quoting the conclusions of two virtually con-temporaneous commissions – one from the USA and the other from Canada. Substantially identical social scientific data were available to each. However, the conclusions they reached were radically different. For example, the Attorney General's Commission on Pornography (1986, p. 326) claimed:

> We have reached the conclusion, unanimously and confidently, that the available evidence strongly support the hypothesis that substantial exposure to sexually violent materials ... bears a causal relationship to antisocial acts of sexual violence ...

By way of contrast, the Fraser Committee (Canada, 1985, p. 99) concluded:

> the research is so inadequate and chaotic that no consistent body of information has been established.

But this is a matter which has consistently refused to lie down. Einseidel (1988) reviews a British, an American and a Canadian official investigation into pornography and points out some of their basic differences in assumptions and conclusions. Furthermore, some researchers have complained vociferously at the 'overinterpretation' of their data (Linz *et al.*, 1987).

But at the micro-political level, there are groups which have been ideo-logically committed to an anti-pornography stance. These are much the same as other 'moral' movements such as those against alcohol, abortion and Sunday trading. Traditionally they are seen as ideologically conservative and have been identified as having certain 'social' and sociological char-acteristics. They have been extensively researched by sociologists and others, but to define their views as 'wrong' simply because of their con-servatism leaves the analysis at a crude level. One classic study of an anti-pornography/anti-violence campaigner is Tracey and Morrison's (1977) of Mary Whitehouse, a monumental figure in the British debate of the 1960s to 1980s. Perhaps as a testament to her 'high profile', a pornographic magazine chose to call itself *Whitehouse*. But of that magazine, more later.

The more traditional conservative opposition to pornography was sup-plemented from the 1970s onwards by a feminist perspective. In theory, at least, the worries about the lewdness of the displays of flesh in pornography were augmented by concern about the material's invocations to sexual violence:

Perhaps one could simply say that erotica is about sexuality, but pornography is about power and sex-as-weapon – in the same way we have come to understand that rape is about violence, and not really about sexuality at all.

(Steinhem, 1983, p. 38)

However, it is a very different matter when one takes the pressure-group activities of the traditional conservatives and the feminist lobby. Here, it may become much more difficult to separate the two in practice, since when applied to policy, the traditional and feminist positions may converge. For example:

At [the] National Viewers' and Listeners' Association, general secretary John Bayer says: 'I don't think topless pictures of women should be in newspapers – they simply aren't suitable material. They create the idea that women are sex objects and the playthings of men.'

Jane Gregory of the Campaign Against Pornography shares this sentiment, and although both organisations believe there should be tighter legal restrictions on the sale of all pornographic materials, neither will comment on whether a distinction should be made between Page 3 and more blatantly rude nude images of women.

(Walker, 1990, p. 50)

There is considerable disparity between both their views and the psychological evidence they are fond of quoting selectively.

To all of this can be added the micro-politics of the pro-'freedom' pressure groups concerned with civil liberties. While these groups may not be neutral with respect to a distaste for pornography, at the same time their over-riding concern is to protect freedoms (Vine 1990a; 1990b).

Not surprisingly, with such a mix of stances, there is a general 'risk' of a selective and partisan use of psychological research. Research has rarely been effectively designed to deal with the social issue of pornography rather than the needs and expediencies of laboratory-based social psychology. The lack of careful analysis on the part of many researchers perhaps encourages the unthinking and selective use of the data by some (see, for example, Baxter, 1990).

The Campaign Against Pornography and Censorship, as we have seen, is one organization which uses 'social scientific' data in its arguments against pornography. Catherine Itzin is a member of this organization who has contributed a number of arguments. The stridency of some of these can be judged from the opening paragraph of Itzin (1990):

Cunt is a term of contempt and abuse, most degrading when used by men against men. It is the language of misogyny. In pornography women are cunts: reduced to their genitals and anuses, posed open and gaping, inviting sexual access. Women in pornography are presented as sexually voracious and sexually insatiable, seeking and enjoying sexual violence and humiliation. This material is mass-produced for the entertainment of men. What does it say about the status and value of women in society?

This hyperbolic style extends to the presentation and interpretation of her own data.

Vine (1990b) expresses considerable doubt over the more obvious advocacy to be found in the public debate on pornography. For example, commenting on the results of Itzin's magazine survey of women's attitudes to pornography, he writes:

So when questionnaires reveal, as Itzin and Sweet say theirs did, 'a strong link between childhood exposure to pornography and sexual experience below the age of consent', just what does that empirical association prove? If you are as certain as these authors that you *already* know the truth, it obviously means that 'early exposure can have a lasting impact on later life'. They tell us that 'more than a quarter of those who first encountered pornography at the age of 13 or under first had sex under 16'. But they also report that 20% of *all* readers who replied lost their virginity before age 16. If so, then seeing porn made very little difference to most women!

(Vine, 1990b, p. 2)

Supplementary to Vine's argument concerning 'certainty about one's views', Lawrence and Herold (1988) found that a strong feminist orientation was related to being antagonistic towards sexually explicit material – as well as infrequent use of the material. Little attendance at church tended to be associated with more favourable attitudes. The point is, of course, that both of these reflect a broad ideological commitment which in itself may be associated with strong theories about pornography – the feminist theory and the fundamentalist 'Christian theory' being obvious examples. It is worthwhile citing a finding of Thompson *et al.* (1990) here. It might be expected that those who believe strongly in the negative effects of pornography (that it dehumanizes women or makes men treat women with less respect) would be strongly in favour of the *greater* regulation of pornography. However, the precise reverse of this emerged in their survey. There is no simple link between believing that pornography has bad effects and wanting greater controls on it. The reasons for this may include the possibility that the solution to the perceived problem is worse than the problem itself.

It should be stressed that not all feminists are comfortable with the control of pornography through censorship. For example:

We suggest that perhaps one reason [why] the feminist debates on pornography have carried such a heavy emotional charge is that they are really about a lot more than simply how best to regulate a particular industry ... much of the debate about pornography has served as a way for women to talk about sex, and about sexual variation, explicitly and publicly for the first time ... This discussion has been infused with a general anxiety among feminists about which forms of sexual desire or behaviour are consistent with feminist politics.

(Ellis *et al.*, 1990, pp. 15–18)

But there may well be a different problem for psychologists opting to study social issues – the no-win situation. For example, Howitt and Cumberbatch's (1990) report on the effects of pornography was commissioned by the government and announced in Parliament. Not only was there the expected media interest but also the pressure of interest groups – for example, correspondence from a feminist group to a government minister in which matters like the appropriateness of the gender of the reviewers and the notion that there is no uncertainty about the effects of pornography were raised. A pornographic magazine chose to undermine the report:

Dear Readers

I want to draw your attention to a move (by the Government) which unless YOU do something will stop the sale of all girlie magazines in Britain ... The rag-bag alliance of feminists, religious bigots, ultra-conservatives and opportunist publicity seekers have decided to mount an attack on the rights of adults to decide how they spend their money. They have persuaded the Government to set up a review of the effect of pornography ... Unlike previous official studies, which concluded there was no evidence to link pornography and sexual violence, no opportunity is being given for submissions to be made. There has to be a substantial risk that every factor will not be given due weight ... *The aim of the 'do-gooders' is to prevent you buying your favourite adult monthly magazines.* They have made their voices heard. If you don't show that you are the majority there is a real threat that this magazine (and similar mags) will no longer be on sale in Britain.

1)   You should write to your M.P. ...
2)   If you really want your opinion considered then also write to:

   The Home Secretary ...

or ring the Home Office ... and speak to the person concerned with Pornography.

If you don't tell them your views, they'll soon be telling you what to read. Please do this for me

Love
Zeta

Whether Zeta was happy with the report is unknown.

Involvement in social issues puts the psychologist in potential conflict with many groups, including other psychologists. The professional training of psychologists may well not help them recognize their own value stances. The social issues approach probably helps highlight these better than typical psychological research, where once the findings are accepted for publication in a journal the whole matter will almost certainly be buried. On the other hand, affecting people's lives by putting them at greater risk of sexual violence or by encouraging censorship, has a longer-term implication for the researcher. They cannot escape this merely with the claim that a psychologist is not responsible for what others do with their research.

Concluding comments

Rape and pornography are most closely related in feminist theory. Pornography has been especially controversial in the last fifty years or so, much of this criticism coexisting with various forms of sexual violence. The feminist upsurge brought to attention domestic violence, sexual violence, and the sexual violence of pornography as part of a coherent 'political' package. Whereas previous attacks on pornography tended to concentrate on its effects on personal sexual morality, they did not involve a 'package' which clearly united so many issues. Indeed, there were considerable changes in the way in which pornography was construed, despite similarities in the vehemence of the opposition to it. The traditional view was closely linked to the family as a primary social unit, which was under threat of breakdown exacerbated by pornography's glorification of unbridled sexuality. The feminist position was radically different. It was not so enamoured of the family, which it saw as the fortress of male power with its violent abuse of women and children. It also relegated women's ambition to domesticity. Eroticism was typically considered bad not in itself, but through its association with themes of male dominance and violence against women.

Unfortunately, in feminist politics, the dividing line between feminism and psychology has not always been drawn. That is to say, because feminist politics claims that pornography is bad, it is not properly subject to the checking procedures characteristic of social sciences. Thus, much of the literature on pornography is accepted or rejected according to whether it supports feminist positions. This is compounded by a trend to find more support wherever it can be squeezed and to dismiss or ignore contradictory findings. There is nothing particularly feminist in this tendency, but it is especially disappointing because of feminism's potential for generating original research and ideas. The traditional, reactionary anti-pornography view was much more stifling and certainly no more 'objective'. Good examples of traditional approaches are found in Eysenck and Nias (1978) and Cline (1974). Nor should we forget that traditional conservatism rejected early social scientific conclusions on pornography's lack of effects. Richard Nixon, the American president who received the first pornography report (Howitt, 1982), dismissed the findings,asking how pornography can have no effects if people can be elevated by great literature.

Sherrard (1990) raises a concern about feminism which is novel but nevertheless worrying. She claims that one kind of feminist epistemology has three basic steps:

> Firstly, that instrumental knowledge is essentially male. Secondly, in contrast, that female knowledge is therefore intuitive, emotional, engaged and caring (together with the implication that it is better, and should replace the former). Thirdly, that these different forms of knowledge derive from different physical bodies.
>
> (Sherrard, 1990, p. 18)

The reason for concern is that she sees these characteristics as being similar to those of prewar German psychology and that these allowed it to be utilized for the political purposes of the Nazis. She warns that the ideas of value-boundedness, qualitative as opposed to quantitative methodology, and considering people as wholes rather than a collection of smaller 'atoms' do not *automatically* produce 'morally better results' (Sherrard, 1990, p.18). There is little quarrel with this warning here. Nothing guarantees that any simple formula can ensure the best outcome. These are matters for vigilance. However, neither should it be assumed that psychology can readily work with politics to produce answers satisfactory to both.

8

TRIBULATIONS OF
REAL-WORLD PSYCHOLOGISTS

When I first chose to study psychology, I came with the belief that
I would be taught more about human nature, instead of which,
I learnt a great deal about white, middle-class, heterosexual
students, and the views of white middle-class heterosexist
'experts'.

(Clarke, 1989, p. 4)

This book has set itself against the short-sighted application of psychology. Psychological techniques, methods, procedures and theory in many ways not only can be but also have been of considerable significance. Nevertheless, the failure to come to terms with the problematic nature of many of the applications of psychology has marred progress. Often, for example, the discipline has limited its own horizons, alienated its own students, and rested content in a snug world of its own. In doing so, psychology has adopted the values, viewpoints and ideologies of particular interest groups. Perhaps, to some extent this is inevitable. But it should not be left without self-examination, self-questioning and awareness. There is evidence that significant sectors of the community (such as feminists and black people) are no longer prepared to accept the 'selective' stance of much of mainstream psychology.

It should not be imagined that most applied psychology, irrespective of its 'objective' sheen, is largely unrelated to social issues. Psychology is sometimes more effective in reproducing and reflecting broader social movements than in providing insights into them. The view that psychology is an ivory-tower discipline is a 'taken-for-granted' assumption which can only be sustained by ignoring psychology's social location. The discipline is socially relevant even when it gives misleading impressions of the nature of people. It provides models of how to view human nature which in themselves have broad social implications. For example, conceptualizations of workers, as we have already seen, have serious implications for how the workforce is treated, and also for the very structuring of organized work hierarchies.

By now it should be clear that psychology has many roles in relation to social issues. Its many objectives may be to a degree mutually incompatible, confused and problematic. The claim that psychology has a role in understanding social issues merely places the discipline where it belongs – helping us understand human experience in all its confusion. Inevitably, psychology's means of understanding the world face continual challenge and revision. They could remain constant only if society were indeed based on invariant principles. There is nothing sacrosanct in psychology's 'peculiar' way of construing the world. The objective is not to unveil nature's truths but to create means of understanding which are relevant to a particular time.

Superficially, at least, psychologists may seem to have the advantages of an intellectually rigourous training, the empirical base of the discipline (despite numerous drawbacks of this), and a commitment to the systematization of knowledge through hypotheses and theory. But these in themselves cannot ensure the superiority of psychological knowledge. No heavenly chart places psychology above the other social sciences, other academic disciplines, the person in the street, committees of people, and religious, political and other points of view. It is wrong to assume that a psychological approach to, say, poverty is intrinsically best. Where would the superiority lie – in the level of understanding? in its pragmatic significance? or elsewhere? The case for psychology is at best a relative one, containing no unchallengeable absolutes in its favour.

Essentials for the social issues approach

Applying psychology to issues of social concern involves the following considerations, at a minimum. They could be used as a checklist, but other things may be overlooked as a consequence. They help ensure, however, that obvious things are not ignored. Raising awareness is a useful function though not the complete answer in every situation. For example, if psychologists have been involved in lobbying, they might be encouraged to temper their comments to the press and other media on the social implications of their research. However, nothing in the following list suggests that they do so, the gaps have to be sought carefully. Essential matters to consider include:

1 Provision of awareness/understanding of the nature of the issues.
2 Provision of data relevant to the issues.

3 Provision of theory relevant to the issues.
4 Provision of a critical stance relevant to the issues.
5 Provision of practical solutions.
6 Explanation of why the issue is construed socially as it is.
7 Provision of the socio-history of the development of relevant ideas.
8 Provision of alternative and possibly radical viewpoints.
9 Possibility of individual and collective lobbying.
10 Provision of services to help deal with the issue in question.
11 Provision of specialized advice.
12 Provision of debate on underlying moral and ethical issues.
13 Provision of policy recommendations.
14 Provision of recommendations concerning appropriate institutional structures.
15 Self-understanding of ideological and personal commitment concerning the issues in question. This is not a reason to exclude oneself from professional involvement, rather to acknowledge the dual role of the psychologist in any area of research or activity.

In other words, psychology should seek to have something to *offer* society on the significant problems facing it. This is a totally different matter from imposing a collective professional view on society. As we have seen, this has been attempted by other professions such as medicine, not necessarily for the general good of any other than that profession. It is not psychology's place to usurp society and claim for itself what it palpably cannot deliver. Every sympathy has to be with Illich (Illich, 1977, pp. 21–2) in his complaint concerning certain professions:

> let us not confuse the public use of expert factual knowledge with a profession's corporate exercise of normative judgement ... The dominant professional provides jury or legislature with his own and fellow-initiates' global opinion, rather than with factual self-limiting evidence and specific skill ... Thus, one sees how democratic power is subverted by an unquestioning assumption of an all-embracing professionalism.

We have already seen that the sort of 'factual self-limiting evidence' of which Illich writes may not be that separable from normative judgement. Rarely, if ever, could psychologists let their data stand without interpretation. (One should not imagine that data are 'pure' knowledge since, for example, the research that is done and how it is done has to be judged against the alternative research which could have been carried out and what alternative methods used.) But at the same time, the distinction between a properly expert judgement and a normative judgement does help keep an important issue in mind. That the distinction is not absolute does not alter this. Often academic psychologists forget that their professional bodies sometimes exert pressure on matters which are not completely the province of the 'scientific'. For example, Tremper (1987), documents cases in which the American Psychological Association chose to advise courts of law on broad matters related to professional concerns.

'Scientific research' is a strange feature of psychology in that it is not so dominant in the training and practice of other professions dealing with people. Teaching, social work, the law, and others lack such a primary ideological commitment to 'science'. But, of course, the presence of both 'science' and practice in psychology is no reason why psychologists should avoid lobbying on 'non-scientific' matters. That would not only put psychologists on a different standing from other professionals but also imply that the work of practising psychologists is more 'scientific' than that, say, of social workers and others who may use research evidence on occasions. Evidence that practising psychologists are 'scientific' in comparison to other professions is not forthcoming. Psychologists have no less reason to lobby on important issues than any other professional groups. It debases 'psychological science' no more than anti-nuclear members in the physical science community undermine their discipline.

Further considerations

There are a number of matters which warrant further discussion. Some of these are obvious. For example, the question of the utility of psychological knowledge to social policy inevitably arises. Others, such as ethics, are no surprise either. Some topics are probably not so predictable. These further issues again raise problems and are not solutions in themselves. The expectation that psychology is a comfortable discipline within which to work is in stark contrast to actuality. The accusation against much psychology, that it is people-phobic, is a consequence of making psychology too easy. It is often less stressful to have a research assistant hand out self-completion questionnaires than to listen to people's accounts of their experiences and difficulties.

The stress of social issues research

Psychological research touching on important social issues will rarely have a calm passage. Tackling matters which are not simply difficult, but controversial, involving moral as well as other questions, will hardly enamour psychologists to each other, let alone to the rest of the community. While a degree of circumspection can be employed, ultimately there is a risk that, by departing from the routine journal fodder, research criticisms will follow. Trivial examples abound from most psychologists' personal experience. For example, Harris (1989, p. 192), whose professional judgement

is that television is a powerful medium with substantial social psychological effects, writes of authors, Freeman and Howitt, who separately have
a different view from his own: 'The negative effects of TV are probably
neither as widespread and serious as suggested by the strongest critics nor
as benign as suggested by the apologists [Freeman and Howitt]'. A certain
lack of symmetry will be observed here – some are strong critics but others
who disagree with oneself are apologists. But this is at the level of 'bad-
mouthing' rather than something likely to distress the 'apologists' unduly.

More extreme examples cannot be shrugged-off so lightly. Not surprisingly, sometimes psychologists who feel 'attacked' for the assumptions
and dangers inherent in their chosen research are outraged. Few of us like
to think that we deliberately set out to do injustice to other people. Scarr
(1988), for example, found that black children brought up by white families
had high levels of achievement. She was disturbed by suggestions that the
study was, in fact, 'fostering' a derogatory view of the child-rearing
abilities of the black community. From one point of view she seems correct
that black children's achievements can be facilitated by placement with
white families. But this may be a very narrowly focused one, dependent
on a blinkered examination of the results of psychological tests. From
another point of view, her message does place the blame for the 'failure'
of black children firmly with the black community, *not* with the broader
community's racism. Her neglecting to acknowledge the risks perhaps
makes her critics' point. Indeed, she implies that because 'the answers to
research questions turn out to be politically palatable to the majority of
social scientists' (Scarr, 1988, p. 57) the objections of other, more critical,
psychologists are in some way unacceptable. This is an argument which
is very difficult to accept in so far as right and wrong are assumed to be
best decided by majorities.

At the same time she makes important observations:

> If questions about minorities and women are framed in terms of
> what is wrong with, deficient about, or needs improvement for these
> underrepresented groups, then the research outcomes for such groups
> are very likely to be negative. If the standard for good behavior is
> always the white male group, then the behavior of women and ethnic
> miniorities is likely to seem negative. If being reared in a single-
> parent family (whose members also happen to be poor, badly
> educated, and housed in slums) is correlated with negative outcomes
> for children, then more Black children than White children appear to
> show deficits. If being more concerned with primary relationships than
> with universal principles of morality is called inferior, then women
> on average appear deficient ... If, on the other hand, one asks how
> women actually solve mathematical problems, how Black males learn
> to read, or how children of lower socioeconomic status ... get jobs, one

may actually learn how to help others to use socially and culturally available means to succeed in the society.

(Scarr, 1988, p. 57)

While it is probably unobjectionable in Western thinking to seek means to enable persons to achieve goals (especially if they are their own goals), this is simply not the same thing as promoting the view that white people are the best to help black people achieve their goals. Individually enabling as this may be, it is not enabling of black people as a group to be masters or mistresses of their own destinies. Quite simply, good intentions are not adequate in research – knowing where the research lies in relation to broader society is a prerequisite of socially sensitive research.

It would be misleading to pretend that psychologists are frequently taken to task for the ideological or value positions they appear to hold. This relative lack of controversy is inherently the consequence of most psychology being aimed at an audience of other psychologists. Since much of this work will merely be extensions of accepted research methods and theory, it is unlikely to receive the devastating attack that research relevant to social issues risks.

The will to apply psychological research

Levy-Leboyer (1988) summarizes several pieces of his research which say something about the failure of commissioning organizations to apply research findings. Naturally, he believes that his research contains valuable insights but in many cases the client organizations were less over-awed at the power of the findings than he believes should have been the case. This reluctance to accept the outcomes of research broadly reflects the 'unpreparedness' of organizations to change their understanding of the nature of the problem. Levy-Leboyer's research and reactions to it are fascinating.

For example, one group of Parisian hospitals was plagued by the high turnover of nursing staff. The personnel department tried to find the 'true' reasons for this by interviewing each of the nurses when they departed from the service. Little or no success was achieved in terms of understanding the problem. Levy-Leboyer's research team was enlisted to find ways of improving the 'departure' interviews so that these 'real' reasons for staff turnover service could be elicited. Levy-Leboyer chose to follow a somewhat different approach. His research team examined a number of hospitals, as well as different departments within these, with 'amazing' results:

> In some departments, turnover was near zero, whereas in others, year after year, it reached a very high percentage. We presented a clear and detailed analysis of these data to the managers. They proposed various explanations for the observed discrepancies: Turnover should be higher in the most stressful wards, in hospital settings far from a

metro station, and in hospitals mainly composed of old buildings where maintenance is a problem. All of these explanations were considered as useful hypotheses, tested through data analysis, and proved totally wrong.

(Levy-Leboyer, 1988, p. 782)

A research initiative was offered by the research team. Departments would be matched on a number of variables then comparisons made between those with high and low turnovers. The personnel people rejected this proposal. They still wanted improvements to the departure interviews! One possible explanation for this sort of response is that anything else would take control over the process away from the personnel managers. It might also take budgetary resources away from them – they might be unable to claim further funds for departure interviewing.

A further example of the mismatch between research and the needs of the funding organization concerns research sponsored by a French telephone department on why telephones were being vandalized. A problem identified by the researchers was the definition of vandalism. This was seen by the organization as any damage to telephone equipment. Background research work showed many delinquents were opposed to wanton damage. Nevertheless, they approved of theft for food and so on. On the other hand, vandals disapproved of robbery but approved of damaging phone equipment because such acts had symbolic value and had no adverse consequences for individual owners as it was a public business. This encouraged the researchers to believe that radically different motivations underlie vandalism and robbery. So far, the research may have been much as the telephone company had expected.

Telephone booths with the highest incomes are the most likely to be damaged. Careful observation helped explain this. The interpretation that thieves rob the booths with the most cash was incorrect. A substantially different process seemed to be involved. Telephone booths full of coins do not work, nor do they always return cash to would-be callers. These Parisian booths gave no prior indication of a full money box. Not surprisingly, users sometimes became very frustrated. Consequently, in an attempt at a do-it-yourself 'repair', some would hit or shake the equipment. Over a half of users would act violently against the equipment following failure of the 'emergency repairs'. They were not delinquents, as such, but a reasonable cross-section of people.

In an attempt to prevent such frustration building up in this way, the researchers prepared a poster. It gave details of locations of another phone and the post office from which a refund could be obtained. This seemed to work well as people read the poster, spent less time in the telephone box, and did not abuse the equipment so much. Surprisingly, the telephone company was not very interested in these findings. Management retained the conviction that the vandals were thieves and so installed telephone equipment which was operated by cards rather than coins! According to Levy-Leboyer (1988, p. 783) this was because:

First, the concept of vandalism kept its ambiguity based on the idea, accepted by our clients without further proof, that young delinquents were responsible both for the theft of money in the coin box and for vandalism. Thus, vandalism should be prevented by hardening the equipment, not by making it more efficient. Furthermore, the research we were commissioned to do was based on a role distribution that we clearly upset. The Post Office Administration was on the 'right' side – they were civil servants dutifully providing their compatriots with a useful service. They were looking for ways to stop the lunatic, socially deviant behavior of people guilty of malignant aggression toward public property. Our analysis reversed the roles. Decent customers, like a homemaker coming from the market or a businessperson on a journey, wanted to make a telephone call. In the fact of inadequate equipment and with no possibility either to complain or to carry out their wish to communicate by phone, they had a right to be angry, and no other way to show their anger ... [W]e failed to modify the attitudes of higher management.

The degree to which psychology and the non-psychological world can be at variance is also demonstrated by Vokey and Read's (1985) experience. Popular music recordings have been alleged to use 'backmasking' – covert messages designed to influence the hearer. The incorporation of a message played backwards on a disc is the typical example. Such claims go back to the 1960s – though the 'demonic' view of music which is associated with backmasking has a far longer history. In the USA, politicians and religious leaders have actively campaigned against such 'messages'. Some go so far as to propose that such recordings should have a 'public health message' along the following lines 'Warning: This record contains backward masking which may be perceptible at a subliminal level when the record is played forward.' The 'messages' impinge on moral concerns. They were claimed to advocate evil, satanism, and the use of drugs. The whole issue of subliminal perception (that is, the perception of messages we are not able consciously to identify) is one of the classic themes of the experimental psychology of the 1950s and 1960s (see, for example, Dixon, 1971). Controls were placed on advertisers in some countries against using such techniques. However, despite this, backmasking begs psychological investigation. The idea that backmasking unconsciously influences the listener would seem to be a simple matter to test empirically. (It might be noted again in passing that 'demonic happenings' are a frequent theme in social outrage – for example, child sexual abuse and satanic rites are a particularly potent combination.)

Vokey and Read designed a number of experiments which put backmasking to proof. It is fallacious to assume that the presence of a message is sufficient evidence of effectiveness. To establish the effects of backmasking ought to involve a psychological investigation as one important contribution. The researchers played simple 'backmasked' passages to people. Listeners were readily able to obtain certain information – for example the sex of the speaker and the language in which the message was spoken. Comprehension of the meaning of 'backmasked' messages was, however, extremely poor. People were unable to tell whether the sentence was a question or a statement. Nor did they provide any evidence of a deeper level of understanding.

Intriguingly, people were asked if they could hear a particular phrase in the backmasked passage. They often 'erroneously' indicated that they could, though no such phrase appeared. This might explain the common view that 'backmasked' messages can be heard on certain records.

Interesting as this may be, from the point of view of our main concerns, it is more important to examine the way in which Vokey and Read's research was treated by the media. For these psychologists the question had been whether backmasking can influence thought. For the journalists the matter was totally different.

> Repeatedly, after devoting considerable effort to clarifying what we had and had not done and what the issues were from a scientific perspective, we would be confronted with such headlines as 'Professors Find no Satanic Messages in Rock Music.' Most readers probably failed to realize that such headlines were true only in the sense that we never looked for satanic messages in rock music. Thus, it is not surprising that we never found any.
>
> (Vokey and Read, 1985, p. 1238)

While our sophistication as members of the psychological community may be overlooked by us, the experience of these researchers implies that the public (to the extent to which they are exemplified by the media) may well totally misunderstand the purposes, methods, and nature of psychological research.

Dempster (1988) complains that one of the most generally established psychological principles – the spacing effect – ought to be applied because there is a significant and consistent body of knowledge from many styles of research supporting it. The spacing effect is that several small 'packages' of study produce better learning than the same total amount of time spent in a single session. While it would appear to be quite a reasonable argument, it is not clear what it means in practice. More importantly, one suspects that few psychology teachers are unaware of the notion of the spacing effect, but how many actually utilize it? Perhaps it is possible to find within the discipline some of the reasons for the apparent reluctance to apply psychology.

The relevance of research

Disproportionate amounts of crime (or prosecutions for crime) involve teenagers (Hagan, 1982). This presents a problem of particular importance and one involving potentially enormous costs. Whatever psychology might have to offer in this area could be of great benefit. However, some of the difficulty of using psychological theory and principles in connection with socially important topics is ably illustrated by Emery and Marholin's (1977) discussion. They looked at the use of 'behaviour modification' principles in the reduction of delinquent behaviour. Irrespective of one's views of the acceptability of using reinforcement and conditioning techniques in changing other humans, one feature of behaviour modification is its relatively precise guiding principles. In a review of studies purporting to modify the behaviour of delinquents using behavioural techniques, it was found that over 90 per cent failed a major fundamental rule of behavioural analysis – the requirement that the behaviour to be changed should be tailored to the needs and wishes of the individual concerned. In other words, simply imposing general outside criteria which are not specifically geared to the particular individual is unsatisfactory. What emerges from this is the recognition of the absence of proper tests of the application of basic psychological theory. Studies which ignore a theory's basic tenets simply are not adequate tests of that theory, though they may be adequate tests of behaviour modification theory as practised.

Furthermore, the top-down approach of psychology (which works for the powerful to control the powerless) may well impose 'incorrect' viewpoints. In the top-down approach the less powerful are typically deemed to *be* the problem rather than to be suffering from it. So if delinquent behaviour 'requires' modification it is assumed that the delinquent is responsible for that behaviour. Consequently, the appropriate way to deal with the matter is to work on the delinquent's behaviour. Aspects of this emerge when we consider what might be termed the 'environmental' or 'ecological' context of delinquency. Emery and Marholin (1977, pp. 868–9) describe an example:

> Dr. Rosenberg, a consultant to a school project in California, was asked to help change the behavior of several children who were deemed 'intolerable'. Rather than attempt to modify the target children's deviant behavior, the consultant chose to teach the children various reinforcement techniques to use in shaping their teachers' behavior ... They learned to discourage negative teacher behavior with remarks like, 'It's hard for me to do good work when you're cross with me.' The children were also taught to reinforce clear explanations on the part of their teachers by following them with comments such as 'Ah, hah! Now I understand! I could never get that before.' Within a few short weeks the teachers who had previously complained about

the target children's incorrigible behavior stopped complaining about the children and found them 'responsive and eager to learn.'

The question of what is appropriate psychological research on social issues is obviously a lot more complex than this. The contribution made by research to the use of psychology in relation to social issues has to be limited. One reason for this is that the role of psychology may be in terms of professional judgement and advice rather than any direct links with research findings. Psychologists may have to intervene or in some way help with practical solutions to imminent or current problems. The time-scale of a research project to evaluate their chosen strategies would probably be far greater than the pressing nature of the problem allows. AIDS is a good example of an urgent matter which was discussed intelligently by the psychological community before there was a substantial research base (see, for example, Batchelor, 1984). However, this is a rather different matter from suggesting that research when it comes can afford to be so consistently sloppy and irrelevant as in that criticised by Emery and Marholin (1977).

Psychology and policy research

Moving beyond practical and technical problems, a much broader question concerns how research can be made relevant to social policy. Policy relevance is not the prime criterion of good psychological research on social issues. Indeed, in general it is probably wise not to place research too centrally within the ambit of policy-makers. Psychology has responsibilities and functions too important to be handed over to those with objectives which are too limited. There is good reason to wonder whether there is much psychological research relevant to social policy. A conspicuous lack of sophisticated discussion of the whole question of policy relevance is typical of psychology. Just what is it about research that makes it policy–relevant? Are there any common factors which help make research applicable by policy-makers? Ruback and Innes (1988) suggest that there are.

In 1990, the British prisons were plunged into uproar by sieges by prisoners at Strangeways Prison, Manchester, and so-called 'copycat' activities at other establishments. Prison overcrowding was blamed for this, despite the fact that some trouble occurred at more commodious modern units. It is fairly natural to seek explanations of the disturbances in terms of the rapidly enlarging prison population, which is typical of the British penal system, though this may be changing. However, it is also a question which merits detailed research. But what ways are there of ensuring that research could be part of a proper dialogue between psychologists and policy-makers?

Ruback and Innes argue that two factors are important when considering the policy relevance of any research. The first is the *number of policy variables* included in the research design. A policy variable is one which the policy-maker can actually change. Variables which are beyond the capacities of the policy-maker to change are not policy-relevant. So, for example, if the policy-maker is in no position to reduce the numbers in prison or to increase the amount of prison accommodation, then research relating the number of prisoners to a given amount of space to unrest is clearly not policy-relevant. In those circumstances, it may be that research which looks at ways of reducing the stress due to overcrowding (for example, by examining the role of leisure activities in reducing tension) may be much more policy-relevant. Policy relevance is not an abstraction but a question of available choices.

Secondly, the *use of independent variables of utility to policy-makers* is necessary so that vast leaps of inference are unnecessary. For example, if research on prison overcrowding concentrated on its effects on calorie intake then this would not seem particularly useful as, say, a measure of stress in that context. Similarly, the research should take place in a relevant ecological context to avoid further jumps of imagination. Consequently, if the research looked at overcrowding in a simulated prison in a psychology laboratory this would not be so ecologically valid as had the research taken place in a real prison. Or, to take another example, research which showed the effects of crowding on how much control incarcerated prisoners feel they have over their environment probably would have little or no interest for the policy-maker.

Clearly research which contains policy variables and has highly utilizable dependent measures is the most likely to be helpful to policy-makers. Research of this sort, however, may not always be psychologically interesting as a result. It may be that, by being tied to the needs of policy-makers, research suits the purposes of psychological ideas and knowl dge very poorly.

In this context, the question of mortality rates in prisons is doubly intriguing. A convenient assumption is that prisoners are at greater risk of death given the possibility of suicide, the concentration of potentially violent people, the risk of AIDS, and the effects of psychological stress in prison. Increases in mortality and other indicators are usually regarded by psychologists as one outcome of extreme stress. The social support literature, for example, suggests this (Howitt *et al.*, 1989). It might be tempting to take mortality rates in prison as evidence or as an indicator of stress in prison.

In the USA there has been some evidence that as prison populations increase death rates increase disproportionately (Cox *et al.*, 1984). But such findings need to be treated with caution. One obvious reason is that prison death rates need to be shown to be greater than those outside prison. Statistically, prisoners are substantially *less* likely to die than non-prisoners. But this is not a proper comparison. Prisoners are likely to consist of a higher proportion of young, black males than is the general population. When adjustments have been made for these disparities, the following seems to be true. Deaths caused by illnesses and illegal killings are significantly lower than expectations; however, suicides are substantially greater.

Now this might be interpreted as suggesting that the stress of prison tends to be directed inwardly, leading to suicide. So prison stress may have different effects on different measures of mortality. The idea that suicide is caused by prison overcrowding, however, is not well founded since about half of suicides occur on the first day of confinement. This is hardly convincing evidence of the special stress of prison crowding, especially as the rate of prison suicides is 29 per 100,000 of the population compared to 20 per 100,000 in similar groups in the non-prison population. Furthermore, there is evidence, according to Ruback and Innes, that suicide is rare in multi-occupied cells but common in single-occupied ones.

So despite the fact that suicide might appear to psychologists as a good but indirect indicator of prison stress, careful penological investigation casts great doubt on its pertinence. The problem for psychologists wanting their research to be applied by policy-makers is as much in their own hands as it can be blamed on the unscientific approach psychologists may feel is typical of policy-makers.

The sort of psychological analysis present by Ruback and Innes is certainly interesting as it disabuses us of misconceptions. It also points us in directions which might illuminate the *understanding* of the process and effects of imprisonment. This might be useful general background for both psychologists and policy-makers. The question still remaining concerns the extent to which a clearer understanding of policy variables might aid better commissioning of policy-relevant research from psychologists and its utilization. To a degree it is also a radically simpler account than that given by Tizard (1990) of the link between research and policy. Nevertheless Ruback and Innes's account is far more optimistic since it gives guidelines of what needs to be done *if* policy is the framework for the research. Tizard reproduces much of the 'science' ideology as if it is given – for example, the worries that psychologists have about value frameworks, the 'problem' of disagreements in the academic community, and the undesirability of advocacy by researchers. Unfortunately, why these are blocks rather than positive assets is not made clear – they are 'self-evident truths'. Why gripe about the neglect of research in policy if one is not prepared to make the case onself? Why should the policy-maker neglect all other matters which guide policy in the absence of a demand for a share of the 'policy-making cake' by researchers?

If policy is what one's research is about, what choice is there but to 'go for it'. However, should one wish to contribute to a 'rational' understanding of society, is policy relevance a major concern?

Finally, Shadish (1984, p. 735) points to broader factors which harness psychology to the community:

If policy research is more instrumentally usable to the extent that it is consistent with extant social structures and ideologies, then a new problem surfaces: Implementable policy research must avoid arid problems caused by flaws in these basic social structures and ideologies.

One is reminded, in this context, of Fox's (1985) claim that psychologists might do well to take on board anarchist principles when examining their ideological positions with regard to global ecology and individual psychology.

Ethics in socially sensitive research

Psychological ethics is intended to deal with a very limited range of dilemmatical situations. Specifically, it protects the immediate participants in the research from tangible harm such as physical injury, stress, humiliation, and the like. It is not geared to dealing adequately with all the possible ramifications of research for inflicting harm. Cynically, it is a means of giving 'moral' credibility to research which otherwise might be refused funding by research committees. Like most self-monitoring by professions, ethics is primarily a protection for the profession, not its clients. So, for example, it is, for the most part, not unethical to make claims based on dubious research about the genetic inferiority of a racial or gender group. However, it is likely to be unethical to lie to a member of that racial or gender group about the purpose of a trivial piece of research. This narrow use of psychological ethics makes it a relatively 'limp' means of guiding social issues research.

Starting from the lack of any clear guidelines in psychological ethics to deal with socially sensitive research, Sieber and Stanley (1988) identify four different aspects of 'scientific' activity which should attract ethical concerns in the social context.

The first aspect is the formulation of the research question. The social implications of research stem not from its 'truth' value but from its links with current social thinking. So, for example, the fact that Freud raised questions of female psychosexual development is an important social fact. Despite being largely dismissed by the modern psychological community, Freud's idea has been absorbed into the thinking of the wider community. Another example is Piaget's claim that there are relatively invariable stages in the development of thinking. This view has been absorbed into the common-sense theories and professional practice of teachers.

The second aspect is the conduct of research and treatment of participants. We have already seen that typically the 'interests' of the individual participating in research are the subject of ethical concerns. This is not surprising given that much psychological research is socially decontextualized. It seems only right and proper that individuals are protected from unnecessary stress or invasions of privacy by psychologists. But what, for example, if a psychologist studies dating behaviour in couples and finds that one of the partners has not revealed that he/she has AIDS? In individualized conceptions of research the same sorts of dilemma may not arise but socially contextualized research is different and does not enable the isolation of individuals from their social context in the same way.

The third aspect is the institutional context. Research by psychologists does not always take place in a purely academic context but may be financed by a company or an institution which is not subject to ethical scrutiny. Sometimes psychologists (academic or otherwise) agree to be contractually bound by an employing or grant-giving organization. It becomes difficult then to guarantee that the research will be ethically sound.

The fourth, and final, aspect is the interpretation and application of research findings. While this issue is dealt with elsewhere, it is worthwhile quoting Sieber and Stanley's (1988, p. 52) example:

> Around the beginning of the 20th century, social scientists considered mental retardation to be the largest and most serious problem in the United States (Davies, 1930). They warned policy makers that, unless retarded individuals were prevented from reproducing, mental retardation would assume greater proportions and have more threatening effects (there would be more crime, alcoholism, prostitution, poverty, and delinquency) and that the number of mentally retarded individuals would increase with each generation, threatening the extinction of Western civilization.

This sort of theme survived well into the second half of the twentieth century. Eysenck (1953), for example, was asking the question in a different form – 'Is Our National Intelligence Declining?' – relatively recently. The point being argued is that intelligence and social class correlate. So, as the intelligence quotient is presumed to be genetically inherited in this formulation, then the higher birth rates in the working class inevitably lead to lowering national intelligence. Or so the claim went. Perhaps the issue is dead given modern evidence of substantial inter-generational gains in average IQ of (see, for example, Flynn, 1989). The curiosity is the basis on which mental retardation was elevated to such an important position in the possible range of issues facing society. Clearly the claim of the centrality of mental retardation for the future of Western civilization has no bearing on current conceptions of major social problems. Social scientists may merely be feeding back to society one dominant ideology. In this case, the question whether our national intelligence is declining simply served to justify elitist social structures and the continued access to privilege through social class and education. We should not forget that the early twentieth century was highly influenced by the ideas of evolution and later genetics.

Both of these could readily be twisted into 'scientific' justification of elitism and make 'talent' appear to be a scarce commodity. All of this may have contributed to the fear of the 'bad gene' and the view that mental retardation would be a growing problem.

Sieber and Stanley (1988, p. 54) claim that it is highly likely that psychological research will raise socially sensitive issues, and often unavoidable, 'if useful theory, knowledge, and applications are to be achieved'. Nevertheless, the bulk of psychology as it is practised falls far short of meeting this description. The socio-phobic nature of most psychology probably explains the lack of a professional 'safety net' of accepted principles guiding socially sensitive research. With changes in the priorities of psychology, pressure may increase for a new sort of ethic – a social ethic rather than a managerial one orientated towards the individual research participant.

Crawford's (1979) discussion of the incompatibility between psychology and more fundamental social values makes an interesting case in point. For example, he contrasts the statement "If my father's son can become President, so can your father's son" (Abraham Lincoln) with "Genetic factors are about twice as important as environmental factors as a cause of IQ differences among individuals" (Arthur Jensen)' (Crawford, 1979, p. 665). The question is, of course, how one decides between the truth value of the two?

Anti-intellectualism and the rejection of psychology

One explanation for the failure of psychological research to be applied is the antagonistic attitude of sections of the community to academic work and other forms of intellectual activity. Consequently, some may reject or question the worth of psychological research irrespective of its precise nature. Shaffer (1977, p. 816) highlights the public treatment given Berscheid's love research (Berscheid and Walster, 1978) by a prominent American politician:

> But the biggest waste has to be $84,000 to find out why or how or if or how long people fall in love. I object to this because no one ... can argue that falling in love is a science. I'm against it because I don't want the answer ... So National Science Foundation – get out of the love racket. Leave that to Elizabeth Barrett Browning and Irving Berlin. Here if anywhere Alexander Pope was right when he observed, 'If ignorance is bliss, tis folly to be wise.'

These comments by US Senator Proxmire may too easily cause concern because of their swingeing rhetorical tone. Berscheid's research on love is readily available. It is discussed in many introductory textbooks (for example, Atkinson *et al.*, 1990) so can be said to have found widespread acceptance among the academic community. Should research be supported which is intrinsically non-applicable, or ideologically offensive to many people if applied? This is not a question of individual scholarship or academic freedom, but one of the purchase of research by the state. If Proxmire's reservations were couched in terms which some reserve for embryological research (or even research on promoting anti-abortion attitudes) the issues might have been more clearly highlighted.

That the psychology establishment does not like attacks on it in no way makes such attacks wrong. It is not normally the function of professional associations to facilitate their own destruction, quite the opposite. So outrage at Proxmire's comments may merely be defensive posturing. It is questionable whether 'anti-intellectual' is the appropriate description. Similar sorts of criticism could be made of the love research from within the academic community. They would then, presumably, be 'intellectual-ism'. Psychologists cannot reasonably be expected to be unfettered by the 'outside world', at the same time seek research funds from that same source, and dismiss criticisms of the research from the outside world. If the research is useless to anyone other than the *cognoscenti* then this raises its own questions. Who wants to fall in love better?

Theory and real-world psychology

Applied psychology has a reputation for being empiricist. This allows its relegation to the lower reaches of status in the profession. The lack of a resolutely theoretical approach leaves it the province of 'number-crunching' hacks. This is a calumny but a convenient one for the determined academic. It is a mistaken view for two reasons.

First, much of what passes for theory in academic psychology is little more than empirical generalization. Few extended and comprehensive theories exist in purely academic psychology. A glance through psychology journals confirms the relative absence of anything other than fairly narrowly based hunches, hypotheses and generalizations.

Second, it is not established that so-called applied psychology lacks theoretical integrity. This is not to suggest that blatant empiricism is anything but common in the applied areas of psychology, since this is also typical of what passes for pure or basic research. Good theory is no less common in real-world psychology than in basic or pure psychology. One need only cite the example of clinical psychology which has developed significant theory out of experience and research in the real world (Freud, Kelly, Ellis, and so on). No suggestion is being made that these famous figures were uninfluenced by the purely academic. However, it is claimed that their theoretical approaches were substantially the outcome of practice. While the case of behaviour therapy may be cited as a counter-example to this, in that it claims to be firmly based on principles of learning theory, exceptions tend to prove the rule. Equally, there is a significant psychology of the workplace which is little dependent on the machinations of laboratory and similar psychological researchers. For example, the best theories of the nature of leadership (see, for example, Fiedler, 1967; Fiedler and Chemers, 1974) have their origins with muddy-booted psychologists, not narrow academics.

One does not do research in the real world in order to emerge with robust findings which can be generalized from one situation to another. To assume that one can is mistaken and flies in the face of evidence (Dipboye and Flanagan, 1979). One should not think that it is easier to generalize from one real-world situation to another than it is from the findings of 'basic' research to the real world. What one might claim is that non-generalizable findings gleaned from real-world situations are more useful than non-generalizable findings from out-and-out laboratory studies, methods being equated as far as is possible.

It would be useful to return to the issue of the effects of prison over-crowding to illustrate how theory can emerge out of field research. The earlier discussion of this chapter dealt with the theory of making research policy-relevant, but at the same time it largely dealt with the effects of imprisonment as an empirical question. Left at that level, a possible criticism is that the image of applied psychology as concerned with little more than the quest for statistical data is left intact by this. So the theory of prison over-crowding should make a marked contrast.

In the USA prison overcrowding has been subject to a number of lawsuits about what appropriate conditions are for prisoners. While such litigation may not be possible in all other countries, the issue clearly overlaps public concerns elsewhere about the size of the prison population. Among the findings that emerged from Cox *et al.*'s (1984, p. 1156) archival and contemporary research were:

1. Increases in population in prisons where facilities are not increased proportionately are associated with increased rates of death, suicide, disciplinary infraction, and psychiatric commitment. Decreases in population are accompanied by decreases in death rates, psychiatric commitments, inmate-on-inmate assaults, and attempted suicides and self mutilations. ... 3. Double cells or double cubicles yielded negative effects on housing ratings, disciplinary infraction rates, and illness-complaint rates relative to singles. ... 7. Spatial density does not seem to be as important a factor as is commonly believed in producing negative effects. Comparisons of one- and two-person units that varied widely in space did not reveal any consistent negative effects related to reduced space.

Findings such as these seem to support prison-reform advocates and others in so far as they suggest that smaller prisons with spaces for the seclusion of individual prisoners would be good for the physical and psychological welfare of inmates and cause fewer managerial problems.

One intriguing outcome from Cox *et al.*'s (1984) research is the theoretical output. They develop out of their findings what they term the 'social interaction-demand model' to explain the effects of prison overcrowding. And, even more importantly, they argue that the model may be relevant to other crowding phenomena in different settings. This is clearly a development which needs attention as the apparent value of theory emerging from so-called applied work may be higher than that coming from decontextualized 'basic' research. Teasing out elements of the model into a simple explanation, the model accounts for the effects of prison density in the following way:

Step One: *Social distance* between people may be affected by the size of housing units which, together with the sheer *number of people* in a given space, forces increased levels of *social interaction.*

Step Two: This increased social interaction increases the *cognitive load* on individuals which is the difficulty of making decisions. Many more individuals may have to be taken into account. Furthermore, increased social interaction can lead to greater *uncertainty* since it is more difficult to anticipate what will happen with more individuals in the group. Furthermore, there will be more *goal interference* with increased social interaction since this means that there is a greater likelihood that individuals will have mutually conflicting goals. Both uncertainty and goal interference can further increase cognitive load.

Step Three: All of the effects in step two can increase *fear/anxiety, frustration,* and *cognitive strain.* These in turn lead to verbal labels such as feeling harassed, stressed, anxious, and the like, or to other responses such as blood pressure increases, aggression, psychiatric symptoms, and rule violations.

So according to Cox *et al.* (1984, pp. 1158–9)

> if high levels of density occur without much uncertainty, goal interference, or cognitive load, few if any negative effects should be observed … From the above considerations it can be easily seen why crowding in prisons might have particularly strong effects. The inmate populations certainly can be characterized as more dangerous than populations in most other environments. Furthermore, the relatively high levels of turnover in prisons and jails ensures the presence of large numbers of unfamiliar inmates. Uncertainty is thus likely to be a major problem in this type of environment.

A question which needs answering, of course, is whether such theory is markedly different from theory emerging in different ways. Certainly there is an extensive literature on the effects of overcrowding (see Stockdale, 1978) which includes ethological ideas which have been subject to much attention (Ardrey, 1966). There is no simple answer to the question. One might choose to judge such theory by the extent to which it generates further research. This is a typical criterion suggested by the academic theorist. But is it a fair criterion? Surely there is a case for claiming that a theory should be judged by its lack of need for further research? If it could be used by prison officials profitably why the need for much further research? New ideas about the worth of theory seem to be needed for real-world psychology. Their work-creating potential for members of the psychology profession seems to be an inwardly looking criterion which serves the needs of the profession rather than the community.

Concluding comments

What conclusions are appropriate for the final chapter of this book? Certainly it will not be claimed that more research is needed. Probably there is a greater need to consolidate the information in psychology than to generate more of it. It might be that there are big gaps in the knowledge generated by psychology which ought to be filled. However, one of the messages of this and previous chapters is that a change of attitude is necessary. This is partly a matter of dissolving the membrane which isolates the psychological community from the rest of society which needs a discipline like psychology to enhance the knowledge base of its work and activities in general. Also important is that the discipline should abandon the defensive elitism that helped build the discipline in the past. It is not a virtue of psychology that it cannot speak to people in terms they understand. The success of psychology should not be judged against the yardstick of the number of jobs for psychologists. The failure of psychology, on the other hand, might be judged by the absence of the discipline in many key areas of activity. Indeed, much of what might have been central to psychology has been usurped by other professions – economics, social work, personnel management, training and communications are examples where psychology might be expected to have been the central rather than a peripheral discipline.

So are there any maxims which could be passed on to future generations of psychologists? Is it possible to consolidate what can be learnt from the past and to encourage psychology to come to grips with important social issues? The following are my candidates for inclusion but they are in need of continual revision:

Maxim one: Accept no maxims.

Maxim two: No particular methods or approaches in psychology are panaceas. However, within psychology there is a body of resources which may be useful sometimes.

Maxim three: The values and beliefs of psychologists are the fuel of good psychology. Cherish your own to the extent that they allow you to challenge them and refine them.

Maxim four: Disagreements with other psychologists are the breeding ground for professional development and learning.

Maxim five: Know yourself. Opportunities for self-learning help calibrate the main research instrument of psychology – the psychologist.

Maxim six: Would your mother truthfully be impressed by what you are doing in the name of psychological research?

Maxim seven: Never have a psychologist for a mother.

Maxim eight: Know a lot about what you are investigating – ensure that no more than one-fifth of this is psychology.

Maxim nine: Never forget that the best psychologists are not psychologists. Always talk to the best psychologists.

Maxim ten: Always have a good breakfast. Then decide whether you are looking forward most to your research or your lunch. If the former skip the latter, and vice versa.

REFERENCES

Abbott, A. (1981). Status and status strain in the professions. *American Journal of Sociology*, 86 (4), 819–35.

Adam, H. and Giliomee, H. (1979). *Ethnic Power Mobilized: Can South Africa Change?* New Haven, Conn.: Yale University Press.

Adorno, T., Frenkel-Brunswik, E., Levinson, D.J. and Sanford, R.N. (1950). *The Authoritarian Personality*. New York: Harper and Row.

Allport, G.W. and Postman, L. (1947). *The Psychology of Rumour*. New York: Holt, Rinehart and Winston.

Amir, M. (1971). *Patterns of Forcible Rape*. Chicago: University of Chicago Press.

Ardrey, R. (1966). *The Territorial Imperative*. New York: Atheneum.

Argyle, M. (1953). The relay assembly test room in retrospect. *Occupational Psychology*, 27, 98–103.

Argyle, M. (1972). *The Social Psychology of Work*. Harmondsworth: Penguin.

Atkinson, R.C. (1977). Reflections on psychology's past and concerns about its future. *American Psychologist*, 32 (3), 205–10.

Atkinson, R.L., Atkinson, R.C., Smith, E.E., Bem, D.J., and Hilgard, E.R. (1990). *Introduction to Psychology*, 10th edn. San Diego: Harcourt Brace Jovanovich.

Attorney General's Commission on Pornography (1986). *Final Report*. Washington, DC: US Government Printing Office.

Auld, J. (1981). *Marijuana Use and Social Control*. London: Academic Press.

Australia (1988). *Report of the Joint Select Committee on Video Material*. Canberra: Australian Government Publishing Service.

Ayllon, T., and Azrin, N. (1968). *The Token Economy: A Motivational System for Therapy and Rehabilitation*. Englewood Cliffs, NJ: Prentice-Hall.

Baartman, H.E.M. (1990). The credibility of children as witnesses and the social denial of the incestuous abuse of children. Paper presented to the 2nd European Conference on Law and Psychology, Nuremberg, 13–15 September.

Bachrach, L.L. (1984). Deinstitutionalization and women: Assessing the consequences of public policy. *American Psychologist*, 39 (10), 1187–92.

Bachrach, L.L. (1989). Deinstitutionalization: A semantic analysis. *Journal of Social Issues*, 45 (3), 161–72.

Bannister, D. (ed.) (1977). *New Perspectives in Personal Construct Theory*. London: Academic Press.

Bannister, D. (ed.) (1985). *Issues and Approaches in Personal Construct Theory*. London: Academic Press.

Banton, M. (1983). *Racial and Ethnic Competition*. Cambridge: Cambridge University Press.

Barker, M. (1981). *The New Racism*. London: Junction Books.

Barlow, G., and Hill, A. (1985). *Video Violence and Children*. London: Hodder and Stoughton.

Baron, L. and Straus, M. (1984). Sexual stratification, pornography and rape in the United States. In N.M. Malmuth and E. Donnerstein (eds), *Pornography and Sexual Aggression*. New York: Academic Press, pp. 185–209.

Baron, L. and Straus, M. (1987). Four theories of rape: a microsocial analysis. *Social Problems*, 34, 467–99.

Baron, L. and Straus, M. (1989). *Four Theories of Rape: A State-level Analysis*. New Haven, Conn.: Yale University Press.

Bartlett, F. (1932). *Remembering: A Study in Experimental and Social Psychology*. Cambridge: Cambridge University Press.

Bass, B.M. (1955). Authoritarianism or acquiescence? *Journal of Abnormal and Social Psychology*, 51, 616–23.

Batchelor, W.F. (1984). AIDS: A public health and psychological emergency. *American Psychologist*, 39 (11), 1279–84.

Baxter, M. (1990). Flesh and blood. *New Scientist*, 5 May, 37–41.

Bean, P. (1974). *The Social Control of Drugs*. London: Martin Robinson.

Bell, S. (1988). *When Salem Came to the Boro*. London: Pan.

Berridge, V. (1984). Drugs and social policy: the establishment of drug control in Britain 1900–30. *British Journal of Addictions*, 79, 17–28.

Berridge, V. (1989). Historical issues. In S. McGregor (ed.), *Drugs and British Society*, London: Routledge, pp. 20–35.

Berridge, V., and Edwards, G. (1981). *Opium and the People*. London: Allen Lane/St Martin's Press.

Berry, B. (1958). *Race and Ethnic Relations*. Cambridge: Riverside Press.

Berscheid, E. and Walster, E.H. (1978). *Interpersonal Attraction*. Menlo Park, Calif.: Addison-Wesley.

Bevan, W. (1980). On getting in bed with a lion. *American Psychologist*, 35 (9), 779–89.

Billig, M. (1979). *Psychology, Racism and Fascism*. Birmingham: Searchlight.

Billig, M. (1981). *L'Internationale Raciste*. Paris: François Maspéro.

Billig, M. (1982). *Ideology and Social Psychology*. Oxford: Blackwell.

Billig, M. (1985). The unobservant participator: Nazism, anti-semitism, and Ray's reply. *Ethnic and Racial Studies*, 8 (3), 444–9.

Billig, M., and Tajfel, H. (1973). Social categorisation and similarity in intergroup behaviour. *European Journal of Social Psychology*, 3, 27–52.

Boring, E.G. (1950). *A History of Experimental Psychology*. New York: Appleton-Century-Crofts.

Bramel, D. and Friend, R. (1981). Hawthorne, the myth of the docile worker and class bias in psychology. *American Psychologist,* 36 (8), 867–78.

Breakwell, G. and Davey, G. (1990). Rushton and race differences. *The Psychologist: Bulletin of the British Psychological Society,* 3 (7), 318.

Brehm, S.S. and Kassin, S.M. (1990). *Social Psychology.* Boston: Houghton Mifflin.

Brent, R. (1989). Sexual abuse of children. *The Psychologist: Bulletin of the British Psychological Society,* 2 (10), 442–3.

Brette, D.J. and Cantor, J. (1988). The portrayal of men and women in US television commercials: A recent content analysis and trends over 15 years. *Sex Roles,* 18 (9–10), 595–609.

British Psychological Society (1988). *The Future of the Psychological Sciences: Horizons and Opportunities for British Psychology.* Leicester: British Psychological Society.

Brown, K. (1985). Turning a blind eye: racial oppression and the unintended consequences of white 'non-racism'. *Sociological Review,* 33 (4), 670–89.

Browne, K. and Saqui, S. (1988). Approaches to screening for child abuse and neglect. In K. Brown, C. Davies and P. Stratton (eds), *Early Prediction and Prevention of Child Abuse.* Chichester: John Wiley and Sons, pp. 57–85.

Browne, K. and Stevenson, J. (1983). *A Checklist for Completion by Health Visitors to Identify Children 'At Risk' for Child Abuse.* Report to the Surrey County Area Review Committee on Child Abuse.

Brownmiller, S. (1975). *Against Our Will: Men, Women and Rape.* New York: Simon and Schuster.

Burgess, A.W. and Holmstrom, L.L. (1979). *Rape: Crisis and Recovery.* Bowie, M.: Robert J. Brody.

Burt, M.R. (1980). Cultural myths and supports for rape. *Journal of Personality and Social Psychology,* 38, 217–30.

Buss, A. (1961). *The Psychology of Aggression.* New York: Wiley.

Butler-Sloss, J. (1988). *Report of the Inquiry into Child Abuse in Cleveland 1987.* London: HMSO.

Campbell, B. (1988). *Unofficial Secrets.* London: Virago.

Canada (1985). *Report of the Special Committee on Pornography and Prostitution.* Ottawa: Supply and Services.

Card, R. (1975). Sexual relations with minors. *Criminal Law Review,* July, 370– 80.

Carter, D.C., Prentky, R.A., Knight, R.A., Venderveer, P.L. and Boucher, R.J. (1987). Use of pornography in the criminal and developmental histories of sexual offenders. *Journal of Interpersonal Violence,* 2 (2), 196–211.

Cattell, R. (1965). *The Scientific Analysis of Personality.* Harmondsworth: Penguin.

Cattell, R.B. and Cattell, N.D. (1969). *High School Personality Questionnaire.* Windsor: National Foundation for Educational Research.

Chester, M.A. (1976). Contemporary sociological theories of racism. In P.A. Katz (ed.), *Towards the Elimination of Racism:* Oxford: Pergamon.

Clark, L.M.G. and Lewis, D.J. (1977). *Rape: The Price of Coercive Sexuality.* Toronto: Women's Press.

Clarke, L. (1989). Academic aliens. *British Psychological Society, Psychology of Women Section Newsletter,* 4, 4–8.

Cline, V.B. (ed.) (1974). *Where Do You Draw the Line? An Exploration into Media Violence, Pornography and Aggression.* Provo, Utah: Brigham Young University Press.

Cohen, S. (1974). *Folk Devils and Moral Panics.* London: McGibbon and Kee.

Commission on Obscenity and Pornography (1970). *The Report of the Commission on Obscenity and Pornography*. New York: Bantam.

Condron, M.K. and Nutter, D.E. (1988). A preliminary examination of the pornography experience of sex offenders, paraphiliac sexual dysfunction and controls. *Journal of Sex and Marital Therapy*, 14 (4), 285–98.

Cook, S. (1985). Experimenting on social issues. *American Psychologist*, 40 (4), 452–60.

Cowan, G.L., Lee, C., Levy, D. and Snyder, D. (1988). Dominance and inequality in X rated vido cassettes. *Psychology of Women Quarterly*, 12, 299–311.

Cox, V.C., Paulus, P.B. and McCain, G. (1984). Prison crowding research. The relevance for prison housing standards and a general approach regarding crowding phenomena. *American Psychologist*, 39 (10), 1148–60.

Cramer, D. (1991). Patients' experience of the therapist relationship: A universal factor of therapeutic change? *The 1990 Principles Congress Proceedings*. Lisse: Swets and Zeitlinger.

Crawford, C. (1979). George Washington, Abraham Lincoln, and Arthur Jensen: Are they compatible? *American Psychologist*, 34 (8), 664–72.

Cresswell, H. (1982). *The Secret World of Polly Flint*. London: Faber.

Cumberbatch, G. (1988). Changing sex behaviour. *The Psychologist: Bulletin of the British Psychological Society*, 1 (2), 47–8.

Cumberbatch, G. and Howitt, D. (1989). *A Measure of Uncertainty: The Effects of the Mass Media*. London: John Libbey.

Daly, M. and Wilson, M. (1988). *Homicide*. New York: Aldine de Gruyter.

Danziger, K. (1985). The origins of the psychological experiment as a social institution. *American Psychologist*, 40 (2), 133–40.

Davies, S.P. (1930). *Social Control of the Mentally Deficient*. New York: Crowell.

Dawes, A. (1990). The effects of political violence on children: a consideration of South African and related studies. *International Journal of Psychology*, 25, 13–31.

Dawson, J.L.M. (1969). Exchange theory and comparison level changes among Australian aborigines. *British Journal of Social and Clinical Psychology*, 8, 104–15.

Dembo, R. (1991). *International Journal of Addictions*, special issue, 25 (3A), 353–76.

Dempster F.N. (1988). The spacing effect: A case study in the failure to apply the results of psychological research. *American Psychologist*, 43 (8), 627–34.

Department of Health and Social Security (1982). *Child Abuse: A Study of Inquiry Reports*. London: HMSO.

Devine, P.G. (1989). Stereotypes and prejudice: Their automatic and controlled components. *Journal of Personality and Social Psychology*, 56 (1), 5–18.

Dilman, I. (1983). *Freud and Human Nature*. Oxford: Blackwell.

Dipboye, R.L. and Flanagan, M.F. (1979). Research settings in industrial and organizational psychology: Are findings in the field more generalizable than in the laboratory. *American Psychologist*, 34 (2), 141–50.

Dixon, N.F. (1971). *Subliminal Perception: The Nature of a Controversy*. New York: McGraw-Hill.

Doherty, M.E., Mynatt, C.R., Tweney, R.D. and Schiavo, M.D. (1979). Pseudodiagnosity. *Acta Psychologica*, 43, 11–21.

Donnerstein, E. (1980). Aggressive erotica and violence against women. *Journal of Personality and Social Psychology*, 39 (2), 269–77.

Donnerstein, E. and Berkowitz, L. (1981). Victim reactions in aggressive erotic films as a factor in violence against women. *Journal of Personality and Social Psychology*, 41, 710–24.

Donnerstein, E., Berkowitz, L. and Linz, D. (1986). Role of aggressive and sexual images in pornography. Unpublished Manuscript.

Donnerstein, E., Linz, D. and Penrod, S. (1987). *The Question of Pornography: Research Findings and Policy Implications.* New York: Free Press.

Dooley, D. and Catalano, R. (1988). Recent research on the psychological effects of unemployment. *Journal of Social Issues*, 44 (4), 1–12.

Drapkin, I. and Viano, E. (1974). *Victimology: A New Focus. Volume 1. Theoretical Issues in Victimology.* Lexington, Mass.: Lexington.

Duck, S. (ed.) (1990). *Personal Relationships and Social Support.* London: Sage.

Dummett, A. (1984). *A Portrait of English Racism.* London: CARAF Publications.

Durkin, K. (1985). *Television, Sex Roles and Children.* Milton Keynes: Open University Press.

Earle, T.C. and Cvetkovich, G. (1990). What was the meaning of Chernobyl? *Journal of Environmental Psychology*, 10, 169–76.

Einseidel, E.F. (1988). The British, Canadian, and U.S. pornography commissions and their use of social science research. *Journal of Communication*, 38 (2), 108–21.

Ellis, K., O'Dair, B. and Tallmer, A. (1990). Feminism and pornography. *Feminist Review*, 36 (Autumn), 15–18.

Ellis, L. (1989). *Theories of Rape: Inquiries into the Causes of Sexual Aggression.* New York: Hemisphere.

Emery, R.E. and Marholin II, D. (1977). An applied behavior analysis of delinquency: the irrelevance of relevant behavior. *American Psychologist*, 32 (10), 860–72.

Evans, J. St.B. T. (1989). Some causes of bias in expert opinion. *The Psychologist: Bulletin of the British Psychological Society*, 2 (3), 112–14.

Evans, R.I. (1980). *The Making of Social Psychology: Discussions with Creative Contributors.* New York: Gardner Press.

Everywoman (1988). *Pornography and Sexual Violence: Evidence of the Links.* London: Everywoman.

Eysenck, H.J. (1953). *Uses and Abuses of Psychology.* Harmondsworth: Penguin.

Eysenck, H.J. (1954). *The Psychology of Politics.* Harmondsworth: Penguin.

Eysenck, H.J. (1957). *Sense and Nonsense in Psychology.* Harmondsworth: Penguin.

Eysenck, H.J. (1973). *The Inequality of Man.* London: Temple Smith.

Eysenck, H.J. (1977). *Crime and Personality.* London: Routledge and Kegan Paul.

Eysenck, H.J. and Gudjonsson, G.H. (1989). *The Causes and Cures of Criminality.* London: Plenum.

Eysenck, H.J. and Nias, D.K. (1978). *Sex, Violence and the Media.* London: Maurice Temple Smith.

Eysenck, H.J. and Wilson, G.D. (1973). *The Experimental Study of Freudian Theories.* London: Methuen.

Eysenck, H.J., and Wilson, G.D. (1978). *The Psychological Basis of Ideology.* Lancaster: MTP Press.

Farr, R. (1989). The international origins of a science: social psychology. *History and Philosophy of Psychology Newsletter* (British Psychological Society), 8, May, 113–21.

Faust, B. (1980). *Women, Sex and Pornography.* Harmondsworth: Penguin.

Fiedler, F.E. (1967). *A Theory of Leadership Effectiveness.* New York: McGraw-Hill.

Fiedler, F.E. and Chemers, M.M. (1974). *Leadership and Effective Management.* San Francisco: Scott, Foreman.

Flynn, J.R. (1989). Rushton, evolution, and race: an essay on intelligence and virtue. *The Psychologist: Bulletin of the British Psychological Society*, 9, 363–6.

Fox, D.R. (1985). Psychology, ideology, utopia, and the commons. *American Psychologist*, 40 (1), 48–58.

Freud, S. (1950). *Totem and Taboo: Some Points of Agreement between the Mental Lives of Savages and Neurotics*. London: Routledge and Kegan Paul.

Freud, S. (1961). *Beyond the Pleasure Principle*. London: Hogarth Press.

Gaertner, S.L. and Dovidio, J.F. (1986). The aversive form of racism. In J.F. Dovidio and S.L. Gaertner (eds), *Prejudice, Discrimination and Racism*. New York: Academic Press, pp. 61–89.

Gale, A. (1990). Applying psychology to the psychology degree: pass with first class honours, or miserable failure? *The Psychologist: Bulletin of the British Psychological Society*, 11, 483–8.

Gelles, R.J. (1979). *Family Violence*. London: Sage.

Gelles, R.J. and Cornell, C.P. (eds) (1985). *Intimate Violence in Families*. London: Sage.

Gergen, K.J. (1982). *Towards Transformation in Social Knowledge*. New York: Springer-Verlag.

Gergen, K. (1985). The social constructionist movement in modern psychology. *American Psychologist*, 40 (3), 266–75.

Gergen, K. and Gergen, M.M. (1984). *Historical Social Psychology*. Hillsdale, NJ: Lawrence Erlbaum.

Geuter, U. (1987). German psychology during the Nazi period. In M.G. Ash and W.R. Woodward (eds), *Psychology in Twentieth-century Thought and Society*. Cambridge: Cambridge University Press.

Gossop, M. (1984). Drug and alcohol dependence. In A. Gale and A.J. Chapman (eds.), *Psychology and Social Problems: An Introduction to Applied Psychology*. Chichester: John Wiley, pp. 231–54.

Graumann, C.F. (ed.) (1985). *Psychologie im Nationalsozialismus*. Berlin: Springer-Verlag.

Griffiths, R. and Pearson, B. (1988). *Working with Drug Users*. Aldershot: Wildwood House.

Gruneberg, M.M. (1987a). *German*. London: Corgi.

Gruneberg, M.M. (1987b). *Spanish*. London: Corgi.

Hagan, J. (ed.). (1982). *Quantitative Criminology: Innovations and Applications*. Beverly Hills, Calif.: Sage.

Hall, S., Critcher, C., Jefferson, T., Clark, J. and Roberts, B. (1978). *Policing the Crisis: Mugging, the State, and Law and Order*. London: Macmillan.

Hare-Mustin, R.T. and Maracek, J. (1988). The meaning of difference: Gender theory, postmodernism and psychology. *American Psychologist*, 43 (6), 455–64.

Harris, B. (1979). Whatever happened to Little Albert? *American Psychologist*, 34 (2), 151–60.

Harris, B. (1986). Reviewing 50 years of the psychology of social issues. *Journal of Social Issues*, 42 (1), 1–20.

Harris, R.J. (1989). *A Cognitive Psychology of Mass Communication*. Hillsdale, NJ: Lawrence Erlbaum Associates.

Hearnshaw, L.S. (1979). *Cyril Burt, Psychologist*. London: Hodder and Stoughton.

Hearnshaw, L.S. (1990). The Burt affair – a rejoinder. *The Psychologist: Bulletin of the British Psychological Society*, 3 (2), 61–4.

Heather, N. (1976). *Radical Perspectives in Psychology*. London: Methuen.

Hechler, D. (1988). *The Battle and the Backlash*. Lexington, Mass.: Lexington.

Hechter, M. (1986). Rational choice theory and the study of race and ethic relations. In J. Rex and D. Mason (ed.), *Theories of Race and Ethnic Relations*. Cambridge: Cambridge University Press.

Henle, M. (1986). *1879 and All That: Essays in the Theory and History of Psychology*. New York: Columbia University Press.

Herbert, C.A. (1989). *Talking of Silence: The Sexual Harassment of Schoolgirls*. London: Falmer Press.

Hewstone, M. and Giles, H. (1984). Intergroup conflict. In A. Gale and A.J. Chapman (eds), *Psychology and Social Problems*. Chichester: Wiley, pp. 275–95.

Hinton, J.W., O'Neill, M.T. and Webster, S. (1980). Psychophysiological assessment of sex offenders in a security hospital. *Archives of Sexual Behavior*, 9 (3), 208–16.

Home Office (1982). *Report of the Expert Group on the Effects of Cannibis*. London: Advisory Council on the Misuse of Drugs.

Home Office (1987). *Criminal Statistics England and Wales*. London: HMSO.

Hothersall, D. (1990). *History of Psychology*. 2nd edn. New York: McGraw-Hill.

Hovland, C. (1954). Effects of the mass media of communication. In G. Lindzey (ed.), *The Handbook of Social Psychology*, Reading, Mass.: Addison-Wesley, pp. 1062–1103.

Howard, G.S. (1985). The role of values in the science of psychology. *American Psychologist*, 40 (3), 255–65.

Howitt, D. (1982). *Mass Media and Social Problems*. Oxford: Pergamon.

Howitt, D. (1990a). Expert opinion: Risky sexual abuse diagnosis. *The Psychologist: Bulletin of the British Psychological Society*, 3 (1), 15–17.

Howitt, D. (1990b). From Bibb Latane to feminist litany. *The Psychologist: Bulletin of the British Psychological Society*, 3 (6), 258.

Howitt, D. (1990c). *Injustice to Children and Families in Child Abuse Cases*. Paper presented to the 2nd European Conference on Law and Psychology, Nuremberg, 13–15 September.

Howitt, D. (1991). Britain's 'substance abuse policy': Realities and regulation in the United Kingdom. *International Journal of Addictions*, 3, 1087–1111.

Howitt, D., Billig, M., Cramer, D., Edwards, D., Kniveton, B., Potter, J. and Radley, A. (1989). *Social Psychology: Conflicts and Continuities*. Milton Keynes: Open University Press.

Howitt, D. and Cumberbatch, G. (1975). *Mass Media Violence and Society*. London: Elek Science.

Howitt, D., and Cumberbatch, G. (1990). *Pornography: Impacts and Influences*. London: Home Office Research and Planning Unit.

Howitt, D. and Owusu-Bempah, J. (1990). Racism in a British journal? *The Psychologist: Bulletin of the British Psychological Society*. 3 (9), 396–400.

Hudson, L. (1972). *The Cult of the Fact*. London: Jonathan Cape.

Husband, C. (ed.) (1982). *'Race' in Britain*. London: Hutchinson.

Illich, I.K. (1977). Disabling Professions. In I. Illich, I.K. Zola, J. McKnight, J. Caplan and H. Shaiken (eds), *Disabling Professions*. Boston: Marion Boyers, pp. 11–39.

Intons-Peterson, M.J. and Roskos-Ewoldson, B. (1989). Mitigating the effects of violent pornography. In S. Gubar and J. Hoff (eds), *For Adult Users Only: The Dilemma of Violent Pornography*. Bloomington: Indiana University Press, pp. 218–39.

Itzin, C. (1990). Pornography and civil liberties. *Index on Censorship*, 9, 12–13.

Itzin, C. and Sweet, C. (1989). Tackling the monsters on the top shelf. *The Independent* 17th April.

Jaffee, D. and Straus, M. (1987). Sexual climate and reported rape: A state level analysis. *Archives of Sexual Behavior*, 16, 107–23.

Jeffery, C.G. (1970). Drug control in the United Kingdom. In R.V. Phillipson (ed.), *Modern Trends in Drug Dependence and Alcoholism*. London: Butterworths, 60–74.

Jones, J.M. (1972). *Prejudice and Racism*. Reading, Mass.: Addison-Wesley.

Jones, R.A. (1987). Psychology, history, and the press. *American Psychologist*, 42 (10), 931–40.

Joseph, G.G., Reddy, V. and Searle-Chatterjee, M. (1990). Eurocentrism in the social sciences. *Race and Class*, 31 (4), 1–20.

Joynson, R.B. (1989). *The Burt Affair*. London: Routledge.

Joynson, R.B. (1990). The Burt affair – a reply. *The Psychologist: Bulletin of the British Psychological Society*, 3 (2), 65–8.

Judson, H.F. (1973). *Heroin Addiction in Britain: What Americans Can Learn from the English Experience*. New York: Harcourt Brace Jovanovich.

Kamin, L.J. (1977). *The Science and Politics of IQ*. Harmondsworth: Penguin.

Kazdin, A.E. (1977). *The Token Economy: A Review and Evaluation*. London: Plenum.

Kimble, G.A. (1984). Psychology's two cultures. *American Psychologist*, 39 (8), 833–9.

Kinder, D. (1986). The continuing American dilemma: White resistance to racial change 40 years after Myrdal. *Journal of Social Issues*, 42 (2), 151–71.

Kinsey, A.C., Pomeroy, W.B., Martin, C.E. and Gebhard, P.H. (1953). *Sexual Behavior of the Human Female*. Philadelphia: W.B. Saunders.

Kitzinger, C. (1989a). Deconstructing sex differences: Rhoda Unger's social constructionism. *Newsletter, Psychology of Women Section, The British Psychological Society*, 4 (Autumn), pp. 9–17.

Kitzinger, C. (1989b). Barbara Sommer: Lifting the curse. *The Psychologist: Bulletin of the British Psychological Society*, 2 (7), 297.

Kitzinger, C. (1990). Bibb Latane: From bystander research to social impact theory. *The Psychologist: The Bulletin of the British Psychological Society*, 3 (2), 72–3.

Klein, D.B. (1970). *A History of Scientific Psychology*. London: Routledge and Kegan Paul.

Klein, S.S. and Simonson, J. (1984). Increasing sex equity in education: roles for psychologists. *American Psychologist*, 39 (10), 1187–92.

Kline, P. (1988). *Psychology Exposed: or The Emperor's New Clothes*. London: Routledge.

Kohn, M. (1987). *Narcomania: On Heroin*. London: Faber and Faber.

Kolarsky, A., Madlafousek, J. and Novotna, V. (1978). Stimuli eliciting sexual arousal in males who offend adult women: an experimental study. *Archives of Sexual Behavior*, 7 (2), 79–87.

Kuper, A. (1988). *The Invention of Primitive Society*. London: Routledge.

Kurdeck, L.A. (1981). An integrative perspective on children's divorce adjustment. *American Psychologist*, 36 (8), 856–66.

Kutchinsky, B. (1976). Deviance and criminality: the case of a voyeur in a peeper's paradise. *Diseases of the Nervous System*, 37, 145–51.

Kutchinsky, B. (1985). Pornography and its effects in Denmark and the United States: a rejoinder and beyond. *Comparative Social Research*, 8, 301–30.

Latane, B. and Darley, J.M. (1970). *The Unresponsive Bystander: Why Doesn't He Help?* New York: Appleton-Century-Crofts.

Lawrence, K. and Herold, E.S. (1988). Women's attitudes toward and experience with sexually explicit materials. *Journal of Sex Research*, 24, 161–9.

Leech, K. (1985). Heroin: leaving it to the market. *New Statesman*, 109, 8–9.

Levy-Leboyer, C. (1988). Success and failure in applying psychology. *American Psychologist*, 43 (10), 779–85.

Lewin, K. (1986). 'Everything within me rebels': a letter from Kurt Lewin to Wolfgang Kohler, 1933. *Journal of Social Issues*, 42 (4), 39–47.

Lindzey, G. (1967). Some remarks concerning incest, the incest taboo, and psychoanalytic theory. *American Psychologist*, 22, 1051–9.

Linz, D. and Donnerstein, E. (1988). The methods and merits of pornography research. *Journal of Communication*, 38 (2), 180–92.

Linz, D., Donnerstein, E. and Penrod, S. (1987). The findings and recommendations of the Attorney General's Commission on Pornography: Do the psychological 'facts' fit the political fury. *American Psychologist*, 42 (10), 946–53.

Livingstone, S., and Green, G. (1986). Television advertisements and the portrayal of gender. *British Journal of Social Psychology*, 25, 149–54.

Lloyd, C. and Walmsley, R. (1989). *Changes in Rape Offences and Sentencing*. Home Office Research Study 105. London: HMSO.

Lloyd, P., Mayes, A., Manstead, A., Mendell, P. and Wagner, H. (1984). *Introduction to Psychology: An Integrated Approach*. London: Fontana.

Longford Committee Investigating Pornography (1972). *Pornography: The Longford Report*. London: Coronet.

Lubek, I. and Apfelbaum, E. (1987). Neo-behaviorism and the Garcia effect: a social psychology of science approach to the history of a paradigm clash. In M.G. Ash and W.R. Woodward (eds), *Psychology: Twentieth Century Thought and Society*. Cambridge University Press.

Lynch, M.A. and Roberts, J. (1982). *Consequences of Child Abuse*. London: Academic Press.

McConahay, J.B. and Hough, J.C. (1976). Symbolic racism. *Journal of Social Issues*, 32, 23–45.

MacDonald, J. (1971). *Rape: Offenders and their Victims*. Springfield, Ill.: Charles C. Thomas.

McDougall, W. (1908). *An Introduction to Social Psychology*. London: Methuen.

McPherson, S. (1990). Some areas of interface between psychology and the guardian *ad litem* programs in juvenile and domestic relations settings. Paper presented to the 2nd European Conference on Law and Psychology, Nuremberg, 13–15 September.

Mahoney, M.J. (1976). *Scientist as Subject: The Psychological Imperative*. Cambridge, Mass.: Ballinger.

Mahoney, M.J. (1987). Scientific publications and knowledge politics. *Journal of Social Behavior and Personality*, 2 (1), 165–76.

Malamuth, N.M. and Ceniti, J. (1986). Repeated exposure to violent and non-violent pornography: Likelihood of raping ratings and laboratory aggression against women. *Aggressive Behavior*, 12, 129–37.

Malamuth, N.M. and Check, J.V.P. (1980). Sexual arousal to rape and consenting depictions: The importance of women's arousal. *Journal of Abnormal Psychology*, 89, 763–6.

Malamuth, N.M., Haber, S. and Feshbach, S. (1980). Testing hypotheses regarding rape: Exposure to sexual violence, sex differences and the 'normality' of rapists. *Journal of Research in Personality*, 14, 121–37.

Malamuth, N.M., Reisin, I. and Spinner, B. (1979). Exposure to pornography and reactions to rape. Paper presented to the 87th Annual Convention of the American Psychological Association, New York.

Malamuth, N. and Spinner, B. (1980). A longitudinal content analysis of sexual violence in the best selling erotica magazines. *Journal of Sex Reseach*, 16, 227–37.

Marshall, W.C. (1988). The use of sexually explicit stimuli by rapist, child, molesters and non-offenders. *Journal of Sex Research*, 25 (2), 267–88.

Matheny, A.P. (1987). Psychological characteristics of childhood accidents. *Journal of Social Issues*, 43 (2), 45–60.

Mayo, E. (1933). *The Human Problems of an Industrial Civilization*. Cambridge, Mass.: Harvard University Press.

Miles, R. (1989). *Racism*. London: Routledge.

Morawski, J.G. and Goldstein, S.E. (1985). Psychology and nuclear war: A chapter in our legacy of social responsibility. *American Psychologist*, 40 (3), 276–84.

Morgan, G. (1985). The analysis of race: Conceptual problems and policy implications. *New Community*, 12 (2), 285–94.

Morin, S.F. (1977). Heterosexual bias in psychological research on lesbianism and male homosexuality. *American Psychologist*, 32 (9), 629–37.

Morris, P. (1990a). 'The *Psychologist* May 1990 Issue – J. Philippe Rushton'. Letter of 27 April 1990 from the British Psychological Society Director of Information.

Morris, P. (1990b). 'The *Psychologist* May 1990 Issue – J. Philippe Rushton'. Letter of 1 May 1990 from the British Psychological Society Director of Information.

Moskowitz, M.J. (1977). Hugo Munsterberg: a study in the history of applied psychology. *American Psychologist*, 32 (10), 824–42.

Murphy, P.M., Cramer, D. and Lillie, F.J. (1984). The relationship between curative factors perceived by patients in their psychotheraphy and treatment outcome. *British Journal of Medical Psychology*, 57, 187–92.

Nelson, B. (1989). Doctor's report ends family nightmare. *Leicester Mercury*, 25 April.

Nelson, B.J. (1984). *Making an Issue of Child Abuse: Political Agenda Setting for Social Problems*. Chicago: University of Chicago Press.

Norden, B. (1990). Campaign against pornography. *Feminist Review*, 35 (Summer), 1–8.

Oremland, E. and Oremland, J. (1977). *The Sexual and Gender Development of Young Children: The Role of Education*. Cambridge, Mass.: Ballinger.

Orne, M. (1962). On the social psychology of the psychological experiment. *American Psychologist*, 17, 776–83.

Overholser, J.C., and Beck, S.J. (1988). The classification of rapists and child molesters. *Journal of Offender Counseling Services and Rehabilitation*, 13, 1715–25.

Owusu-Bempah, J. (1990). Personal communication.

Padgett, V.R., Brislin-Slutz, J.A. and Neal, J.A. (1989). Pornography, erotica, and attitudes toward women: the effects of repeated exposure. *Journal of Sex Research*, 26 (4), 479–91.

Page, S. (1989). Misrepresentation of pornography research: psychology's role. *American Psychologist*, 44 (3), 578–80.

Parker, I. (1989). *The Crisis in Modern Social Psychology and How to End It*. London: Routledge.

Parton, N. (1981). Child abuse, social anxiety and welfare. *British Journal of Social Work*, 11, 391–414.

Parton, N. (1985). *The Politics of Child Abuse*. London: McMillan.

Paull, J. (1980). Laws of behavior: Fact or artifact? *American Psychologist*, 35 (12), 1081–3.

Pfafflin, S.M. (1984). Women, science and technology. *American Psychologist*, 39 (10), 1183–6.

Phillips, A.S. and Bedeian, A.G. (1989). PMS and the workplace. *Social Behavior and Personality,* 17 (2), 165–74.

Phizacklea, A. and Miles, R. (1980). *Labour and Racism.* London: Routledge and Kegan Paul.

Piaget, J. (1952). *The Origins of Intelligence in Children.* New York: International Universities Press.

Pinkney, A. (1984). *The Myth of Black Progress.* Cambridge: Cambridge University Press.

Pion, G.M. and Lipsey, M.W. (1984). Psychology and society: the challenge of change. *American Psychologist,* 39 (7), 739–54.

Potter, J. (1982). ' ... Nothing so practical as a good theory.' The problematic application of social psychology. In P. Stringer (ed.), *Confronting Social Issues: Some Applications of Social Psychology,* Volume 1. London: Academic Press, pp. 23–49.

Powell, G.E. and Chalkley, A.J. (1988). The effects of paedophile attention on the child. In B. Taylor (ed.), *Perspectives on Paedophilia.* London: Batsford.

Power, R. (1989). Responses to social problems. In S. McGregor (ed.), *Drugs and British Society.* London: Routledge, 129–42.

Pride, M. (1987). *The Child Abuse Industry.* Winchester, Ill.: Crossway.

Rappoport, L. (1984). Dialectical analysis and psychosocial epistemology. In K.J. Gergen and M.M. Gergen (eds), *Historical Social Psychology.* Hillsdale, NJ: Laurence Erlbaum, pp. 103–24.

Rappoport, L. and Kren, G. (1975). What is a social issue? *American Psychologist,* 30, 838–41.

Ray, J.J. (1974). *Conservatism as Heresy.* Sydney: ANZ Books.

Ray. J.J. (1985). Racism and rationality: A reply to Billig. *Ethnic and Racial Studies,* 8 (3), 441–3.

Reason, P. and Rowan, J. (eds) (1981). *Human Inquiry: A Sourcebook of New Paradigm Research.* Chichester: John Wiley.

Reich, W. (1933/trans. 1946). *The Mass Psychology of Fascism.* New York: Orgone Institute Press.

Riegel, K.F. (1978). *Psychology Mon Amour.* Boston: Houghton Mifflin.

Roethlisberger, F.J. and Dickson, W.J. (1939). *Management and the Worker.* New York: Wiley.

Rokeach, M. (1960). *The Open and Closed Mind: Investigations into the Nature of Belief Systems.* New York: Basic Books.

Rose, S., Kamin, L.J. and Lewontin, R.C. (1984). *Not in Our Genes.* Harmondsworth: Penguin.

Ross, E.A. (1908). *Social Psychology: An Outline and Sourcebook.* New York: MacMillan.

Ruback, R.B. and Innes, C.A. (1988). The relevance and irrelevance of psychological research. *American Psychologist,* 43 (9), 683–93.

Rushton, J.P. (1987). Toward a theory of human multiple birthing: Sociobiology and r/K reproduction categories. *Acta Geneticae Medicae et Gemellologiae,* 36, 289–98.

Rushton, (1990). Race differences, r/K theory, and a reply to Flynn. *The Psychologist: Bulletin of the British Psychological Society,* 5, 195–8.

Russell, D.E.H. (1988). Pornography and rape: A causal model. *Journal of Political Psychology,* 9 (1), 41–73.

Russo, N.F. and Denmark, F.L. (1984). Women, psychology, and public policy: selected issues. *American Psychologist,* 39 (10), 1161–5.

Ryder, R. (1989). Child abuse. *The Psychologist: Bulletin of the British Psychological Society*, 2 (8), 333.

Samelson, F. (1974). History, origin myth and ideology: 'Discovery' of social psychology. *Journal for the Theory of Social Behavior*, 4, 217–31.

Samelson, F. (1986). Authoritarianism from Berlin to Berkely: on social psychology and history. *Journal of Social Issues*, 42 (1), 191–208.

Sampson, E.E. (1981). Cognitive psychology as ideology. *American Psychologist*, 36 (7), 730–43.

Sandelands, L.E. (1990). What is so practical about theory? Lewin revisited. *Journal for the Theory of Social Behavior*, 20 (3), 235–62.

Sanders, W.B. (1980). *Rape and Woman's Identity*. Beverly Hills, Calif.: Sage.

Sandfort, T.G.M. (1988). *The Meanings of Experience: On Sexual Contacts in Early Youth, and Sexual Behavior and Experience in Later Life*. Utrecht : Homostudies.

Sandfort, T.G.M. (1989). Studies into child sexual abuse: An overview and critical appraisal. Paper presented at the 1st European Congress of Psychology, 2–7 July, Amsterdam.

Sanford, N. (1986). A personal account of the study of authoritarianism: A comment on Samelson. *Journal of Social Issues*, 42 (1), 209–14.

Sarason, S.B. (1981). *Psychology Misdirected*. New York: The Free Press.

Scarr, S. (1988). Race and gender as psychological variables: social and ethical issues. *American Psychologist*, 43 (1), 56–9.

Scott, J.E. and Cuvelier, S.J. (1987). Sexual violence in *Playboy* magazine: a longitudinal content analysis. *Journal of Sex Research*, 23, 534–9.

Sears, D.O. and Kinder, D.R. (1971). Racial tensions and voting in Los Angeles. In W.Z. Hirsch (ed.), *Los Angeles: Viability and Prospects for Metropolitan Leadership*. New York: Praeger.

Shadish, W.R. (1984). Policy research: Lessons from the implementation of dein-stitutionalization. *American Psychologist*, 39 (7), 725–38.

Shaffer, L.S. (1977). The Golden Fleece. Anti-intellectualism and social sciences. *American Psychologist*, 32 (10), 814–21.

Shedler, J., and Block, J. (1990). Adolescent drug use and psychological health: A longitudinal inquiry. *American Psychologist*, 45 (5), 612–30.

Sherif, M. (1966). *Group Conflict and Cooperation*. London: Routledge and Kegan Paul.

Sherrard, C. (1990). The embodiment of fascism. *History and Philosophy of Psychology Newsletter* (British Psychological Society), 11, 15–19.

Sieber, J.E. and Stanley, B. (1988). Ethical and professional dimensions of socially sensitive research. *American Psychologist*, 43 (1), 49–55.

Signorelli, N. (1985). *Role Portrayal and Stereotyping on Television* Westwood, Conn: Greenwood Press.

Skinner, B.F. (1972). *Beyond Freedom and Dignity*. London: Cape.

Skinner, B.F. (1976). *Walden Two*. London: MacMillan.

Slade, J.W. (1984). Violence in the hard-core pornography film. *Journal of Communication*, 34 (3), 148–63.

Smart, C. (1984). Social policy and drug addiction: A critical study of policy development. *British Journal of Addiction*, 79, 31–9.

Smith, D.D. (1976). The social content of pornography. *Journal of Communication*, 26, 16–33.

Sniderman, P.M. and Tetlock, P.E. (1986a). Reflections on American racism. *Journal of Social Issues*, 42 (2), 173–87.

Sniderman, P.M. and Tetlock, P.E. (1986b). Symbolic racism: Problems of motive attribution in political analysis. *Journal of Social Issues*, 42 (2), 129–50.

Soble, A. (1986). *Pornography, Marxism, Feminism and the Future of Sexuality*. New Haven, Conn.: Yale University Press.

Sommers, E.K. and Check, J. (1987). The empirical investigation of the role of pornography in the verbal and physical abuse of women. *Violence and Victims*, 2 (3), 189–209.

Stagnar, R. (1986). Reminiscences about the founding of SPSSSI. *Journal of Social Issues*, 42 (1), 35–42.

Steinhem, G. (1983). *Outrageous Acts and Everyday Rebellions*. New York: Holt, Rinehart and Winston.

Stermac, L.E. and Quinsey, V.L. (1986). Social competence amongst rapists. *Behavioral Assessment*, 8, 171–85.

Stockdale, J.E. (1978). Crowding: Determinants and effects. In L. Berkowitz (ed.), *Advances in Experimental Social Psychology*, Volume 11. New York: Academic Press.

Szasz, T. (1986). The case against suicide prevention. *American Psychologist*, 41 (7). 806–12.

Szasz, T. (1990). The theology of therapy: the breech of the First Amendment through the medicalization of morals. *Changes*, 8 (1), 2–14.

Tajfel, H. (ed.) (1978). *Differentiation between Social Groups: Studies in the Social Psychology of Intergroup Relations*. London: Academic Press.

Tajfel, H. and Fraser, C. (eds) (1978). *Introducing Social Psychology*. Harmondsworth: Penguin.

Teff, H. (1975). *Drugs, Society and the Law*. Farnborough: Saxon House.

Thompson, C.H. (1934). The conclusions of scientists relative to racial differences. *Journal of Negro Education*, 3, 494–512.

Thompson, M.E., Chaffee, S.H. and Oshagan, H.H. (1990). Regulating pornography: A public dilemma. *Journal of Communication*, 40 (3), 73–83.

Thurstone, L.L. and Chave, E.J. (1929) *The Measurement of Attitudes*. Chicago: University of Chicago Press.

Tizard, B. (1990). Research and policy: Is there a link? *The Psychologist: Bulletin of the British Psychological Society* 3 (10), 435–40.

Tracey, M. and Morrison, D. (1977). *Whitehouse*. London: Macmillan.

Tremper, C.R. (1987). Organized psychology's efforts to influence judicial policy-making. *American Psychologist*, 42 (5), 496–501.

Tyler, A. (1986). Scourges of the mind. *New Statesman*, 111, 21–3.

Ungar, R.K. (ed.) (1986a). *Representations: Social Constructions of Gender*. New York: Baywood.

Ungar, R.K. (1986b). Looking toward the future by looking at the past: social activism and social history. *Journal of Social Issues*, 42 (1), 215–17.

Uzoka, A.F. (1979). The myth of the nuclear family. *American Psychologist*, 34 (11), 1095–1106.

van Naerssen, A.X., van Dijk, M., Hoogeveen, G., Visser, D. and van Zessen, G. (1987). Gay SM in pornography and reality. *Journal of Homosexuality*, 13 (2–3), 111–19.

Vaughan, G. (1964). The effect of the ethnic grouping of the experimenter upon children's responses to tests of an ethnic nature. *British Journal of Social and Clinical Psychology*, 3, 66–70.

Vine, I. (1990a). How does pornography affect behaviour? University of Bradford, unpublished manuscript.

Vine, I. (1990b). How not to understand pornography. University of Bradford, unpublished manuscript.

Viney, L.L., Westbrook, M.T. and Preston, C. (1985). The addiction experience as a function of the addict's history. *British Journal of Clinical Psychology*, 24, 73–82.

Vokey, J.R. and Read, J.D. (1985). Subliminal messages: Between the devil and the media. *American Psychologist*, 40 (11), 1231–9.

Walker, L. (1990). Happy birthday. *Amateur Photographer*, 17 November, pp. 50–1.

Watson, J.B. and Raynor, R.R. (1920). Conditioned emotional reactions. *Journal of Experimental Psychology*, 3, 1–14.

Weinberg, R.A. (1979). Early childhood education and intervention: Establishing an American tradition. *American Psychologist*, 36 (8), 856–66.

West, D.J. (1985). *Sexual Victimisation*. Aldershot: Gower.

Westland, G. (1978). *Current Crises in Psychology*. London: Heinemann Educational.

Whitehouse, M. (1967). *Cleaning Up T.V.* Blandford: London.

Whitehouse, M. (1971). *Who Does She Think She Is?* London: New English Library.

Williams, B. (1979). *Report of the Committee on Obscenity and Film Censorship*. London: HMSO.

Williams, S. (1988). *Psychology on the Couch*. Hemel Hempstead: Harvester-Wheatsheaf.

Wilson, W.C. (1973). Pornography: the emergence of a social issue and the beginning of psychological study. *Journal of Social Issues*, 29 (3), 7–17.

Wittig, M.A. (1985). Metatheoretical dilemmas in the psychology of gender. *American Psychologist*, 40 (7), 800–11.

Woolfson, R.C. (1982). Psychological correlates of solvent abuse. *British Journal of Medical Psychology*, 55, 63–6.

Wrench, J. (1990). New vocationalism, old racism and the careers service. *New Community*, 16 (3), 425–40.

Young, J. (1984). Heroin hoax. *New Statesman*, 108, 13–14.

Zola, I.K. (1977). Healthism and disabling medicalization. In I. Illich, I.K. Zola, J. McKnight, J. Caplan and H. Shaiken (eds), *Disabling Professions*. Boston: Marion Boyars, pp. 41–67.

AUTHOR INDEX

Abbott, A., 5, 167
Adam, H., 115, 167
Adorno, T., 110, 111, 167
Allport, G.W., 117, 167
Amir, M., 50, 167
Apfelbaum, E., 42, 175
Ardrey, R., 165, 167
Argyle, M., 37, 167
Atkinson, R.C., 28, 29, 35, 63, 64, 161, 167
Atkinson, R.L., 28, 29, 35, 63, 64, 167
Attorney General's Commission on Pornography, 123, 129, 138, 139, 140, 167
Auld, J., 68, 167
Ayllon, R., 11, 167
Azrin, N., 11, 167

Baartman, H.E.M., 73, 168
Bachrach, L.L., 2, 168
Bannister, D., 67, 168
Banton, M., 96, 104, 168
Barker, M., 108, 168
Barlow, G., 123, 131, 168
Baron, L., 134, 136, 168
Bartlett, F., 117, 168
Batchelor, W.F., 2, 156, 168
Baxter, M., 131, 134, 135, 141, 168
Bean, P., 56, 168
Beck, S.J., 133, 177
Bedeian, A.G., 11, 168, 177
Bell, S., 93, 168
Berkowitz, L., 136, 171
Berridge, V., 55, 56, 61, 168
Berry, B., 108, 168
Berscheid, E., 161, 168
Bevan, W., 22, 168
Billig, M., 6, 47, 48, 49, 99, 102, 114, 121, 168, 169, 173
Block, J., 64

Boring, E.G., 6, 169
Boucher, R.J., 129, 169
Bramel, D., 39, 169
Breakwell, G., 101, 169
Brehm, S.S., 37, 38, 62, 63, 64, 169
Brent, R., 89, 169
Brette, D.J., 131, 169
Brislin-Slutz, J.A., 130, 177
British Psychological Society, 14, 169
Brown, K., 96, 169
Browne, K., 80, 81, 82, 83, 169
Brownmiller, S., 122, 126, 169
Burgess, A.W., 124, 125, 169
Burt, M.R., 130, 169
Buss, A., 137, 169
Butler-Sloss, J., 93, 169

Campbell, B., 93, 94, 169
Cantor, J., 131, 169
Card, R., 79, 169
Carter, D.C., 129, 169
Catalano, R., 2, 171
Cattell, N.D., 67, 169
Cattell, R.B., 67, 102, 169
Ceniti, J., 126, 176
Chaffee, S.H., 142, 180
Chalkley, A.J., 79, 177
Chave, E.J., 110, 180
Check, J.V.P., 126, 128, 176, 179
Chemers, M.M., 163, 172
Chester, M.A., 104, 169
Clark, J., 75, 172
Clark, L.M.G., 49, 50, 169
Clarke, L., 147, 170
Cline, V.B., 145, 170
Cohen, S., 56, 75, 170
Commission on Obscenity and Pornography, 123, 170

Condron, M.K., 129, 130, 170
Cook, S., 116, 170
Cornell, C.P., 74, 172
Cowan, G.L., 131, 170
Cox, V.C., 157, 163, 164, 170
Cramer, D., 6, 8, 121, 170, 173, 176
Crawford, C., 161, 170
Cresswell, H., 88, 170
Critcher, C., 75, 172
Cumberbatch, G., 2, 122, 123, 124, 131, 134,
    136, 137, 139, 143, 170, 173
Cuvelier, S.J., 131, 178
Cvetkovich, G., 2, 171

Daly, M., 76, 77, 170
Danziger, K., 51, 170
Darley, J.M., 120, 121, 175
Davey, G., 101, 169
Dawes, A., 2, 170
Dawson, J.L.M., 105, 170
Dembo, R., 54, 170
Dempster, F.N., 154, 170
Denmark, F.L., 2, 30, 178
Department of Health and Social Security,
    83, 170
Devine, P.G., 116, 170
Dickson, W.J., 36, 178
Dilman, I., 3, 170
Dipboye, R.L., 163, 170
Dixon, N.F., 153, 170
Doherty, M.E., 90, 171
Donnerstein, E., 130, 136, 138, 171
Dooley, D., 2, 171
Dovidio, J.F., 107, 108, 172
Drapkin, I., 49, 171
Duck, S., 63, 171
Dummett, A., 98, 171
Durkin, K., 131, 171

Earle, T.C., 2, 171
Edwards, D., 6, 55, 61, 168
Edwards, G., 55, 61, 168
Einseidel, E.F., 140, 171
Ellis, L., 143, 171
Ellis, K., 122, 171
Emery, R. E., 155, 156, 171
Evans, J. St. B.T., 90, 91, 171
Evans, R.I., 120, 171
Everywoman, 137, 171
Eysenck, H.J., 3, 111, 145, 123, 160, 171,
    172

Farr, R., 6, 172
Faust, B., 122, 172
Feshbach, S., 126, 176
Fiedler, F.E., 163, 172
Flanagan, M.F., 163, 170
Flynn, J.R., 101, 160, 172
Fox, D.R., 159, 172

Fraser, C., 114, 180
Frenkel-Brunswick, E., 110, 111, 167
Freud, S., 3, 29, 44, 172
Friend, R., 38, 39, 169

Gaertner, S.L., 107, 108, 172
Gale, A., 26, 172
Gebhard, P.M., 73, 74, 174
Gelles, R.J., 74, 172
Gergen, K., 27, 29, 30, 54, 60, 70, 172
Gergen, M.M., 54, 172
Geuter, U., 47, 172
Giles, H., 115, 173
Gilionee, H., 115, 167
Goldstein, S.E., 2, 176
Gossop, M., 69, 172
Graumann, C.F., 47, 172
Green, G., 131, 175
Griffiths, R., 64, 65, 172
Gruneberg, M.M., 11, 172
Gudjonsson, G.H., 4, 171

Haber, S., 126, 176
Hagan, J., 155, 172
Hall, S., 75, 172
Hare-Mustoin, R.T., 30, 172
Harris, B., 6, 40, 41, 173
Harris, R.J., 149, 173
Hearnshaw, L.S., 42, 173
Heather, N., 21, 173
Hechler, D., 75, 173
Hechter, M., 96, 173
Henle, M., 42, 110, 173
Herbert, C.A., 71, 173
Herold, E.S., 142, 175
Hewstone, M., 115, 173
Hill, A., 123, 131, 168
Hinton, J.W., 128, 173
Holmstrom, L.L., 124, 125, 169
Home Office, 63, 77, 173
Hoogeveen, G., 132, 180
Hothersall, D., 6, 173
Hough, J.C., 107, 175
Hovland, C., 9, 173
Howard, G.S., 43, 173
Howitt, D., 6, 58, 72, 84, 104, 119, 121, 122,
    123, 124, 131, 134, 136, 137, 139, 143, 145,
    157, 170, 173, 174
Hudson, L., 16, 174
Husband, C., 96, 174

Illich, I.K., 148, 174
Innes, C.A., 156, 178
Intons-Peterson, M.J., 130, 174
Itzin, C., 131, 141, 174

Jaffee, D., 136, 174
Jeffery, C.G., 59, 174
Jones, J.M., 102, 174

Jones, R.A., 99, 174
Joseph, G.G., 113, 114, 174
Joynson, R.B., 42, 174
Judson, H.F., 54, 174

Kamin, L.J., 45, 102, 174, 178
Kassin, S.M., 37, 62, 63, 64, 169
Kazdin, A.E., 11, 174
Kimble, G.A., 23, 24, 25, 174
Kinder, D., 107, 174, 179
Kinsey, A.C., 73, 79, 174
Kitzinger, C., 11, 120, 33, 174
Klein, D.B., 6, 174
Klein, S.S., 2, 174
Kline, P., 19, 25, 174
Knight, R.A., 129, 169
Kniveton, B., 6, 121, 173
Kohn, M., 53, 174
Kolarsky, A., 128, 175
Kren, G., 1, 177
Kuper, A., 28, 175
Kurdeck, L.A., 2, 175
Kutchinsky, B., 131, 132, 133, 175

Latane, B., 120, 121, 175
Lawrence, K., 142, 175
Lee, C., 131, 170
Leech, K., 60, 175
Levinson, D.J., 110, 111, 167
Levy, D., 131, 170
Levy-Leboyer, C., 151, 152, 153, 175
Lewin, K., 109, 174
Lewis, D.J., 49, 50, 169
Lewontin, R.C., 45, 178
Lindzey, G., 72, 73, 175
Linz, D., 138, 175
Lipsey, M.W., 2, 177
Livingstone, S., 131, 175
Lloyd, C., 127, 134, 175
Lloyd, P., 37, 175
Longford Committee Investigating
    Pornography, 123, 175
Lubek, I., 42, 175
Lynch, M.A., 79, 175

McConahay, J.B., 107, 175
MacDonald, J., 50, 175
McDougall, W., 99, 102, 175
McPherson, S., 78, 175
Madlafousek, J., 125, 175
Mahoney, M.J., 23, 42, 176
Malamuth, N., 126, 128, 131, 176
Manstead, A., 37, 175
Maracek, J., 30, 172
Marholin, D., 155, 156, 171
Marshall, W.C., 133, 176
Martin, C.E., 73, 79, 174
Matheny, A.P., 2, 176
Mayes, A., 37, 175

Mayo, E., 36, 37, 39, 176
Mendell, P., 37, 175
Miles, R., 98, 106, 176
Morawski, J.G., 2, 176
Morgan, G., 98, 176
Morin, S.F., 36, 45, 176
Morris, P., 100, 101, 176
Morrison, D., 140, 180
Moskowitz, M. J., 6, 176
Murphy, P.M., 8, 176
Mynatt, C.R., 90, 171

Neal, J.A., 130, 177
Nelson, B., 91, 176
Nelson, B.J., 74, 176
Nias, D., 3, 123, 145, 171
Norden, B., 120, 177
Novotna, V., 125, 175
Nutter, D.E., 129, 130, 178

O'Dair, B., 143, 171
O'Neill, M.T., 128, 173
Oremland, E., 79, 177
Oremland, J., 79, 177
Orne, M., 52, 177
Oshagan, H.H., 142, 180
Overholser, J.C., 133, 177
Owusu-Bempah, J., 29, 104, 119, 174, 177

Padgett, V.R., 130, 177
Page, S., 138, 177
Parker, I., 16, 17, 18, 177
Parton, N., 74, 83, 177
Paull, J., 20, 21, 22, 177
Paulus, P.B., 157, 163, 164, 170
Pearson, B., 64, 65, 172
Penrod, S., 138, 171
Pfafflin, S.M., 31, 177
Phillips, A.S., 11, 177
Phizacklea, A., 106, 176
Piaget, J., 113, 177
Pinkney, A., 96, 177
Pion, G.M., 2, 177
Pomeroy, W.B., 73, 79, 174
Postman, L., 117, 167
Potter, J., 6, 9, 121, 173, 177
Powell, G.E., 79, 177
Power, R., 66, 177
Prentky, R.A., 129, 169
Preston, C., 67, 180
Pride, M., 91, 92, 93, 177

Quinsey, V.L., 133, 179

Radley, A., 6, 121, 173
Rappoport, L., 1, 52, 177
Ray, J.J., 48, 49, 104, 177, 178
Raynor, R.R., 40, 180
Read, J.D., 154, 180

Reasom, P., 16, 178
Reddy, G.G., 113, 114, 174
Reich, W., 110, 178
Riegel, K.F., 16, 178
Roberts, B., 75, 172
Roberts, J., 79, 175
Roethlisberger, F.J., 36, 178
Rokeach, M., 112, 178
Rose, S., 45, 178
Roskos-Ewoldson, B., 130, 174
Ross, E.A., 99, 102, 103, 178
Rowan, J., 16, 178
Ruback, R.B., 156, 178
Rushton, J.P., 99, 100, 178
Russell, D.E.H., 125, 126, 178
Russo, N.F., 2, 30, 178
Ryder, R., 89, 178

Samelson, F., 41, 110, 111, 112, 113, 178
Sampson, E.E., 36, 178
Sandelands, L.E., 8, 178
Sanders, W.B., 124, 178
Sandfort, T.G.M., 71, 72, 80, 84, 178
Sanford, N., 110, 111, 167, 178
Saqui, S., 80, 82, 83, 169
Sarason, S.B., 16, 178
Scarr, S, 150, 151, 178
Schiavo, M.D., 90, 171
Scott, J.E., 131, 178
Searle-Chatterjee, M., 113, 114, 174
Sears, D.O., 107, 179
Shadish, W.R., 2, 158, 179
Shaffer, L.S., 161, 179
Shedler, J., 64, 179
Sherif, M., 115, 179
Sherrard, C., 145, 179
Sieber, J.E., 159, 160, 161, 179
Signorielli, N., 139, 179
Simonson, J., 2, 174
Skinner, B.F., 3, 179
Slade, J.W., 131, 179
Smart, C., 60, 179
Smith, D.D., 131, 179
Sniderman, P.M., 107, 179
Snyder, D., 131, 170
Soble, A., 131, 179
Sommers, E.K., 126, 179
Spinner, B., 131, 176
Stagnar, R., 6, 179
Stanley, B., 159, 160, 161, 179
Steinhem, G., 141, 179
Stermac, L.E., 133, 179
Stevenson, J., 80, 81, 169
Stockdale, J.E., 165, 179

Straus, M., 134, 135, 168, 174
Sweet, C., 131, 174
Szasz, T., 27, 28, 65, 179, 180

Tajfel, H., 114, 115, 169, 179
Tallmer, A., 143, 171
Teff, H., 57, 60, 180
Tetlock, P.E., 107, 179
Thomson, C.H., 99, 180
Thompson, M.E., 142, 180
Thurstone, L.L., 110, 180
Tizard, B., 158, 180
Tracey, M., 140, 180
Tremper, C.R., 149, 180
Tweney, R.D., 90, 171
Tyler, A., 61, 64, 180

Ungar, R.K., 33, 180
Uzoka, A.F., 29, 180

van Diyk, M., 132, 180
van Naerssen, A.X., 132, 180
van Zessen, G., 132, 180
Vaughan, G., 104, 180
Venderveer, P.L., 129, 169
Viano, E., 49, 171
Vine, I., 141, 142, 180
Viney, L.L., 67, 180
Visser, D., 132, 180
Vokey, J.R., 153, 154, 180

Wagner, H., 37, 175
Walker, L., 141, 180
Walmsley, R., 127, 134, 175
Walster, E.H., 161, 168
Watson, J.B., 40, 180
Webster, S., 128, 173
Weinberg, R.A., 2, 180
West, D.J., 78, 79, 180
Westbrook, M.T., 67, 180
Westland, G., 19, 20, 180
Whitehouse, M., 122, 180
Williams, B., 123, 180
Williams, S., 23, 180
Wilson, G.D., 3, 111, 171, 172
Wilson, M., 76, 77, 181
Wilson, W.C., 122, 123, 181
Wittig, M.A., 31, 32, 181
Woolfson, R.C., 67, 181
Wrench, J., 109, 181

Young, J., 61, 181

Zola, I.K., 69, 70, 181

SUBJECT INDEX

abuse
   responses to, 79
   types of abusers, 78
accident prevention, 2
advocacy, 32
AIDS, 2, 157, 160
Albert B., 40
American Psychological Association, 6
   divisions, 24
   Division of Experimental Psychology, 24
anthropology, 3
anti-drugs campaigns, 66
anti-intellectualism, 161
antisemitism, 48
applied psychology, 4, 9, 11
   myth of, 5–8
   types of, 10–13
applied research, 14
at risk, 78
Attorney General's Commission on
    Pornography, 138
authoritarian personality, 111–12
automatic thought processes, 116
avoiding the obvious, 104
backmasking, 153–4
barbiturates, 64
basic research, 11, 13–14, 36
behaviour modifications, 155–6
Berlin, Irving, 161
Berscheid, 161
biological racism, 97, 99–102
black children, 150
black community, 150
black psychologists, 45
blaming the victim, 105
boomerang effect, 66
British School Health Service Group, 69
British system, 58

brittle-bone disease, 91
Browning, Elizabeth Barrett, 161
Burt, Cyril, 9, 42

Caffey, 74
Campaign Against Pornography, 141
Canadian soldiers, 56
cannabis, 61–2
capitalism, 38
Cartesian, 21–3
change, 17
chic, 18
child abuse
   physical and sexual, 71–94
child development, 2
Chinese whispers, 117
civilization, 3
clinical psychology, 162
cocaine, 57
cognitive anxiety, 68
cognitive innatism, 115
Collins, Jackie, 23
Colwell, Maria, 75
compensatory education, 2
consensual sexual contact, 80
contents of pornography, 131–3
controlled processing, 118
controlled thought processes, 116
convergence, 75
counselling, 2
crime, 4
criminal charges, 61–2
critics, 16–20
cult, 43
cultural racism, 102–5
cultural spillover theory, 134

Darwin, Charles, 99
death rates in prison, 157

deinstitutionalization, 2
delinquency, 155
demographic studies, 133–6
Descartes, 21
determinism, 24–5
diagnosticity of signs, 90
discovering laws, 16
discrimination, 31
divorce, 2, 136
drug abuse, 54–70
drug users, 59

Earthling, 20–1
elementism, 24
emperor's new clothes, 19
enlightenment, 27
epistemic differential, 24
epistemology, 7–8
ethics, 101, 159–61
eurocentrism, 113–19
experimental psychologists, 16
experimental psychology, 25, 136

false positives, 83–9
feminism, 120–45
feminist, 138, 140–44
feminists, 30, 131
Festival of Light, 75
field study, 24
First International Opium Convention, 57
fixed reality, 33
Forum, 129
Francis, Dick, 23
Fraser Committee, 140
Freeman, 150
Freud, 159
fundamentalist christian, 142

Galton, Francis, 99
Garcia, John, 42
gender, 30
  bias, 32
  inequality theory, 134
  politics, 93–4
Genovese, Kitty, 121
glue sniffers, 67
God, 20–1
good intentions, 151
guidance, 2

Hague Convention, 57
hardware, 9–10
harm, 72
Harrison Act, 57–8
Hawthorne Effect, 36–7
healing characteristics, 8
Henderson, Dr. P., 69
heterosexual bias, 36
High School Personality Questionnaire, 67

Hitler, 46
holism, 24
homosexuality, 36
hospital, 151–2
Howitt, D., 150
human welfare, 22

ideological commitment, 17
ideology, 32
  of application, 9
  of modernity, 36
idiographic, 24
illness, 70
incest, 72–3
  taboo, 72
indoctrination, 43
infanticide, 76–7
inside-out model, 4
institutions for paupers, 76
intellectualism, 32
Intelligence, National, 4
interrogates, 13
intraprofessional status, 5
Introduction to Psychology, 28–9
investment good, 22

Jensen, Arthur, 161
Jewish psychologists, 109–13

K–strategy, 100
Kempe, Henry, 74

laboratory, 18, 24
  experiment, 16
laws of behaviour, 20–1
leadership, 163
Lewin, Kurt, 8
liberalism, 75
Librium, 64
Lincoln, Abraham, 161

madness, 27
malaise in social psychology, 17
malicious child abuse reports, 78
Maoris, 30
marginalizing racism, 104
marijuana, 63, 68
Marxism, 38
mass communications research, 9
mass media, 154
mathematical, 26
maxims, 166
mental illness, 2
metacognition, 90
metatheory, 31
Mexico City earthquake, 18
Minneapolis, 137–8
misdirection of theory, 120–25
misogyny, 141
Mogadon, 19

moral movements, 140
moral panic, 56
moral tone, 63
Moseley, Winston, 121
multiple causation, 31
Munsterberg, 6

national intelligence, 160
National Science Foundation, 161
natural laws, 16
nature, 21–2
Nazi Germany, 46–7
Nazis, 109–10, 145
negative tests, 19
new racism, 105–9
Nixon, President Richard, 145
nomothetic, 24
normal men, 128
nuclear family, myth of, 29
nuclear issues, 2

objectivism, 24
objectivity, 30, 32
obstacles to progress, 15–34
operant conditioning, 3
opium, 55
oppression, 45
organizational cultures, 26
orthodoxy, 32
outside-in approach, 4
overcrowding, 163–5

paedophiliac, 72
Pearson, 99
Peeping Tom, 132
Penthouse, 129
perceptual experience, 68
phobias, 40
Playboy, 129
Playgirl, 135
policy, 139
    research, 156
    variables, 156–7
political thinking, 4
pornography, 4, 120–45
    theory, 135
positivism, 20–23, 33
    defined, 21
post-modernist, 33
practitioner psychology, 12
premenstrual syndrome, 11–12
prevention of abuse, 80–3
primal horde, 29
primitive society, 28
prison, 156–8
    crowding, 158
    overcrowding, 163–5
    sieges, 156
productivity, 26

professional errors, theories
    of, 89–94
professional purity, 5
professional socialization, 26
Professorships in Nazi Germany, 47
Proxmire, Senator, 161–2
pseudo-retreat, 129
pseudodiagnosticity, 90
pseudosexual, 126
psychoanalysis, 43
psychotherapy, 7
public status, 5
publications, 26
punditry, 136–9
punishments, 61
pure psychology, 4, 9
pure research, 11

R-strategy, 100
race differences, 45
racial prejudice, 48
racism, 95–119
    definition of, 95–6
    socioeconomic, 96
radical chic, 18
radical psychology, 18
rape, 49–50, 122
    myths, 130, 133
    as normal, 125–7
    offenders, 128–30
    rates and pornography, 134–6
readership, 23
real-world psychology, 15, 162–5
real world, 2–5
relevance, 155–6
rogue doctors, 58
roman men, 76
Ross, E., 102–4
rules for radicals, 17–18
Rush, 65

satanism, 153–4
schism, 32
scholarship, 32
science, 19–20
scientific
    approaches to social science, 30
    cultures, 9
    knowledge, 27
    methods, 26
    values, 24
screening for abuse, 80–3
Secret World of Polly Flint, 88
self, 30
    -prescription, 58
    -serving, 6
service provision, 2
sex equality, 2
sexually transmitted diseases, 73

Shanghai Conference, 57
smoking, 4
social
  anthropology, 28
  constructionist, 27–31
  disorganization theory, 134
  issues approach, 147–9
  issues research, 12
  policy research, 11–12
  problems research, 12
  responsibility, 101
  science, 23
  work, 75
  workers, 65
social identity theory, 115
sociality, 68
Society for the Study and Cure of the
    Inebriated, 56
Society for the Study of Social Issues, 6,
    24–5
socio-technologies, 9–10, 12
South Africans, 104
spacing effect, 154
Spearman, 99
stepparent, meaning of, 77
stimulus generalization, 41
stress in research, 149–51
subjective probability, 91
subjectivity, 32
subjects, 50–2
subliminal perception, 153
suicide, 27–8, 158
symbolic racism, 105–8

taken-for-granted character, 30
taking sides, 45–50
telephone vandalism, 152–3
tender-mindedness, 23
testing, 7
therapist, 8
time, 68
tough-mindedness, 23
training, 43
turnover, 151
two cultures in psychology, 23–5

unemployment, 2
utility of variables, 57
utopia, 3

Valium, 64
value-free, 42
value judgement, 32, 35
values, 35–52
vandalism, 151–2
varieties of psychologists, 23–5
victimology, 46, 49–50
Vietnam War, 75
violence, political, 2

war, 3
white families, 150
Whitehouse, Mary, 140
will to apply research, 151–4
winning formula, 26
women psychologists, 45
Wundt, 6